The Ethics of Cultural Studies

The Ethics of Cultural Studies

Joanna Zylinska

continuum
LONDON • NEW YORK

Continuum
The Tower Building, 11 York Road, London, SE1 7NX
15 East 26th Street, New York, NY 10010

British Library Cataloguing-in-Publication Data
A catalogue record for this book is available from the British Library.

ISBN: 0–8264–7523–X (hardback)
        0–8264–7524–8 (paperback)

Library of Congress Cataloging-in-Publication Data
Zylinska, Joanna, 1971–
    The ethics of cultural studies/Joanna Zylinska.
        p. cm.
    Includes bibliographical references and index.
ISBN 0–8264–7523–X (hard)—ISBN 0–8264–7524–8
1. Culture—Study and teaching—Moral and ethical aspects. 2. Social ethics. I. Title.

HM623.Z95 2004
174'.9306—dc22

2004058294

Typeset by Fakenham Photosetting Limited, Fakenham, Norfolk
Printed and bound in Great Britain by MPG Books Ltd, Bodmin, Cornwall

Contents

Acknowledgements

The origins of this project lie with my time at Bath Spa University College. It was at Bath that, together with Mark Devenney, I organized an international conference 'Cultural Studies: Between Politics and Ethics' in July 2001. I would like to express my gratitude to all the conference participants, as well as my colleagues at Bath Spa – especially Paul Bowman, Mark Devenney and Alan Marshall. I am also grateful to my colleagues and friends at the University of Surrey, Roehampton – Anita Biressi, Lyndie Brimstone, Darren O'Byrne, Paul Rixon and John Seed – for supporting this project, and for awarding me a period of sabbatical leave which enabled me to make significant progress on the manuscript. I would like to thank my colleagues and students at Goldsmiths College, in particular Sarah Kember and Angela McRobbie, for encouraging me to keep the ethical enquiry open and for suggesting some new ways in which it could be developed. I am also indebted to many others who have commented on my ethical encounters throughout the process of writing this book: Caroline Bainbridge, Dave Boothroyd, Judith Butler, Simon Critchley, Jeremy Gilbert, Dorota Glowacka, Chris Hables Gray, Gary Hall, Dorota Kolodziejczyk, Heather Nunn, Stelarc and Ewa Ziarek. The electronic journal *Culture Machine* <www.culturemachine.net> has provided a hospitable space for testing some of my earlier ideas on ethics, politics and culture.

Parts of this book have been published as articles. An earlier version of Chapter 2, entitled 'An Ethical Manifesto for Cultural Studies ... Perhaps', acted as an opening to the special issues of *Strategies: Journal of Theory, Culture and Politics* 14:2 (November 2001), which I co-edited with Mark Devenney. Chapter 3 was first published as 'Mediating Murder: Ethics, Trauma and the Price of Death' in *Journal for Cultural Research* 8:3 (July 2004). Chapter 5 was originally written as a contribution to the 'Close Encounter with Judith Butler' panel organized by Ewa Ziarek at the 27th Annual Conference of the International Association for Philosophy and Literature, Writing Aesthetics, at the University of Leeds, 26–31 May 2003. An earlier, shorter version of this chapter came out in *Cultural Studies* 18:4 (2004) under the title 'The Universal Acts: Judith Butler and the Biopolitics of Immigration'. All of the above are reprinted here by permission of Taylor & Francis, who have asked for a link to their journal website to be listed here <www.tandf.co.uk/journals>. Chapter 7 originally appeared as my contribution to my edited collection on the work of performance artists Stelarc and Orlan, *The Cyborg Experiments: The Extensions of the Body in the Media Age* (London and New York: Continuum: 2002).

I would also like to thank the British Academy for enabling me to present some of this work at two international conferences – a Culture

Machine-hosted seminar on deconstruction and cultural studies at the American Comparative Literature Conference, San Diego, 4–6 April 2003, and the plenary roundtable 'The Body – Virtual or Material?' at the 28th Annual Conference of the International Association of Philosophy and Literature, 'Virtual Materialities', Syracuse University, 9–25 May 2004 – by awarding me two Overseas Conference Grants.

Preface

There has been a great resurgence in debates on ethics outside the strictly delineated discipline of philosophy. Terms such as 'business ethics', 'professional ethics', 'medical ethics' or 'bioethics' have now become part of everyday parlance. Ethics is also a burgeoning field within both the humanities and the social sciences – a development some have labelled 'the ethical turn'.[1] However, apart from Jennifer Daryl Slack and Laurie Anne Whitt's 'Ethics and Cultural Studies', which appeared as their contribution to the renowned *Cultural Studies* collection edited by Lawrence Grossberg, Cary Nelson and Paula Treichler (1992), there has been very little work that directly investigates the relationship between cultural studies and ethics.[2]

This is not to say that ethics is unimportant for cultural studies. On the contrary, the argument of this book starts from the premise that an ethical sense of duty and responsibility has *always* constituted an inherent part of the cultural studies project. And yet, when declaring the field's overt political commitment, cultural studies' theorists have frequently avoided addressing ethical questions directly, as the problem of ethics, with rare exceptions, has been seen as being more the domain of disciplines such as philosophy, political theory or deconstruction-oriented literary theory. Nevertheless, I will argue here that the interdisciplinary multinational project of cultural studies has always had ethical underpinnings. In its questioning of inherited traditions and cultural prejudices and its interest in 'marginal voices', cultural studies develops precisely from a recognition of, and respect for, specificity, locatedness and what the philosopher Emmanuel Levinas has called 'the infinite alterity of the other' (even if this relationship is not always adequately theorized or reflected on). This will allow me to claim that, if it is to continue with its political agenda, cultural studies needs to address explicitly its relationship to ethics, and that its politics *cannot* in fact be thought *without* ethics.[3]

With this book I thus hope to cast light on the increasing importance of ethics to contemporary humanities and social sciences. At the same time, I want to suggest that ethics needs to become – or even perhaps is already in the process of becoming – another 'focal point' of cultural studies' debates, situated alongside issues of politics, identity, representation, interdisciplinarity, pedagogy and institutionalization. In this way, *The Ethics of Cultural Studies* is intended as a contribution to the ongoing investigation of cultural studies, its duties, tasks and responsibilities. Given the instability of the cultural studies' foundations, and the fact that cultural studies itself seems to have been perceived as something of an earthquake within the academic landscape, perhaps I can be excused for hoping that this book might start some new tectonic movements in its still young geological formation.

The short 'seismic history' of cultural studies has already been well documented and goes like this.[4] Silently developing in the sedimented layers of traditional academic disciplines such as English, history and philosophy, cultural studies suddenly burst out with great force in the 1970s and 1980s, in a series of eruptions that radically transformed the University with its recognized disciplinary divisions, with the epicentre of the earthquake shifting from the UK to the US, Australia and other places around the globe. Even though cultural studies has now become an established presence on both sides of the Atlantic – one can think here of numerous undergraduate and postgraduate programmes, research centres and publishers' lists – its somewhat concealed murmur of discontent reminds us that the ground beneath our feet is far from secure.

It is precisely in terms of tectonic metaphors, conveying a sense of organic mutation at work not only in the academy but also within some larger social structures, that the cultural studies project has been described by one of its foremost practitioners. Reflecting 'the rapidly shifting ground of thought and knowledge, argument and debate about a society and about its own culture', cultural studies is for Stuart Hall 'the sort of necessary irritant in the shell of academic life that one hopes will, sometimes in the future, produce new pearls of wisdom'. He sees it as 'a point of disturbance, a place of necessary tension and change' (1996b: 337). But it is not only the disruptive aspect of cultural studies, its shaking up of the traditional foundations of knowledge and its legitimating institutions, that Hall perceives as constitutive of this new–old discipline. The sense of tension, irritation and disruption is accompanied by a radical transformation of the understanding of the notion of 'culture' and its relation to the other spheres of life, including art, education, politics and economy. The transformative project of cultural studies, as delineated by Hall and the other members of the Centre for Contemporary Cultural Studies at Birmingham (where the academic foundations of cultural studies first took shape), thus has an explicitly articulated political dimension, one that is activated not just by a commitment to a theoretical understanding of the world but also to the reordering of its social arrangements. Commenting on the complexities of the structures and dynamics of racism at the end of the twentieth century, Hall postulates: 'the work that cultural studies has to do is to mobilize everything that it can find in terms of intellectual resources in order to understand what keeps making the lives we live, and the societies we live in, profoundly and deeply antihumane in their capacity to live with difference' (1996b: 343).

Even though I find Hall's use of the term 'antihumane' somewhat problematic (as it rests on the seemingly unquestioned assumption that human beings deserve a certain treatment due to the very nature of their humanness), I do embrace his argument regarding the profound inability of many sectors of contemporary Western societies to live with difference, even if, in their official discourses of democracy and liberalism, 'difference' seems to find a propitious breeding ground. While it is 'other', pre-modern, less individualized and more tribal societies that are often described as lacking 'tolerance' and ability to celebrate cultural difference, pluralism and freedom, I agree with Hall that the Occident is not really able to engage with radical alterity without attempting to annul, squash or domesticate it in one way or another. This does not mean that difference is always first recognized and then violated. Some of the most violent forms of relating to difference involve not noticing it in the first place, or attempting to reduce it to conceptual categories already in our possession. But before the reader dismisses my argument at this point with an impatient sigh: 'Not *another* book on cultural difference!',[5] let me propose what on the surface may seem like a preposterous claim: namely *that cultural studies itself has not yet really engaged with difference*. What I want to argue in *The Ethics of Cultural Studies* is that, in spite of its interest in postcolonialism, multiculturalism, fluid sexualities and youth subcultures, *cultural studies has yet to think its own relationship to alterity*. And it is precisely through an engagement with *the thinking of alterity* in cultural studies, without reducing this alterity to a sequence of already known and concretized others (racial minorities, the working classes, gays and lesbians, women, and so on), that the ethical dimension of cultural studies indicated in my title will be posited. In this way, I hope to somewhat shift the orientation of the cultural studies project from its original, more clearly articulated political grounding (as summed up by Stuart Hall in his article 'Race, Culture, and Communications: Looking Backward and Forward at Cultural Studies', from which I quoted earlier).

Significantly, Hall's remark on cultural studies' opposition to the inhumane aspects of everyday life is more than a diagnosis of late-capitalist Western societies' inability to come to terms with any forms of alterity that challenge or undermine their self-image. His description of the cultural studies project also has a normative dimension: it entails a sense of mobilization and obligation, a call to responsibility and action. This is another point I want to develop in this book – that the cultural studies project, focused on the exploration of our 'insurmountable allergy' (Levinas, 1986: 346) towards the forms of difference that we cannot comprehend or master, is, in its very premises, *normative*; i.e. that it involves an ethical injunction, an obligation and a call to responsibility.

In Chapter 1, which I have titled 'A User's Guide to Culture, Ethics and Politics', I set an encounter between cultural studies, continental philosophy and political theory in order to explain the working of this injunction. Referring to the writings of Emmanuel Levinas, Jacques Derrida and Ernesto Laclau, I propose there a reflection on cultural studies' engagement with ethical positions as well as an investigation of its ethical tasks. This point is developed further in Chapter 2, in which I explore what we can actually understand by 'responsibility' in cultural studies. In Chapters

3 to 8, the book's ethical perspective is foregrounded through a series of interventions (rather than mere illustrations). In these chapters I put the 'ethical injunction of cultural studies' to the test by examining a number of everyday events that demand a responsible response from us. I look there at 'moral panics' connected with race, rap and hip-hop (Chapter 3), '9/11' and its media representations (Chapter 4), the current discourses around asylum and immigration in Western multicultural democracies (Chapter 5), Polish anti-Semitism in the context of the newly expanded European Union (Chapter 6), and technological experiments with the body in art (Chapter 7) and medicine (Chapter 8). To allow for different points of entry and different uses of the volume, each chapter constitutes an independent entity, drawing on a variety of events from the media, popular culture, art and politics.

There are however a number of thematic threads that connect these chapters. As issues of 'identity and difference' have always featured prominently on the cultural studies' agenda, it is perhaps unsurprising that they should have come to occupy a significant position in the book, especially since the Levinas- and Derrida-inspired ethical perspective I develop here consists of formulating a response to, and taking responsibility for, difference. (A User's Guide that follows should make this position clearer.) It should also become clear throughout the course of the book that ethics for me does not amount simply to a logical working out of rules that could then be applied to specific cases; rather, it emerges from the lived experience of corporeal, sexuate beings. This is why the analysis of 'the body' and the processes of 'embodiment' – another set of key terms in the book – is also necessary for my ethical enquiry, from looking at the abject, emaciated or dead bodies of asylum seekers which do not seem to matter very much at all to the official democratic 'body politic', through to the exploration of new forms of corporeal emergence at the crossroads of information sciences and biotechnology. Last but not least, the theme of 'violence' – explicitly foregrounded in the title of Chapter 4 that deals with representations of the events of death and trauma in the media – plays an important role in my study. This is because, even though ethics might be seen as an attempt to curb or overcome violence (see Freud, 1985), violence is also, as I hope to show here, *foundational* to ethics (as it is to all processes of identification, interpretation and meaning-making).

One of the driving forces behind this study is my own political commitment to transforming the world according to the principle of justice (even if, for now, the 'content' of this principle needs to be put in suspension). But as well as presenting an account of the already established positions in thinking about politics in cultural studies, I intend to query here a number of the more traditional definitions of politics, while also delineating some possible new ways of practising 'the political'.

Notes

1   As examples of this 'ethical turn' one can cite the following volumes: *Moral Spaces: Rethinking Ethics and World Politics*, ed. David Campbell and Michael J. Shapiro (1999b), *Ethics After the Holocaust: Perspectives, Critiques, and Responses*, ed. John K. Roth (1999), *The Turn to Ethics*, eds Marjorie Garber *et al.* (2000), *An Ethics of Dissensus: Postmodernity, Feminism, and Radical Democracy*, Ewa Plonowska Ziarek (2001), *What Happens to History: The Renewal of Ethics in Contemporary Thought*, ed. Howard Marchitello (2001b), or *Mapping the Ethical Turn: A Reader in Ethics, Culture, and Literary Theory*, eds Todd F. Davis and Kenneth Womack (2001), to name but a few.

2   As an exception, I should mention here Rey Chow's *Ethics After Idealism* (1998), which is an attempt to stage an encounter between cultural studies and cultural theory (with a particular emphasis on deconstruction) under the aegis of ethics. For Chow ethics is a reading practice which 'must carry with it a willingness to take risks … to destroy the submission to widely accepted, predictable and safe conclusions' (1998: xxii), but her ethical perspective is not conceptually developed throughout the book (although it is interestingly 'performed' in a number of her textual analyses). Chow's eponymous 'ethics after idealism' is presented as arising from an encounter between Slavoj Žižek's 'ethics of limits' and Gayatri Spivak's 'affirmative ethics' (33–54); however, its philosophical foundations remain unexplored.

3   Some of the ideas included in this paragraph come from an introduction to the special issue of *Strategies: Journal of Theory, Culture & Politics* on the subject of 'Cultural Studies: Between Politics and Ethics' (2001), which I co-edited with Mark Devenney.

4   Of course, any attempt to tell a linear 'story of origin' falls prey to the narrative tactics of the story-teller, to his/her conclusions, generalizations and omissions. My own brief account of cultural studies' birth out of the tectonic movements that took place in academia in the 1970s is no exception. Indeed, I am aware that a fixed point of cultural studies' origin cannot be unequivocally located. For example, as Raymond Williams suggests, we should perhaps go beyond the 'Birmingham story' and look at adult education in the UK in the 1930s and 1940s as the site of cultural studies' birth (quoted in Gary Hall, 2002: 78). Bearing these reservations in mind, I would like to refer those readers who are interested in hearing other such stories of cultural studies' emergence to Tom Steele's *The Emergence of Cultural Studies 1945–65* (1997), Graeme Turner's *British Cultural Studies* (2002) and Adrian Rifkin's 'Inventing Recollection' (2003).

5   This weariness with the exploration of difference seems to be a growing sentiment among a number of thinkers 'on the left'. Slavoj Žižek and Alain Badiou have both recently called for a return to 'oneness', which they see as a necessary condition of political action. Badiou, for example, claims that in the universe there are only differences. He says, 'Infinite alterity is quite simply what there is. Any experience at all is the infinite deployment of infinite differences. … There are as many differences, say, between a Chinese peasant and a young Norwegian professional as between myself and anybody at all, including myself'. And then he adds, 'As many, but also, then, neither more nor less' (2001: 25–6). What Badiou seems to be doing here is emptying the philosophy of difference of its meaningfulness, i.e. reducing it to the absurd, to banality, to vacuity. As it is such an obvious and commonplace thing to notice that people are different from each other, it is really a waste of time (and of political energy) to go on about these differences – it is boring, facile and counter-productive. And yet, I want to postulate in this book that the philosophy of difference has a lot to offer. A sometimes all-too-easy turn to 'multiplicities', out of which political unity will nevertheless emerge, seems to happen at the expense of the ethics of incalculable alterity, but the cost of this turn does not seem to have always been thought through.

1

A User's Guide to Culture, Ethics and Politics

WELCOME TO THE CULTURE CLUB: *C-USERS AND ABUSERS*

'Culture' has become a hot commodity in Western economies. From 'youth culture', through to 'black culture', 'street culture', 'beauty culture', 'enterprise culture' and 'management culture', the word 'culture' seems to embrace a wide spectrum of customs, behaviours, political viewpoints and ways of being, increasingly connected to the capitalist machinery of production and consumption. The *use of culture* presupposed in the title of this chapter reflects this change in the notion of 'culture' that occurred in late twentieth-century Western capitalist societies. As Bill Readings observes in *The University in Ruins*, the concept of culture as a unifying regulatory ideal that provided a foundation to the modern university and, by extension, the modern nation state, has been replaced by the perception of culture in terms of 'excellence', a unit of a virtual scale which can be measured with performance indicators (1996: 117–18). And, it goes without saying, different performance indicators can be applied to different self-contained 'units' – depending on whether we are talking about, or rather measuring, youth or business culture. 'Culture' seems to refer now to everything and nothing in particular, turning the emergent discipline of cultural studies into a decentred investigation of a referent which is itself lacking. Rather than being studied as an object, culture can only be *used*; it can be performed, produced and consumed but not studied in the conventional sense, because its researcher is unable to separate herself from her object of study. 'As Madonna knows', concludes Readings, 'culture is made up of roles and their combinations' (117).

Readings has a number of reservations concerning this turn of events. Even though he acknowledges cultural studies' self-reflexivity when it comes to its analysis of cultural ideologies and positions, he wonders to what extent cultural studies can become something other than a nostalgic investigation of a world that once was. He argues that the study of cultural identification and participation which cultural studies promotes has in fact been disallowed by the disappearance of the very object (i.e. 'culture') in which the dispossessed are to be encouraged to participate. Significantly, Readings's dissatisfaction with cultural studies' unavoidable and thus tragic quietism[1] strangely coincides with the critique of cultural studies by the conservative supporters of 'tradition' and 'value' in education. The proponents of more established discipline-based scholarly models have reacted with fear and anger to this academic development, whose object of study – culture defined 'as a whole way of life' – has been seen as unsubstantial. Immersing the 'cultural critic' – the student, the researcher – in the very field of study has been seen as a recipe for losing sight of both 'objectivity' and 'value'. That there is an inherent contradiction between these two terms escapes those who want to continue with the unreformed Matthew Arnold-inspired model of humanities education, a model which promotes the study of 'the best which has been thought and said in the world', for the benefit of us all (see Bloom, 1994; Rorty, 1996).

Questioning the nature of established 'cultural values', cultural studies has examined the ideological assumptions that have shaped our thinking about the world, but it has also proposed a reengagement with the ordinary and the everyday in an attempt to bring about a fairer and more just society. It is in this sense that the critical project of cultural studies has had, from its inception, a political agenda. For Stuart Hall,

> [i]t is a serious enterprise ... and that is inscribed in what is sometimes called the 'political' aspect of cultural studies. Not that there's one politics already inscribed in it. But there is something *at stake* in cultural studies, in a way that I think, and hope, is not exactly true of many other very important intellectual and critical practices. Here one registers the tension between a refusal to close the field, to police it and, at the same time, a determination to stake out some positions within it and argue for them. (1999: 99)

But cultural studies' politicality is often overlooked by its critics – one can mention here such diverse thinkers as Harold Bloom, Todd Gitlin, Nicholas Garnham, Francis Mulhern, Richard Rorty, Slavoj Žižek, Manuel De Landa and Richard Dawkins. Due to its engagement with 'the ordinary people's' cultural practices such as reading glossy magazines, watching soap operas and going to football, cultural studies has often been portrayed as a sign of a general 'dumbing down', and of pandering to society's lowest common denominator in an attempt to attract the maximum number of gullible students on board (see Ferguson and Golding, 1997; Philo and Miller, 2001). And it is precisely this apparent contradiction between the seriousness of its political project and the tacky gaudiness of the popular culture it has examined that has led to many misconceptions about cultural studies, disseminated in both the academic and mainstream press.[2]

The guide to culture, ethics and politics presented here can thus perhaps be seen as one possible response to both Bill Readings's questioning of cultural studies' tasks and responsibilities in the light of the disappearance of 'culture' as an object of study, and the right-wing critique of cultural studies as a sign of a social and educational malaise.[3] Even though I began by tentatively embracing Readings's conclusion regarding the *use* of culture as 'excellence', of 'everything and nothing', I am interested in finding out to what extent the impossible object of culture is itself performed and thus reinstated – while also being simultaneously mis-*used* and ab-*used* – through numerous acts of cultural participation. This guide does not therefore follow the sound logic and rhetoric of user manuals. I am equally interested in users' rational *and irrational* investments, motivations and desires when it comes to enacting their 'cultural roles'; i.e. in their (explicit or implicit) ethical justifications and political orientations which shape their being-in-culture. It is thus not only 'culture as such' that I talk about here; cultural studies' political engagements and interventions are another one of my focal points. Acknowledging the danger involved in what can be described as a cultural studies' 'turn to ethics' – which can stand for a departure from, or even atrophy of, its political commitment – I argue that every political decision has to be underpinned by an ethical investment.

DESCRIPTION v NORMATIVITY: *OR, 'HOW THINGS ARE' AS OPPOSED TO 'HOW THEY SHOULD BE'*

Drawing on the work of the philosopher Emmanuel Levinas and the political theorist Ernesto Laclau, I postulate that an ethical framework of cultural studies is not to be imposed from outside (through reference to post-Marxism or deconstruction, for example – important as they are for my analysis), but rather that ethical normativity *is always already present* in numerous cultural studies' articulations, projects and interventions. Normativity does not stand here for a set of preconceived rules and regulations, but rather for a certain sense of obligation and responsibility which organizes the political horizon of cultural studies, without filling it with a universal content. But it is through an encounter with Laclau's post-Marxism and Levinas's ethics that this 'foundation-less normativity' of cultural studies will become evident.

The distinction between description and normativity – or, in other words, between 'how things are' and 'how they should be' – is not entirely tenable, for reasons I will explain below. I thus want to refrain from first describing cultural studies as a discipline which has been defined more explicitly in political terms and only then accompanying it by my own 'ethical' correction. Instead, I hope my *description* of cultural studies' ethical engagement is performative (in the sense given to this term by J. L. Austin in his speech-act theory developed in *How to Do Things with Words* (1962)):[4] it simultaneously brings about an event, it establishes a certain idea of ethical *normativity*. But, to complicate matters even further, this idea of ethical normativity also needs to be presupposed in the event to allow any statements about cultural studies, its activities, orientations and politics. (More on this later.)

In his contribution to *Contingency, Universality, Hegemony* Ernesto Laclau develops a critique of this very opposition between descriptiveness and normativity from his reading of Marxism. He argues that Marxism was never a purely descriptive science, as the 'objective' historical process it recognized already had a normative dimension. This is to say that Marxism was premised on an ethical investment (i.e. the idea of justice and common good), even if it lacked a separate ethical argument. To paraphrase Laclau – whose work is important for me here because his rigorous investigation of the notion of 'politics' ties in with an ethical enquiry[5] – we can say that the description of the cultural studies project can never be *just* a neutral description of what is going on in the discipline. Its very condition of possibility is a *normative* element governing, from the very beginning, whatever apprehension of 'facts' as facts there could be. To describe cultural studies, in Simon During's words, as a field which 'accepts that studying culture is rarely value-free, and so, embracing clearly articulated left-wing values ... seeks to extend and critique the relatively narrow range of norms, methods, and practices embedded in the traditional past-fixated, canon-forming humanities' (During, 1999: 27), is already to presuppose a certain value inherent in the idea of the left-wing critique, in the transformation of the traditional model of education and in the concept of social justice which informs this transformation.

Cultural studies has never attempted to position itself as value free – in fact, it is precisely its declared 'politicality' that is often used to distinguish it from a number of allegedly more 'objective' disciplines. And it is the (broadly defined) Marxist legacy, with its interest in the material and its commitment to social justice, that has by and large informed this politics. While cultural studies may not always have relied on a unified theory of society or the kind of a progressive notion of history that informs traditional Marxism, it has nevertheless retained a belief in the possibility of social change to be found in Marx and Engels's writings. As During explains, 'engaged cultural studies is academic work (teaching, research, dissemination, etc.) on contemporary culture from non-elite or counter-hegemonic perspectives ("from below") with an openness to the culture's reception and production in everyday life, or more generally, its impact on life trajectories' (1999: 25). It is this 'from below' approach that drives my own study of cultural studies' ethical commitment. Rather than *introduce* ethics *into* cultural studies, and in this way impose ethics from above in the form of a prescriptive framework intended to complement its politics, I want to *trace* an ethical dimension *in* a number of cultural studies' articulations, practices and interventions. This will also allow me to show that the political commitment of cultural studies already works against a certain normative horizon. However, I also claim that its numerous acts of political practice simultaneously *perform*, propose and develop an ethics of cultural studies. I realize that there is something quite daunting, perhaps even irritating, about performative logic – as the element which is presupposed as a horizon (i.e. ethics) is simultaneously in the process of being established. But the notion of performativity is extremely helpful in explaining how cultural concepts and entities that are often seen as 'eternal' and 'universal' actually originate, and how we all contribute to the production of this idea of universality. The ethics of cultural studies is thus both *presupposed* and *proposed* in the book; it relies on a normative order already in place for an ethical proposal to be put forward.

PERFORMATIVITY: *THE POLITICAL ACTS*

Distinctions between 'theory' and 'practice', 'ethics' and 'politics', 'value' and 'fact' or, putting it crudely, between 'thinking about how things should be' and 'doing something about it', collapse when we analyse them through the notion of performativity, which – by describing the status quo – simultaneously establishes a certain reality. This process is, 'theoretically' at least, interminable. To illustrate what I mean by this, let me refer to the example of gender, first introduced into debates on performativity by Judith Butler. According to Butler, gender can be thought of as having a 'performative character', or as being established (and simultaneously always dis-established, unworked) in the performative process. When we are born into the world, we adopt a number of gender codes that are passed on from our parents, educators and earlier generations – such as 'pink for the girls, blue for the boys', 'girls shouldn't sit like that', 'boys don't cry', and so on – while also adjusting them to some extent. Gender does not therefore correspond to some pre-existing essence of identity but is rather produced, or performed, through a sequence of acts which are, at the same time, old (i.e. recognizable) and new (i.e. contributing to the development of the 'reality' of gender). As Butler explains, 'Performatives do not merely reflect prior social conditions, but produce a set of social effects, and though they are not always the effects of "official" discourse, they nevertheless work their social power not only to regulate bodies, but to form them as well' (1997: 158–9).

Performativity is consequently an empowering concept in politics because it not only explains how change happens but also shows that change is possible even when we are functioning within the most congealed, oppressive and totalitarian social and cultural structures.[6] In relation to gender, it means that patriarchal family structures, oppressive gender roles that prevent women from accessing highly paid jobs while preventing men from expressing their affectivity, and homophobic regulations regarding gay parenthood and gay couples' legal situation when it comes to inheritance, can all be altered. And it is precisely the series of oppositions between 'ethics' and 'politics', 'normativity' and 'description', 'theory' and 'practice', and 'thinking what to do' and 'actually doing it', that performativity puts into question by indicating that the first set of terms is already implicated in the second as its condition of possibility. This means that, to engage in any practice, to undertake any form of political action, we need to be guided by some prior belief (what Laclau terms 'an ethical investment'), which belongs to the order of 'universals'. For example, students participating in rallies against higher education fees are usually informed by the belief that education is a common good and a right that should be free for all, or that introducing fees will perpetuate class distinctions in society, a state of events which they consider unwelcome. (Of course, students may go to a demonstration because it is something to do on an afternoon and because their friends are also going, and they do not necessarily have to believe that education should be free, or care one way or another. This does not negate the fact that they need to maintain some sort of relationship to the values underpinning an 'anti-fees demo', even if this relationship is one of disagreement – and thus they are acting against their beliefs – or apathy.)

It is in the sense explained above that my description of cultural studies' ethical orientation simultaneously delineates an ethical proposal, while also relying on a normative order *already in place* for an ethical proposal to be developed. (I discuss this point further in the next few sections, drawing on the work of Ernesto Laclau.)

DECONSTRUCTION: *WORK (ALWAYS) IN PROGRESS*

That said, the normative order already in place is not *ethical per se*; it is not endowed with some universal transcultural value. Its normative character stems, as Laclau explains, from an ethical investment that we as members of a certain community (be it 'students', 'cultural studies practitioners', 'the West' or 'anti-globalization protesters') made at some point, and which by now may have receded into our unconscious. Laclau does thus recognize the need to affirm some 'universalist' terms (such as the legitimacy of the discourse of equality or people's right to their self-determination) and some political values of the Enlightenment project, such as freedom, justice or commitment to reason. But what he also calls for is a 'different modulation' of Enlightenment values, one that will allow us to see them as contingent and pragmatic constructions (see Laclau, 1990: 187-9). These values, according to Laclau, need to be seen as being 'in deconstruction', i.e. we need to 'abandon the aspiration to [their] single foundation' (1990: 125) and accept their radically open character. This is not all: we must also become aware of the 'constitutive outside' that establishes these very values (by being what they are not).

References to deconstruction, evoking a spectre of Jacques Derrida, usually without calling him by name, are frequent in Laclau's writings. As Laclau's work on hegemony, politics and ethics has influenced some of the ideas presented here, Laclau's debt to Derrida is also, inevitably, my own.

But it is not only through Laclau that my encounter with Derrida's thought has taken place. My earlier work on and in cultural studies – developed from my original academic affiliation as a scholar of English and American literature – already carried a Derridean inscription (see Zylinska, 2001). This has crystallized through my involvement with the online academic journal *Culture Machine*, which promotes and develops new work at the crossroads of cultural studies and cultural theory.[7] The case for cultural studies' engagement with deconstruction has been made most persuasively by Gary Hall, one of *Culture Machine*'s founding editors, in his book *Culture in Bits* (2002). A member of the generation of scholars in the humanities and social sciences whose whole university education has been shaped by 'Theory', Hall proposes there a cultural studies 'which is thought through the work of Jacques Derrida as much as that of Raymond Williams, Stuart Hall or the "Birmingham School"' (1). For him deconstruction offers a productive way of thinking through some of the problems in contemporary cultural studies – including the relations between theory and politics, culture and society, the cultural and the economic, Marxism and post-Marxism, essentialism and anti-essentialism, agency and structure, textuality and lived experience, the subject and the social – without attempting to resolve any of those relations in a dialectical manner. As Hall remarks, a dialectical resolution of these conceptual oppositions organizing cultural studies – including the opposition between theory and politics, which he sees as privileged by political economists, and which consequently implies all the other oppositions – is not only impossible, it is also politically and intellectually disabling. Instead, he sees cultural studies as necessarily existing in a creative tension between these conflicting concepts – not in a liberal fashion, where each position is equally valid, but rather in a state of mutual transformation, where our notions of 'theory', 'politics', 'activism', 'transformation' and 'the world' are pushed beyond their traditional delimitations and forced to rework their relationship with one another outside the comfort of systemic philosophy (94). In this sense, argues Hall, 'if there is something called "cultural studies", knowledge of what it might be is already displaced, deconstructed, as if by itself, without deconstruction, since ... cultural studies is "in deconstruction" as the condition of its very possibility (and of course impossibility)' (3).

I postulate in this book that a relationship between ethics and politics is one of the structuring oppositions of cultural studies. And it is putting deconstructive strategies to work across the politico-ethical spectrum that I am particularly interested in here. Derrida's deconstructive thinking enables me to explore the tension between academic theory and political practice in cultural studies, between the playful celebration of cultural forms and our responsibility for and towards 'culture'. But it is more in the form of 'writing in sympathetic ink' rather than 'applying Derrida' to my study of ethics that the deconstructive inscription manifests itself. I thus do not attempt to 'use' Derrida's writings for my reading of cultural studies' work on politics in order to 'deconstruct' the latter,[8] nor do I rely on deconstruction as an *external* validating framework for the examination of the processes occurring *within* cultural studies. Derrida's presence in the book is rather that of a ghostly figure, popping out unexpectedly from behind a chair, appearing as if out of the blue at the turn of a page and allowing us to develop a sense of premonition that he is just about to return again, and that perhaps he has never left us in the first place. This is not to say that I always articulate my invitation to him, that I acknowledge (or even *am able to* acknowledge) his presence, his haunting, in other words that I always directly quote from Derrida and 'use' him to authorize our ethical ruminations. Instead, I envisage a number of deconstructions taking place here, *apparently* unprovoked, *as if* unexpected – but they always require an act of listening, an openness to what may come about.

'Deconstruction' is for me a vital political strategy that remains attentive to the working of the performative, while also allowing us to traverse the sedimented (or naturalized) layers of oppositions that organize our social universe. Judith Butler argues that 'For Derrida, the force of the performative is derived precisely from its decontextualization, from its break with a prior context and its capacity to assume new contexts' (1997: 147). But it will also help us articulate some new ethical claims that cannot be ultimately constrained by the normative order; it will offer 'a way to think performativity in relation to transformation, to the break with prior contexts, with the possibility of inaugurating contexts yet to come' (Butler, 1997: 151–2).[9] Laclau explains the working of deconstruction in the following way:

> Deconstruction consists in discovering the undecidability of things which are presented as being either joined or separated. So deconstruction involves two kinds of operation. On the one hand, it shows that between two things which have been portrayed as being essentially linked there is in fact some kind of undecidability which prevents them from being assembled together. On the other hand, deconstruction also involves showing that between two things which are originally presented as separated there is a certain amount of contamination. (2002: unpag.)

Contamination is always at work in establishing the sequence of oppositions that shape our political imaginary as well as our identities, collective and individual ones. Our idea of being a man implies the sense of not being a woman; our sense of belonging to the West, to civilization, to democracy, depends on acknowledging at the same time that we are not Eastern, savage or politically irrational and unruly. The determination of these 'positive' identities relies therefore on the simultaneous production of a set of oppositional concepts. The emergence of these 'positive' identities to which we lay claim involves an operation of what Derrida terms 'violence'; it is based on the suppression and denigration of one set of terms for the sake of the elevation of the other. But this mechanism also involves another type of suppression – a 'forgetting' of the fact that our own identity and sense of belonging is premised on a lack, on not being somebody else, but also, perhaps, on simultaneously desiring that otherness which we do not have or maybe even comprehend, but which we attempt to make fit into our own conceptual spectrum.

IDENTITY: *VIOLENT FOUNDATIONS*

Robert Young argues that this violence of 'Western humanism', as he terms it – implying the identitarian categories mentioned above – is not accidental to Western culture; it is in fact intrinsic to it (1996: 249). But in doing so he is also talking about the process of loosening these strict identitarian categories initiated by the postcolonial critique – a process which is also a deconstruction, because as a result of it the significance of the terms 'West', 'whiteness' and 'humanism' is revealed as being always already contaminated by the notions of 'East', 'blackness' and 'barbarism'. This recognition of the contamination and fragmentation of the subject marks for Young the end of ethical universalism, which was premised on an unproblematic idea of the human. If we recognize that human beings 'are not unitary essences but products of a conflictual psychic and political economy', that they are fragmented, intrinsically unstable and co-dependent in the processes of identification in which they participate, '[i]t is precisely this inscription of alterity within the self that can allow for a new relation to ethics: the self has to come to terms with the fact that it is also a second and a third person' (1996: 248). Thinking about identity in relational terms also implies acknowledging its intrinsic incompleteness: if my identity is implicated in, even dependent on, that of a second and a third person, then the fullness of being, or the sense of one's own wholeness and mastery, can only ever be a fantasy. As Stuart Hall puts it, 'There is always "too much" or "too little" – an over-determination or a lack, but never a proper fit, a totality' (1996a: 3). It is the investigation of the link between this inscription of alterity within the self and a new relation to ethics posited by Young that I now want to turn to.

'TURN TO LEVINAS': *RESPECT!*

Analyses of the departure from a totalized model of selfhood have proliferated not only in cultural studies but also in English literature, the social sciences, psychology and philosophy. But it was originally within the academic tradition perhaps best described as 'continental philosophy' that the recognition of the intrinsic alterity of the human self was situated in an explicitly *ethical* context, mainly through an engagement with the work of the Lithuanian-born French philosopher Emmanuel Levinas. What I want to argue here, however, is that Levinas's thought is immensely important for all kinds of work on ethics and politics, on being in the world, on enjoying it and on attempting to transform it according to the principle of justice, and that the significance of Levinas's project is consequently not limited to philosophy considered as a discrete academic discipline. My point is thus to show that cultural studies – which has so far drawn more explicitly on disciplinary methods and approaches proposed by media communications, sociology, English literature and history – has a great deal to gain from an engagement with Levinas's work.

This is not to claim that I attempt to 'discover' Levinas for cultural studies, and that no one before me has pointed to the 'usefulness' of Levinas's philosophy for culture and politics. But it is this 'usefulness' and 'appropriation' that is also contested here. I am aware of what Barbara Johnson has termed, somewhat dismissively but perhaps also justifyingly, 'a Levinas effect' (2000: 62) in the contemporary humanities, which reduces any interaction between human beings to an encounter between the dominant self and the oppressed other. Not only does the original power relation remain intact in this encounter (as the colonial, masculine, heterosexual, etc. self is only confirmed in its position of domination), but any debates on colonialism, gender inequality or homophobia end up being reduced to 'victimhood studies'. This 'Levinas effect' can perhaps also be observed in cultural studies, with frequent talk about the need to replace domination with respect, knowledge with responsibility and any sense of political unity with the celebration of cultural difference. (One does not need to be a reader of Levinas to be familiar with these propositions.) What I therefore attempt to do in this book is postulate a more rigorous engagement with Levinas's work on ethics. This engagement goes beyond reflecting any dispersed 'Levinas effect', an effect which either sidesteps any actual reading of Levinas or reduces it to 'moral soundbites'.

The reason for my own 'turn to Levinas' is a certain *amour fou*, a passion for Levinas's work, which constantly manages to challenge my understanding of the concepts of justice and the good, of ethics and politics, of vulnerability and violence. I have been returning to Levinas's work on ethics and politics when thinking about media representations of murder and '9/11', about the Holocaust and European anti-Semitism, about feminism and technological experiments in medicine and art. I should perhaps also admit that my reading of Levinas has had something of Jacob's wrestling with the angel about it: not necessarily in its heroism but rather in its stubbornness. Often finding myself puzzled by Levinas's reduction of femininity to fecundity and domesticity, by what sometimes seems like a conflation of ethics and religion, or by some aspects of his politics which allowed him to dismiss the Israeli-Palestinian conflict by saying 'in alterity we can find an enemy. .... There are people who are wrong' (quoted in Campbell, 1999: 39), I have nevertheless been captivated by his idea of ethics 'before ontology', a demand on being that goes beyond any set of rules. But *The Ethics of Cultural Studies* is a product of two loves: it also arises out of a passion I have had for the academic developments that have occurred over the last few decades under the heading of 'cultural studies'. The book is thus an attempt to bring together these two loves in an effort to articulate an ethical dimension of cultural studies. It is therefore not a case of 'bringing ethics to cultural studies' but rather of staging an encounter between the philosoph-ical tradition as developed by Levinas (and continued, in many forms and disguises, by such thinkers as Jacques Derrida and Ernesto Laclau – though the latter probably would not identify his work as a 'continuation' of the Levinasian thread) and the interdisciplinary project of cultural studies, which provides a privileged point of access to the relation between 'politics' and 'theory' (see Gary Hall, 2002: 11). What allows me to think that this encounter between cultural studies and Levinas is not only desirable but is in fact already taking place is their shared interest in the other, in his or her alterity, destitution and wretchedness. But what Levinas can help us with when it comes to developing a politics of cultural studies is the recognition that the other is always already moral, and thus that our politics cannot be thought without or outside ethics.

LEVINAS'S ETHICS: *MY PLACE IN THE SUN ISN'T REALLY MINE*

Levinas's thought can be said to have been born out of a sense of disappointment with 'the complacency of modern philosophy', which 'prefers expectation to action, remaining indifferent to the other and to others, refusing every movement without return' (1986: 347). The problem with [first] philosophy, according to Levinas, is that its wisdom is reduced to self-consciousness, as a result of which '[i]dentical and non-identical are identified. The labour of thought wins out over the otherness of things and men' (1989a: 78). One can notice here the invoca-tion of Marx's critique of Western idealism as a project whose premises were based only on understanding the world, not on transforming it.[10] (Incidentally, this passage from Marx's *Theses on Feuerbach* often serves as a starting point for the discussion of cultural studies' political engagement on many undergraduate cultural studies courses.) Levinas's project thus begins with a call for action, for direct involvement, for the examination of lived lives. His philosophy is directly indebted to Husserl's phenomenology, which links the production of meaning with our lived experience, as well as pointing to the fact that our consciousness is an intentionality which is always in contact with objects outside of itself. For Levinas, phenomenology is 'a way of becoming aware of where we are in the world' (Levinas and Kearney, 1986: 15).

It is not only discovering our place in the world but also accounting for it that constitutes the main premise of Levinas's thought. My 'place in the sun' is for Levinas always a usurpation, it is never *originally* mine; instead, it belongs to the Other whom I may have oppressed, starved or driven away from my home, my life and my space (see Levinas, 1989a: 82-5). My being in the world thus requires justification; I need to keep asking myself if my existence is not already a usurpation of someone else's place. This is not to say that Levinas would not recognize that, for example, some of us will spend our lives in celebratory self-aggrandizement, not really worrying too much about our place in the world, about the origin of the goods supposed to satisfy our consumerist pleasure (be it the latest digital cameras, cars or replica football kits), about global market mechanisms instantiated in the process of their production and distribution, or about the implications their manufacture will have on the planet's resources. But no matter how much we buy, inject and absorb into our own selfhood, for Levinas we always find ourselves standing before the face of the Other, which is both our accusation and a source of our ethical responsibility. It is both mine and the Other's mortality, our being in the world as 'being-towards-death', that inscribes our lives in an ethical horizon; and it is the Other's death in particular that challenges me and calls for my justification. Levinas writes:

> [I]n its mortality, the face before me summons me, calls for me, begs for me, as if the invisible death that must be faced by the Other, pure other-ness, separated, in some way, from any whole, were my business. It is as if that invisible death, ignored by the Other, whom it already concerns by the nakedness of its face, were already 'regarding' me prior to confronting me, and becoming the death that stares me in the face. The other man's death calls me into question, as if, by my possible future indifference, I had become the accomplice of the death to which the other, who cannot see it, is exposed; and as if, even before vowing myself to him, I had to answer for this death of the other, and to accompany the Other in his moral solitude. The Other becomes my neighbour precisely through the way the face summons me, calls for me, begs for me, and in so doing recalls my responsibility, and calls me into question. (1989a: 83)

I perhaps need to mention here that we should not be tempted to reduce Levinas's thought to a politics of guilt, echoing the Judaeo-Christian obsession with disobedience, sin and God's wrath. Even though the Judaic tradition does inform Levinas's work in more than one way, and even though references to the idea of God feature prominently in his writings, God is not the *principle* of ethics for Levinas, nor does He provide a *positive content* in Levinas's ethical theory. Rather than as a religious project, Levinas's philosophical work should be seen as, first of all, an opening within the edifice of Western philosophy, or as a way of thinking that poses a challenge to the traditional (Greek) mode of philosophizing which shapes our concepts of time, space, truth, good and evil. What Levinas is attempting to achieve in his writings – predominantly in his two major volumes *Totality and Infinity* and *Otherwise Than Being* – is a postulation of ethics as a first philosophy, situated *before* ontology. This 'before' should not be understood in a temporal sense: from a linear temporal perspective (i.e. the concept of time that organizes our conceptual universe) ontology cannot be preceded, as there *is* nothing before being. However, if ontology (i.e. a 'philosophy of being') is seen as a 'philosophy of power' and 'injustice' (Levinas, 1969: 46) that tries to reduce any idea of the other to the terms and categories possessed by the same (which amounts to describing to what extent the other *is* or *is not* like me), ethics should be read as a different mode of thinking, one which 'precedes' ontology in its relation to knowledge and justice. Instead of attempting to thematize and conceptualize the other as always already known, ethics points to the radical and absolute alterity of the other which collapses the familiar order of Being and calls the self to respond to this alterity. This possibility, as well as necessity, of responding to what Levinas defines as an incalculable alterity of the other is the source of an ethical sentiment. Refusing to assert the self's primacy, Levinas focuses on the vulnerability of the self when facing the other, who is always already 'absolutely other', and who cannot be fully grasped by the self. This other-ness can evoke different reactions in the self. But even though the other can be ignored, scorned or even annihilated, he or she has to be first of all addressed (responded to) in one way or another. Levinas accounts for this 'pre-temporal responsibility' in the following way:

> Responsibility for the Other, for the naked face of the first individual to come along. A responsibility that goes beyond what I may or may not have done to the Other or whatever acts I may or may not have committed, as if I were devoted to the other man before being devoted to myself. Or more exactly, as if I had to answer for the other's death even before *being.* A guiltless responsibility, whereby I am none the less open to an accusation of which no alibi, spatial or temporal, could clear me. It is as if the other established a relationship or a relationship were established whose whole intensity consists in not presupposing the idea of community. A responsibility stemming from a time before my freedom – before my (*moi*) beginning, before any present. ... A responsibility for my neighbour, for the other man, for the stranger or sojourner, to which nothing in the rigorously ontological order binds me .... (1989a: 83–4)

ETHICS AND RESPONSIBILITY: *THE WRETCHED STRANGER IS MY MASTER*

There is something profoundly difficult about attempting to understand Levinas's idea of the other who puts me in question and makes me responsible.[11] The Other's position before us is somewhat paradoxical: he is 'the stranger or sojourner', the widow and the orphan, but at the same time the master and the lord, 'whom one approaches as "You" in a dimension of height' (Levinas, 1969: 75). Yet this difficulty is precisely what Levinas is highlighting with this paradox. To explain its working we need to look at the instances in which ethics takes place. For Levinas, an original relation with an exterior being always occurs in discourse, and it is in discourse that ethics is sited. In order to explicate this idea, Levinas refers to the philosophy of dialogue developed by Martin Buber. But he also takes issue with the formalism and symmetry of the 'I-Thou' relationship in Buber's work, a relationship that subsumes the heterogeneity of the speaking beings into the primordial communicative project instantiated by dialogue. Levinas argues that the discursive relationship between the self and the other is not reciprocal. It is not an exchange between equals, nor should it be seen as organized by a prior idea of communicative success or spiritual unity. Instead, discourse always comes from the other, because 'It is not I, it is the other that can say *yes*. From him comes affirmation; he is at the commencement of experience' (Levinas, 1969: 93).[12] In this way, Levinas points to the fact that I am not the source of meaning in the world, that I am born into the universe in which meanings – coming from the other – circulate, and that I can only *respond* (in fact, I have to respond) to what precedes me. This response (even if performed in the greatest arrogance and self-illusion about one's originality and self-sufficiency) is also already a welcome, it is an opening to, and a recognition of, the other, of his destitution, wretchedness and suffering, but also of his infinite alterity. It is in this sense that ethics for Levinas is primordial, and that it is inevitable.

Let us reiterate that this inevitability does not mean that the other cannot be annihilated – it is precisely the possibility of killing the Other, and the fact that 'the Other is the sole being I can wish to kill' (Levinas, 1969: 198) that make the relationship between us ethical. The *physical* possibility of taking the Other's life does not therefore contradict what Levinas describes as 'an *ethical* impossibility of murder' (198; emphasis added). If 'Murder exercises power over what escapes power' and if 'I can wish to kill only an existent absolutely independent, which exceeds my powers infinitely', my attempt at the total negation of Infinity only confirms it (198). Levinas's philosophy is thus a blow to human self-aggrandizement; it is a philosophy of humility, but not in a traditional Christian sense, more in a sceptical sense of the recognition of one's limitations. We may of course ignore these limitations, but to do so would be both tragic and foolish. Thus this 'respect for the other', celebrated in some cultural studies' approaches and embraced by multiculturalism, must not be reduced to the decision of a self-contained ego: it needs to spring from a recognition of the fact that 'Over him I have no power' (Levinas, 1969: 39). It is the relation with the Other that 'introduces me to what was not in me' and it is the Other that founds my idea of reason. In this way, the Other allows for a passage from the 'brutal spontaneity of one's immanent destiny' to the idea of infinity which 'conditions nonviolence' and thus 'establishes ethics' (Levinas, 1969: 203–4).

With Levinas we are thus introduced into an entirely new conception of the ethical, a conception which engages with, but also departs from, the ethical model developed by Immanuel Kant. The significance of Kant's work on ethics must not be forgotten – his was one of the first ethical systems in Western philosophy to be freed of the need for a positive metaphysical foundation. Morality for Kant had to come from *our* reason, rather than from any external concept of the good, and it did not involve any non-universalizable principles.[13] Levinas's ethics is also foundation-less, which means that it is not based on any prior principle to which I can refer in order to verify my obligation and my morality. But for Levinas it is the Other who is the source of both my reason and my obligation. Obligation thus *happens to me*, it precedes me. This obligation is free of any specific content – Levinas does not therefore give us a list of commandments, he does not tell us how to live and act. It is obligation *as such*, rather than an obligation *to do something*, that is the source of ethics. John Caputo explains that what Levinas calls ethics does not actually *exist*, but 'is a kind of hyperbolic demand on existence' (1993: 120). Caputo finds a way out of what some see as a 'religious impasse' of Levinas's philosophy by reading his Other as a 'prophetic hyperbole, as a great as if' (18), which is 'a poetic ... name for that fact, as it were, of obligation, of heteronomy, that we do not belong to ourselves, that we are always already held first in the grip of something I know not what, *je ne sais quoi*, something *heteros*, something absolutely *heteros* – almost' (83).[14]

POWER STRUGGLE: *AGAINST TOTALITY*

Levinas's work contests the 'self-centered totalistic thinking that organizes men and things into power systems, and gives us control over nature and people' (Wild, 1969: 17). In a similar vein, cultural studies has always taken issue with the actions of those whom Levinas terms 'totalizers', who 'are satisfied with themselves and with the systems they can organize around themselves as they already are' (Wild, 1969: 17). The cultural studies' project has, from its inception, been premised on the critique of the idea of totality which is enacted in our socio-political life. Significantly, Levinas's analysis of the notion of power developed in *Totality and Infinity* starts from the questioning of self-power – and this is precisely the point at which cultural studies can, perhaps even should, turn to Levinas. This is not to dismiss the self-critical work that has already taken place in cultural studies – one can think here of the problematization of the West as a meaningful unity, of the exposition of the power mechanisms organizing the position of the cultural critic or of cultural studies' engagement with psychoanalysis which pointed to the intrinsic limitations of the 'knowing subject' – but rather to remind us that this process of self-investigation must be interminable. An encounter with Levinasian ethics allows us to cast light on an ethical injunction that arises out of our positioning in the world *in the face of the other*, whose alterity precedes me and defies my conceptual grasp. This ethical injunction does not come *from* Levinas (which is why cultural studies does not *need* Levinas to make its project 'complete'), but Levinas's work can help us articulate this injunction and understand its inevitability. It can also allow us to rearticulate the cultural studies project in the discourse of responsibility, which will protect it against the self-aggrandizing rhetoric of some forms of left politics. (The next chapter will discuss the cultural studies project in the context of responsibility.) This is not to say that, via Levinas, cultural studies will become less political, that its turn to ethics will necessarily involve a departure from its political engagement. On the contrary, I suggest that it is *only* through its openness to the ethical that cultural studies can understand, and meaningfully perform, its politics.

DECISION: *BETWEEN POLITICS AND ETHICS*

This brings me back to Ernesto Laclau's explication of politics through his reference to an ethical investment that we as members of a particular community made at some point in our lives. Laclau postulates that singular political actions are always 'enveloped' in a universal ethical dimension. He explains this by looking at the aims and desires behind a number of such actions. One could assume, claims Laclau, that the achievement of the desired aims through particular interventions – such as participation in a strike for a rise in wages or in a factory occupation for improvements in working conditions – would put an end to the workers' movement. However, he argues that these aims can be read in a broader context as representing a desire for achieving 'something that utterly transcends them: the fullness of society as an impossible object which – through its very impossibility – becomes thoroughly ethical. The ethical dimension is what *persists* in a chain of successive events in so far as the latter are seen as something which is split from their own particularity from the very beginning' (Butler, Laclau and Žižek, 2000: 84). The ethical is for Laclau an infinite horizon against which particular political claims can be made – and it is *only* against this horizon of infinity, or, better, universality, that these particular claims can be asserted. This is to say, first, that the authors of these claims need to 'rise above' the level of real material conditions and reach for the immaterial, the not-yet, and, second, that their specific aims have to be formulated against the idea of justice that transcends these claims, i.e. that they need to evoke a sense of the universal to claim this particularity.

It is perhaps something of a commonplace to state that political action – be it participation in anti-capitalist protests, in demonstrations in support of student grants or affirmative action or in 'pro-choice' rallies intended to give women control over their bodies – requires a decision. But to acknowledge the inevitability of decision in our political lives does not necessarily amount to being transparent about the mechanisms involved in the decision-making process. As explained above, every decision needs to transcend the particularity of a given political claim and situate itself against the idea of universality, of what Laclau terms a 'full' (i.e. just, satisfied, whole) society. Yet at the same time Laclau recognizes that this fullness of society is nothing but a myth, and that the social is open and unfixed (1990: 28). Society as a stabilized entity is impossible as its constitution is intrinsically antagonistic, and there is nothing that can ensure the ultimate resolution of all social antagonisms. This is why, although it will be positioned against the horizon of universality (as its point of reference or comparison), the decision we make can be 'grounded on no a priori principle external to the decision itself' (Butler, Laclau and Žižek, 2000: 84). This is precisely where the radicality of our political actions – and, by extension, of the cultural studies project that concerns us here – springs from.

However, Laclau is quick to point out that the question regarding the grounds for choosing one particular option rather than a different one is not actually so relevant, as any decisions we are likely to take will always be context-bound. As he explains in *New Reflections on the Revolution of Our Time*, the denial of such a limited context, i.e. the assertion of full contingency of any decision, 'would only make sense for an inhabitant of Mars':

> It is true that in the *final instance* no objectivity can be referred back to an absolute ground; but no important conclusion can be drawn from this, since the social agents never act in that final instance. They are therefore never in the position of an absolute chooser who, faced with the contingency of all possible courses of action, would have no reason to choose. On the contrary, what we always find is a limited and given situation in which objectivity is *partially* constituted and also *partially* threatened; and in which the boundaries between the contingent and the necessary are constantly displaced. (1990: 27)
>
> . . .
>
> [T]he Cartesian illusion of an absolute starting point must also be given up, since the person making ethical judgements is never an abstract individual, but a member of a certain community that already believes in a number of principles and values. (1990: 243)

The above provides a useful response to all those who deny the significance of deconstruction (or, more broadly, poststructuralist theory) for cultural studies and cultural politics. The opponents of deconstruction and post-Marxism claim that if there are no external grounds for a decision that would be justified by the existence of a certain notion of God, truth or human values, then we will end up with chaos, 'postmodern nihilism' and relativism, and a political impasse. What Laclau argues, in turn, is that even though we do not have a universal ground on which we can base our decisions, we always operate in a specific situation, and that our scope of available options is usually limited by the situation in which we find ourselves. Laclau's contingency (in a similar vein to Derrida's 'undecidability') does not thus mean being forever stuck between equally valid options without knowing which one to choose. Contingency already inheres an ethical *injunction to choose*, to make a decision. Even though Laclau acknowledges the limitedness of every 'context' in which we find ourselves, as if 'carved' from the horizon of infinity, he also recognizes that this limitedness gives us a reason to choose and helps us make a decision. The content of this decision is not prescribed in advance; it is only the *need* to choose, to respond to the options before us (even if by withdrawal, apathy and doing nothing whatsoever), that is being pointed out here. (One can make a link here with the Levinasian ethics which is instantiated by the Other's call, as an invitation to respond and a simultaneous impossibility of *not* responding.)

Even though we never *fully* operate within the horizon of infinity, we can never be *ultimately* sure about the rightness of our choice, as there is no pre-given, universal framework to legislate it. Laclau states, 'As with anything else, the limits of moral opinions are essentially open and no final closure can be granted by any kind of ethical discourse' (1990: 243). The acknowledgement of this horizon of infinity, and of the fact that at no moment in time will we be able to grasp all the available options, makes Laclau advise vigilance towards our own position in the world. Our decision-making process must never therefore be separated from an investigation of the construction of the conditions of possibility that inform our decision. It is precisely this openness of the ethical that allows for the political to take place. As I mentioned earlier, for Laclau society is not 'all that is': it is rather a temporary stabilization of power, or a collection of 'the sedimented forms of "objectivity"' (1990: 35). A harmonious society is impossible because antagonism – which inheres destabilization – is its constitutive element. As Laclau explains, 'The moment of antagonism where the undecidable nature of the alternatives and their resolution through power relations becomes fully visible constitutes the field of the "political"' (1990: 35). Social relations for Laclau are always power relations, and the constitution of any social identity is itself an act of power.

ARTICULATION: *THERE IS NOTHING OUTSIDE DISCOURSE*

In order to explain how the process of social change actually occurs, i.e. how the sedimented power structures are loosened up to allow for the emergence of other forms of social organization, Laclau introduces into his work the notion of articulation. Articulation names a process of the creation of something new out of a dispersion of elements (1990: 183); it describes 'any practice establishing a relation among elements such that their identity is modified as a result of the articulatory practice' (Laclau and Mouffe, 1985: 105). Laclau and Mouffe relate this notion to the concept of 'discourse', which for them names a structured totality resulting from articulation (Laclau and Mouffe, 1985: 105). It is worth stressing here that for Laclau *all* social practice is articulatory; i.e. that it has a discursive character. Articulation involves a temporary stabilization of signifiers, a meaningful arrangement whose conditions of possibility lie within the signifying system of which we all partake. Again, this does not mean that these conditions are prescribed in advance – indeed, the temporary links between different concepts (e.g. that between sovereignty and divinity in medieval political systems, or between freedom and democracy) are not necessary, and they occur at the expense of temporarily excluding the possibility of some other links being established. The process of establishing these links between concepts allows for the transformation of social reality and for the creation of new modes of being. It is in this sense that social transformation has a discursive character, which does not mean that everything is being 'reduced' to discourse, only that the role of signifying structures in making reality available and meaningful to us is recognized as crucial. It is not to say, either, that discursive change 'leads to' change in reality – instead, it is to highlight the foundational role of articulation in effecting change in the world.[15] As Laclau explains, 'if contingency penetrates all identity and consequently limits all objectivity, in that case there is no objectivity that may constitute an "origin": the moment of creation is radical – *creatio ex nihilo* – and no social practice, not even the most humble acts of our everyday life, are entirely repetitive. "Articulation", in that sense, is the primary ontological level of the constitution of the real' (1990: 184). For Laclau articulation is capable of establishing reality, not merely describing it. It is precisely through an engagement with Laclau's notion of articulation (developed as it was from the Marxist theories of Louis Althusser and Antonio Gramsci) that Stuart Hall has introduced this concept to cultural studies, as a 'remedy' against cultural studies' early Marxist reductionism and essentialism. According to Jennifer Daryl Slack, articulation quickly became 'one of the most generative concepts in contemporary cultural studies' (1996: 112), leading to what has sometimes been described as its 'linguistic' or 'discursive turn'.[16]

While the possibility of establishing some new social conjunctures can be a source of political hope, it is the ethical horizon against which political acts are being performed that interests me here. Significantly, this radical articulatory moment – creation *ex nihilo* – is described by Levinas as always taking place against the horizon of infinity, which is a constitutive ground of ethics. Creation *ex nihilo*, claims Levinas, 'breaks with the system, posits a being outside of every system, that is, where freedom is possible' (1969: 104). Expressing a multiplicity which is not united in a totality, this radical moment of creation points to the self's opening onto the idea of infinity, of which it is not the cause, and which is introduced into it through an ethical relationship with the other. This idea of infinity coming from the other is the guarantee of the self's freedom and of the possibility of breaking through the sedimented relations of power.

ANTAGONISM IN THE PLURAL: *THE END OF CLASS POLITICS?*

The constitutive nature of power relations is one point that cultural studies has taken on board as a result of its engagement with Marxism.[17] The intrinsic antagonism of the social, which is shaped by competing particularist claims, is not something that can be appeased or resolved. Instead, cultural studies has focused on attempting to understand the nature of these plural antagonisms while acknowledging that they cannot be hierarchized through the privileging of class as a dominant category of social inequality. This interest in different social identities, and in the power mechanisms involved in their production, has sometimes led to cultural studies being accused of losing a real political purchase and of becoming reduced to 'victimhood' or, to use Slavoj Žižek's term, 'bias' studies (Butler, Laclau and Žižek, 2000: 230–3). What gets overlooked in these criticisms is the fact that cultural studies' interest in different forms of marginalization is not just about the celebration of the oppressed. This type of critique pushes the centre, i.e. those occupying more dominant cultural positions, to look at and question their own relation to power (see Gilroy, 2000; Giroux, 2000c). But the charge that is really being raised against cultural studies in these attacks is its disavowal of class politics and its dispersal of the political struggle into a number of particularist battles defined 'only' in terms of cultural positions. Incidentally, they are the same charges that have been raised against the work of Ernesto Laclau and Chantal Mouffe, whose ideas have become increasingly important in cultural studies.[18] Laclau and Mouffe's post-Marxist position, first elaborated in their *Hegemony and Socialist Strategy* (1985), is developed from the close reading of the concept of hegemony as it was used in traditional Marxism. Jeremy Gilbert explains that

> once it is realized that the structure of society is the product of the political interaction of competing forces – the struggle for hegemony – rather than an expression of underlying economic laws, the deterministic verities of classical Marxism (the base/superstructure metaphor, the

'false consciousness' model of ideology, the notion of the inevitable and implacable progressive development of the productive forces, class essentialism) become untenable. This might seem like a sufficient explanation for why people should be looking for a position which can understand the specificities of given formations in such work: its radically conjunctural mode of analysis emphasizes the specific, the local and the contingent at the expense of any notion of historical necessity. (2001: 192)

Laclau and Mouffe's 'superseding of class' has not been a rejection *tout court* or even a 'correction' of Marx, but rather a historicization of his theory and its extension to the field of different historical and political experiences – in the sense that the society Marx lived in was to a large extent a class society, while ours cannot be predominantly defined in class terms (see Laclau, 1990: 161–3). Still, Laclau and Mouffe's post-Marxist position has been seen by some as a betrayal of 'real' politics and as a co-optation by capitalism, with its rhetoric of cultural identities and cultural differences. They defy their opponents by insisting that their argument allows for a radicalization of Marxism without abandoning its political commitment, and that their conclusions regarding the contingency of history and the superseding of class as a dominant social category are not at all pessimistic. Abandoning an aspiration to a single foundation of the social and pointing to the radical historicity and contingency of social relations entails the acknowledgement of the fact that these relations 'can be radically transformed through struggle' (Laclau, 1990: 35–6). And if power is the condition for society to be simultaneously possible and impossible, and if power struggles cannot be classified a priori in terms of their significance, 'social transformation means building a new power, not radically eliminating it' (31). However, even though there is no external legitimating framework for this transformation, the process itself has to occur against a horizon of justice. This is precisely where ethics is needed – provided ethics is understood here not as a set of rules but rather in the sense delineated in this chapter, as a demand on being and a call to response and responsibility.

ETHICS BEFORE POLITICS: *LOOKING OUTSIDE*

It is in this sense that ethics is crucial – one can perhaps even say foundational – to cultural studies. This way of understanding ethics should prevent us from reducing it to mere 'moral outrage', to compassion or sympathy for the victim. Ethics as I understand it is not a sentiment; it is not a post-factum reaction to an event. Instead, ethics is foundational and prior to being – as explained by Levinas – and thus, since it precedes ontology, it also precedes politics. (This is of course not to say that ethics is 'more important than' politics, only that it precedes, and makes demands on, the order of being.) As we can never escape ontology, it is politics that gives a name to our everyday actions to transform the world. Socio-political trans-formation occurs at the material level, which is the level of society and the state, but also of the everyday and the minuscule. But if politics and social transformation are about eradicating injustices of power (see Laclau, 1990: 31), the decision as to what action to take and how to respond responsibly to an event that we are faced with is already inscribed in the horizon of ethics. Should we refuse to acknowledge the ethical dimension in every political act, we risk reducing politics to an application of a rule, a software programme for repairing the world.

But we must also not forget that ethics does not amount to a closed system of morals, and that any such system in existence at any moment in time is always a result of a hegemonic struggle. Our task, cultural studies' task, consists thus in responding to the congealed system of values – through 'argumentative moments' and interventions – while remembering that there can be no closed ethical system which will be permanently filled with universal content. Cultural studies needs to assert the contingency and historicity of all values as well as reflect on its own ethicity, its own rela-tion to values (be it equality, recognition or respect for cultural difference). It is therefore not enough to claim, as Douglas Kellner does, that cultural studies remains in close relation to ethics because in the 1970s and 1980s it developed 'an ethical critique of all cultural forms that promoted oppression and domination while positively valorizing texts and representations that produced a potentially more just and egalitarian moral order' (Kellner, un-dated). This 'approach' assumes that values are already *firmly* in place, and that the task of cultural studies consists merely in comparing the current cultural practices against this template of values that all human beings at a given time allegedly share. What remains unquestioned in this approach is the very constitution of these values, as well as cultural studies' relation-ship to them, and, hence, to power. Ien Ang contends that the moral(istic) critique of oppression – of racism, for example – will simply not do, because it does not take account of the deeper, more pervasive sense of identity panic and identity (de)formation at work in the culture that produces this critique (2000: 5). It is thus not 'culture as such' that is found to entail an intrinsic 'moral dimension' – as Kellner would like it. Rather, a performative and contingent character of morals in culture has to be asserted and examined by cultural studies. This of course does not amount to moral 'relativism' – itself 'an invention of the fundamentalists', according to Laclau – but it involves the investigation of the sedimented power structures that have authorized certain morals, and looking at what remains *outside* such established moral discourses, at what disrupts them and challenges their legitimacy.

The Civic Quarter Library

Borrowed

Customer   Wajgan, Harim

	Due Date
The ethics of cult	17/7/2009,23:59
The student's guid	17/7/2009,23:59
Ethics for the inf	17/7/2009,23:59
Research ethics fo	17/7/2009,23:59

22.05.2009 15:16:55

Notes

1 For a more positive interpretation of Reading's critique of cultural studies, where cultural studies is mobilized as a place from which the university can rethink its own institutional and intellectual tasks rather than wallow in self-pity over its ruinous state, see Gary Hall's *Culture in Bits*, especially the section titled 'This is Excellent' (2002: 118–22).

2 I have already acknowledged in the Preface to this book that one needs to be wary of such straightforward narratives of cultural studies' origin, but I also recognize the usefulness of many such accounts when working out one's own position in and on the field. In addition to the texts mentioned in Note 1 to the Preface, I would like to direct those readers who are interested in debates over the role, position and definition of 'culture' in cultural studies to Jessica Munns and Gita Rajan's edited collection, *A Cultural Studies Reader* (1995) and John Storey's *What Is Cultural Studies?* (1996).

3 Henry Giroux takes issue with both the 'neo-conservative' and 'progressive' positions on education and cultural studies in the US in his article 'Cultural Politics and the Crisis of the University'; he also provides a useful summary of these positions. What he finds disturbing is

> the common ground shared by a growing number of conservatives and progressives who attempt to reduce pedagogy to technical formalism or a reified methodology, on the one hand, or narrowly define politics and pedagogy within a dichotomy that pits the alleged 'real' material issues of class and labor against a fragmenting and marginalizing concern with the politics of culture, textuality, and difference, on the other. (2000a: unpag.)

4 Austin divides all speech acts into constative and performative ones, i.e. statements perceived as true or false descriptions of facts ('It is raining'), and statements which accomplish something through speech itself ('I pronounce you man and wife'). In *Limited Inc* (1988), Derrida performs a deconstruction of this opposition and argues that performativity is in fact the feature of all utterances, not just select ones. I discuss this point in detail in Chapter 3; however, for the time being I just want to draw the reader's attention to Austin's original conclusion regarding the performative function of language; i.e. its ability to perform deeds at the very moment of their utterance. The concept of performativity will be important for me in this and other chapters.

5 It was Simon Critchely who both drew attention to the ethical dimension of Laclau's work and called on Laclau to articulate his own understanding of the relationship between ethics and politics more explicitly. See their debate in *The Ethico-Political Issue*, vol. 4 of *Culture Machine* (Zylinska: 2002b).

6 'Consider the situation in which racist speech is contested to the point that it does not have the power to effect the subordination that it espouses and recommends; the undetermined relation between saying and doing is successfully exploited in depriving the saying of its projected performative power. And if that same speech is taken up by the one to whom it is addressed, and turned, becoming the occasion of a speaking back and a speaking through, is that racist speech, to some extent, unmoored from its racist origins? ... That the utterance can be turned, untethered from its origin, is one way to shift the locus of authority in relation to the utterance' (Butler, 1997: 92–3).

7 Since its foundation in 1999 *Culture Machine* (http://www.culturemachine.net) has positioned itself as seeking out and promoting the most provocative of new work, and analyses of that work, in culture and theory from British and international authors. But it is volume 6 (2004) in particular, co-edited by Dave Boothroyd, Gary Hall and myself, that explores and articulates the relationship between cultural studies and deconstruction.

8   Quoting extensively from Derrida's essay, 'As If I Were Dead' (1996), Gary Hall (2002:62) explains the difficulty involved in any attempt to 'apply' deconstruction to any academic work, as follows:

> Jacques Derrida has insisted on numerous occasions that deconstruction is not a theory or program that can be simply 'applied' to a given text or object:
>
>> it cannot be applied because deconstruction is not a doctrine; it's not a method, nor is it a set of rules or tools; it cannot be separated from performatives, from signatures, from a given language. So, if you want to 'do deconstruction' – 'you know, the kind of thing Derrida does' – then you have to perform something new, in your own language, in your own singular situation, with your own signature, to invent the impossible and to break with the application, in the technical, neutral sense of the word. (217)
>
> But if '[d]econstruction cannot be applied', neither can it 'not be applied'. Derrida readily acknowledges that if, 'on the one hand, there is no "applied deconstruction" ... on the other, there is nothing else' precisely because 'deconstruction doesn't consist in a set of theorems, axioms, tools, rules, techniques or methods':
>
>> If deconstruction, then, is nothing by itself, the only thing it can do is apply, to be applied, to something else, not only in more than one language, but also with something else. There is no deconstruction, deconstruction has no specific object, it can refer to, apply to, for example, the Irish problem, the Kabbalah, the problem of nationality, law, architecture, philosophy, amongst other things. It can only apply. (218)

9   An excellent explanation of this process can be found in Derrida's classic essay, 'Structure, Sign and Play in the Discourse of the Human Sciences' included in his *Writing and Difference* (1978).

10   In his interview with Richard Kearney, Levinas explains: 'In Marx's critique we find an ethical conscience cutting through the ontological identification of truth with an ideal intelligibility and demanding that theory be converted into a concrete praxis of concern for the other' (Levinas and Kearney, 1986: 33).

11   In his writings Levinas distinguishes between *autrui* (the personal other, the you, translated by Alphonso Lingis as Other) and *autre* (other). Lingis explains that this translation, undertaken with Levinas's permission, regrettably sacrifices the possibility of reproducing Levinas's own use of capital or lower-case letters with both these terms in the French text (Levinas, 1969: 24–5). Levinas frequently alternates between the two within any one paragraph.

12   This point will be taken up by Derrida, who will inscribe his deconstructive thinking in the framework of affirmation, a 'multiple yes'. We can already see this in 'Structure, Sign and Play', where he counterpoises the thought of the negative (which he associates with a nostalgia, or perhaps even melancholia, for the lost or impossible presence of the absent origin) with the Nietzschean 'affirmation of the play of the world ... the affirmation of a world of signs without fault, without truth, and without origin which is offered to an active interpretation' (1978: 292). His essay on Joyce, 'Ulysses Gramophone: Hear Say Yes in Joyce' (1992d), develops this point further.

13   Catherine Chalier provides a thorough and elegant account of Kant's and Levinas's ethical positions, and of the points of convergence between their theories, in *What Ought I to Do? Morality in Kant and Levinas* (2002).

14   For a thoughtful engagement with Caputo's ethics of obligation, which exposes its limitations without denying its appeal, see William Connolly (1999). Connolly argues that Caputo's other is always a needy other, a state of events which can be disabling for politics. Arguably, something of the triumphalism of Levinas's Other as master gets lost in Caputo's account.

15   This does not mean that the world does not exist without us but that it only exists 'for us' if we can make sense of it, if we relate to it through the systems of meaning at our disposal. Even such experiences as 'pain' or 'love' are never entirely pre- or extra-linguistic. For us to recognize them as 'pain', to *know* what is happening to us – even if we are in the deepest throes of suffering – we need to have an *idea* of what pain 'is'.

16   Exposing the reductiveness of Marxist economism and the contingency of all social identities, the concept of articulation has allowed cultural studies practitioners to engage with different positionalities outside the strict class paradigm – such as race, gender, sexuality and age. It has also allowed for the rethinking of the strict distinction between 'politics' and 'culture', and for developing a new form of 'cultural politics' – to the dismay of both traditional right-wing thinkers (such as, for example, Harold Bloom or Lynn Cheney) and traditional left-wing critics (including Terry Eagleton and Todd Gitlin) (see Giroux, 2000a).

17   The articulation of this problematic through the discourse of power took place in cultural studies predominantly via the work of Michel Foucault.

18   In her Postscript to the *Cultural Studies* collection edited by Grossberg, Nelson and Treichler (1992), Angela McRobbie argues for the significance of Laclau and Mouffe's post-Marxism for cultural studies on two principal grounds: 1. its recognition of the unavoidability of conflict in society, without locating this conflict solely in class terms (this allows cultural studies to engage with a series of equivalent claims to do with sexuality, gender, race, etc.); 2. the fact that its politics is not rooted in a fixed notion of agency but rather that it espouses partial, fluid identities. Post-Marxist ideas have become important for the 'newer' generation of cultural studies scholars in the UK, including Paul Bowman and Jeremy Gilbert (see Bowman, 2001; Gilbert, 2001).

2

Ethics and Cultural Studies

IDLE STUDENTS AND TABLOID PRINCESSES

Richard Dawkins, author of the celebrated *The Selfish Gene* and the first Charles Simonyi Professor of the Public Understanding of Science at Oxford University, is deeply committed to the propagation of science. For over thirty years now he has been trying to attract the uninitiated on both sides of the Atlantic to the recognition of scientific wonders, which have frequently been occluded by myth, superstition and ill-will. But Dawkins's popularization of science is not compromised by what is commonly known as 'dumbing down'. Indeed, the premises of his project, recently delineated in his book *Unweaving the Rainbow*, are extremely serious:

> 'Fun' sends the wrong signals and might attract people to science for the wrong reasons. Literary scholarship is in danger of being similarly undermined. Idle students are seduced into a debased 'Cultural Studies', on the promise that they will spend their time deconstructing soap operas, tabloid princesses and Tellytubbies. Science, like proper literary studies, can be hard and challenging but science is – like proper literary studies – also wonderful. (1998: 23)

In order to promote his scientific project, Dawkins constructs a series of springboards for his argument which allow him to differentiate the wonders of science from the horrors and offences of some other disciplines and areas of enquiry. Adopting the much coveted role of the not-necessarily-first Professor of the Public Mis-Understanding of Cultural Studies, he attacks the 'idle students' of popular culture whose minds have been desensitized, barring them from the recognition of the true beauty of proper science and good literature. A number of very serious decisions have been taken here. Dawkins knows in advance, in a somewhat mock-Leavisite manner, what counts as 'proper literary studies' (the book abounds with references to Coleridge and Keats), while at the same time he fears that this propriety will be contaminated by the fun of a 'debased "Cultural Studies"'. While science and 'proper literary studies' are undoubtedly both hard and wonderful, cultural studies, masquerading in 'the meaningless wordplays of modish francophone *savants*', seems to have no other function than to 'impress the gullible' (Dawkins, 1998: 41).

This type of argument is part of a long tradition of 'cultural studies bashing', an attitude that was reinvigorated through the so-called 'Sokal affair' of 1996.[1] As Jennifer Daryl Slack and M. Mehdi Semati argue, critical responses of this kind 'can best be understood in the context of conflicts between the sciences and the humanities in conjunction with anti-liberalism, anti-intellectualism and conflicts among the left over what constitutes a legitimate politics' (2000: 216). What is most significant about these attacks is the insubstantiality of the target they adopt and rely on. Slack and Semati explain that this method works 'by fixing an indeterminate target, to give an illusion that something which is in fact concrete and ridiculous (like the figure of a ghost) is under attack' (217). For this purpose, the identity of cultural studies has to be both pre-decided and excluded from investigation '*to garner support for what is already known*' (234, emphasis added): indeed, the vehemence of such arguments depends on the refusal to engage with, or perhaps the misunderstanding of, the debates *within* cultural studies concerning its legitimacy, its disciplinary boundaries and its political commitment.

This is not to say that to retain its political force as an 'intervention'[2] cultural studies has to resist *out of principle* both identification and institutionalization. Cultural studies has already developed an identifiable 'tradition', with all its accompanying institutions and power structures: university departments, research centres, publishers' outlets, conferences, grant awarding bodies, etc. A number of scholars would probably scoff at Dawkins's caricatured view of cultural studies, and – with a kind of satisfaction and relief associated with 'homecoming' – welcome the positioning of their books in the 'cultural studies' section of academic and mainstream bookshops and publishers' catalogues. As an example of one such acceptance of cultural studies in the academic community, let me refer to Judith Halberstam's Introduction to her extremely interesting book *Female Masculinities*. According to its author, this book 'will be immediately recognized as a work of cultural studies' (1998: 13). Although Halberstam problematizes further the strict definitions of gender – and of masculinity in particular – prevailing in cultural studies, she has no doubt that what she describes as her 'queer methodology', attempting 'to combine methods that are often cast as being at odds with each other', clearly belongs to this old–new discipline that Dawkins perceives as fit only for idle students and equally idle scholars. However, her apparently innocent remark in passing (i.e. Halberstam's book is not so much *about* cultural studies as about the construction of masculinity as natural in our culture through its association with, on the one hand, physical maleness, and, on the other, prosthetic extensions to the body *à la* James Bond), which quickly asserts the validity and acceptance of cultural studies as an academic discipline, seems to coincide strangely with Dawkins's dismissal of it. As far as the response to the discipline of cultural studies is concerned, these two approaches situate themselves at the opposite ends of the emotive spectrum. What they share is *an unquestioned decision, made in advance, about what cultural studies is.* This decision consequently allows both Dawkins and Halberstam to progress with their different arguments (i.e. the defence of science and of gender construction respectively). It seems to me that Halberstam's taken-for-grant-edness of cultural studies – even if expressed in the form of an 'aside', and featuring in an explicitly political contribution to transgender debates – can itself be seen as a somewhat dangerous (perhaps even irresponsible) pre-empting of the need to go about tracing the foundations and orientations of cultural studies. By assuming a prior knowledge of what cultural studies is, Halberstam inadvertently allows for the usurpation of this 'knowledge' (as an attitude which in fact constitutes a substitute of 'knowledge') by those who are ready to launch a conservative attack on what they both fear and loathe.

It is this act of making a decision about what cultural studies is in advance, without attending to the ideas, debates and traditions of the disci-pline that can certainly be 'hard and challenging', even if it does not need to exclude 'fun', that I am interested in exploring in this chapter. Arguing for the ethical orientation of the '(anti?)discipline' of cultural studies, I want to ground my ethical investigations in the concept of responsibility. As well as investigating the responsibilities that cultural studies has or provides, I want to explore our responsibility towards cultural studies, a responsibility which manifests itself in an attitude of enquiry and respect which will not allow us to decide in advance what cultural studies is, and which will also, therefore, save it from pre-closed attacks of the Richard Dawkins kind.

CULTURAL STUDIES AND ETHICS

By introducing the notion of responsibility to debates on cultural studies, I do not intend to attempt to turn the tide of 'fun' Dawkins and other critics associate with cultural studies, and impose instead a sense of solemnity and seriousness in to this oft denigrated area of academic enquiry. My argument is that a sense of duty and responsibility has always constituted an inherent part of the cultural studies project, and already manifested itself in the early adult education movement, the work of the Birmingham Centre for Contemporary Cultural Studies and in the writings of Raymond Williams, Richard Hoggart and Stuart Hall. In all of these, the critique of the status quo – where critique does not stand merely for criticism or polemic but rather, as Richard Johnson explains, for 'procedures by which other tradi-tions are approached both for what they may yield and for what they inhibit' (1995: 575) – has been connected 'with political causes in the broader sense' (577). Johnson's formulation is akin to the pronouncements made by a number of other cultural studies theorists and practitioners – one can think here of Stuart Hall's conviction that cultural studies should develop 'intellectual and theoretical work as a political practice' (1999: 103) or Tony

Bennett's more recent proposal for 'cultural policy studies' (see 1998). And yet when declaring the field's overt political commitment, cultural studies' theorists frequently avoid addressing ethical questions up front, even if, one could suppose, the whole issue of the responsibility of cultural studies, its duties, engagements and flirtations, has always been played out in the area *between* politics and ethics.[3] By situating the discussion of cultural studies in an ethical framework I thus intend to cast light on what, to some extent, has remained latent in its direct investigations and programmes, while at the same time providing a justification for them. So, rather than attempting to *bring ethics to* cultural studies, I want to argue that the interdisciplinary multinational project of cultural studies *has always had* ethical underpin-nings. This perspective will allow me to challenge the populist view of cultural studies as a debased academic discipline. As well as retracing the ethical dimension of cultural studies and its links with more overtly political discourses, I will also attempt to interrogate the nature and the possible justification of cultural studies' current responsibilities.

I would like to begin this process of 'retracing' ethics in cultural studies by turning to an article which, for the first time, inscribed the work conducted within cultural studies in the discourse of ethics. Originally presented at an international conference 'Cultural Studies Now and in the Future' held at the University of Illinois in 1990, the essay in question, 'Ethics and Cultural Studies' by Jennifer Daryl Slack and Laurie Anne Whitt, was subsequently included in the *Cultural Studies* anthology edited by Lawrence Grossberg, Cary Nelson and Paula Treichler. The significance of this essay should not be underestimated. Slack and Whitt set themselves the ambitious task of demonstrating that ethical commitment – even if not formulated in clearly recognizable philosophical terms – has always defined the cultural studies project. To prove this point, they go back to what they term 'the Marxist-humanist' origin of cultural studies as delineated by Richard Hoggart, E. P. Thompson and Raymond Williams. Slack and Whitt see the three 'founding fathers' of cultural studies as united in their ethical commitment to opposing 'the instrumental reduction of the human' (1992: 576) to a dispossessed and disempowered social mass. People, or here, specifically, the working class, are seen as 'a group of atomistic individuals recognized as possessing intrinsic, non-instrumental value' (577). It is this intrinsic value of the human, and of singular human life, that the early project of cultural studies is engaged in recognizing and protecting. Williams's conviction that 'culture is ordinary' and Thompson's analysis and critique of class struggle are intended to defend all those whose intrinsic human value has been obscured through unfair social and economic practices. Slack and Whitt assert that this kind of ethical atomism is continued in further developments in cultural studies, where the locus of human value is extended to include people of different races, genders and subcultures. The expanded scope of 'social others' does not challenge the individualist humanist assumptions organizing the cultural studies thinking in the 1970s and early 1980s. The real change comes, according to Slack and Whitt, with what Stuart Hall described as the structuralist turn in cultural studies, which shifts the focus of attention and analysis away from dispossessed individuals toward the larger social structures within which these individual subjects are constructed. As a result moral agency, which was previously found in individual human beings, is now dispersed throughout social formations such as the state, church, family, education system, etc.

At this point there occurs a radical and somewhat unexpected twist in Slack and Whitt's story. In their linear discussion of the development of ethical thought in cultural studies the two authors turn to postmodernism, which for them stands for 'the loss of criteria for moral judgement' (581) and, consequently, has 'serious and disturbing implications for a politics and ethics' (582). Slack and Whitt see postmodernism as a kind of anti-Hegelian *Aufhebung* in which the two trends of cultural studies identified by Stuart Hall as 'culturalism' and 'structuralism' collapse into moral vacuum, resulting in the withdrawal, even impossibility, of ethics in cultural studies. They declare that 'postmodernism leaves us normatively adrift, thereby vitiating the possibility of a politics and an ethics that can motivate the interventionist moment of cultural studies' (582). Accepting at face value the dour conclusions regarding the impossibility of ethics from a postmodern perspective, they add a fourth (prosthetic) leg to the Hegelian tripod by proposing a turn to a 'new totality'. Opposing the 'old totalities' which are presumed to be bad and oppressive, Slack and Whitt argue for a 'concept of totality that has been carefully thought through in terms of a "unity in difference"' (584). It is in environmentalism, which expands its scope of subjects from the human to the non-human and which embraces our planet 'as a whole', that they find an ethical grounding for the new project of cultural studies.

> The ecosystem replaces the individual as the fundamental moral datum, or unit of moral analysis, in terms of which we do our thinking about what is morally right and wrong. ... [T]o do so is consistent with the project of cultural studies and in many respects represents an extension rather than a rejection of its normative commitments. It is also a move for which cultural studies has been well prepared, given the persistent and dynamic tension throughout its history between atomism and holism. (572)

Now I do not want to argue against the importance of this turn to environmentalism, or eco-culturalism. Indeed, a number of projects conducted under the generic term of bioethics have been embarked upon since the publication of Slack and Whitt's essay, and have been accompanied by a wide body of cultural studies' publications on the subject.[4] What concerns me here is rather the validity of, and justification for, this turn, positioned as an escape from the moral snares of postmodernism. Even though it is not my aim to present an apology for postmodernism here, I nevertheless feel that this 'third moment' in Slack and Whitt's account of cultural studies' development (a narrative which is symptomatic of many accounts of the politics of cultural studies in the early 1990s) needs to be revisited in order to search for a few of the ghosts that threaten to haunt the ethical universe of their 'new totality'. Tellingly, Slack and Whitt rely on a very narrow, almost caricatured version of 'postmodernism' as a state of moral confusion and the 'devaluation of all values'.[5] But at the same time this definition of postmodernism needs to involve a certain openness and conceptual vagueness against which more 'focused' political and ethical propositions can be formulated. Let me repeat once again that it is not my intention to 'correct' Slack and Whitt's view of postmodernism, or to defend postmodernism as a viable ethical option. A veritable rag-bag of ideas, postmodernism does not seem to me to be a particularly useful concept when it comes to explaining the project of cultural studies. What I would like to look at instead is a cultural ethics and politics 'after postmodernism' – 'after' not in the sense of moving 'beyond' postmodern discourse in the temporal sense, but rather as a taking into account of the problems regarding individual agency, totalization and the (im)possibility of maintaining a unified political project – in order to trace some new forms of the ethical and the political in cultural studies.[6] Such an engagement with some of the assumptions of postmodernism – be it in the form of their rejection or incorporation – disallows a return to the concepts of 'atomism' and 'holism' as we know them. Instead, this kind of engagement (which, in a way, is impossible *not* to maintain, even if it takes a form of outright rejection or 'forgetting') results in a radical shake-up of the foundations of the ethical discourse of, and in, cultural studies. It is the consequences of this shake-up that I want to discuss below.

THE CULTURAL STUDIES OF DIFFERENCE

One must see oneself as others do. The other's view cannot be totally alien or external, since it has constituting effects. ... One can never be fully at home with, or trusting of, oneself. Decentred, partially estranged, multiple, overdetermined subjectivity is not a postmodernist conceit. Colonized and culturally, racially, or sexually defined 'others' have long been familiar with it.

Jane Flax, 'Race/Gender and the Ethics of Difference'

While I share Slack and Whitt's concern about the ethical and political implications of cultural studies, I do not embrace their conviction that some time in the early 1990s cultural studies suddenly *stopped* being an ethical project and that it had *lost* its political commitment. What they describe as 'the ceaseless production and celebration of a radically relativized difference' seems to be an easy – one could even say 'unethical' – dismissal of an important process of cultural studies' opening to multiple differences that have not yet been identified or named in any programmatic way. It seems to be precisely this undecidability of the cultural studies' project that Slack and Whitt are anxious about and that they sum up with the negative term 'relativism'. But rather than agree with their conclusion that, with postmodernism, cultural studies has been deprived of 'the possibility of a politics and an ethics that can motivate the interventionist moment in cultural studies', I would like to propose a slightly different conclusion: perhaps cultural studies has yet to *become* ethical? Instead of seeing it as abandoning its political and ethical commitment for the sake of the 'ceaseless production and celebration of ... difference', perhaps we could conclude that cultural studies has yet to 'teach itself ethics'? I realize that by stating this I have arrived at a contradiction: while this chapter starts with the claim that cultural studies *has always been* ethical I am now concluding that it *has yet to become* ethical. This is actually a key 'aporia' (i.e. a difficulty, a paradox, a passage 'without a passage' which one nevertheless has to attempt to traverse) that I will attempt to disentangle in the further part of my argument.

Let me assure the reader at this point that by stating that cultural studies *has yet to become* ethical I am not single-handedly dismissing the important work conducted in cultural studies over the course of the last few decades by Stuart Hall, Lawrence Grossberg, Henry Giroux, Paul Gilroy, Angela McRobbie or Trinh T. Minh-ha, to name but a few of those whose work has taken the ideas developed in early cultural studies in some new directions. What I am proposing instead is that the ethical project of cultural studies – the realization of which can be found in the work of the above mentioned theorists, in the early Marxist-humanist tradition of British Cultural Studies that Slack and Whitt refer to, and in many contemporary reworkings of this project from the perspective of 'culture and science studies' – can only be seen as a project-in-the-making, one whose conceptual boundaries and agendas are always open to change. And even if this openness deprives cultural studies of the unified 'project' through which it can be defined – a 'loss' for which cultural studies has been attacked by, for example, Nicholas Garnham (1997) or Douglas Kellner (1997) – it actually constitutes an ethical moment that radicalizes cultural studies' aims and agendas.

I want to explain the consequences of describing cultural studies as an open-ended project by referring to the thinking of Emmanuel Levinas. As mentioned in the previous chapter, Levinas is a philosopher readily associated with the question of 'ethics'. Yet this 'turn to Levinas' should not be seen here as an attempt to 'bring philosophy into cultural studies', or to draw on external disciplinary frameworks in order to remedy an alleged 'lack' within cultural studies. Levinas's work is important for my project because of his understanding of ethics outside, or beyond, the traditional discourse of moral philosophy, and because, as I explained in 'The User's Guide to Culture, Ethics and Politics', it embraces the most ordinary events of everyday life: he is interested in workaday encounters with what he defines as 'the alterity of the other', encounters which challenge the familiar and the ordinary. His philosophy thus situates itself in close proximity to cultural studies' conceptualization of culture as 'a whole way of life', and to its interest in the material, the quotidian and the ordinary. Ethics, for Levinas, is not something imposed from outside or above; instead, ethics is *unavoidable*. An ethical event occurs in every encounter with difference. Levinas's project is thus aimed at undermining the guiding principles of traditional Western philosophy, which 'from its infancy ... has been struck with a horror of the other that remains other – with an insurmountable allergy' (Levinas, 1986: 346). Challenging what he perceives as the totality of our culture which most frequently results in egocentrism and violence, Levinas sets out the principles of his ethical project in his major work *Totality and Infinity*. He describes this book as 'a defence of subjectivity'. However, subjectivity here should not be understood 'at the level of its purely egoist protestation against totality, nor in its anguish before death, but as founded in the idea of infinity' (Levinas, 1969: 26). For Levinas, infinity springs from 'the relationship of the same with the other' (26), a relationship which is irreducible to the terms and conditions delineated by the self. This irreducibility of the other to the self creates conditions for the emergence of an ethical moment. Of course, the sentient self can react to the other by either welcoming or rejecting him or her. But this possibility, as well as necessity, of responding – i.e. reacting – to what Levinas defines as an incalculable alterity of the other is the source of an ethical condition (even if not a guarantee of its positive fulfilment). Refusing to assert the self's primacy, Levinas focuses on the vulnerability of the self when facing the other, who is always already 'absolutely other', and whose otherness can evoke different reactions in the self. In this sense, responsibility, which is one of the key terms of Levinas's ethics, does not mean that the other cannot be ignored, scorned or even annihilated, but rather that he or she has to be addressed (responded to) in one way or another. The ethical conditions arise out of this *possibility* of acknowledging and welcoming the alterity which, according to Levinas, is always already part of the self's experience.

It is this challenge to the Western philosophy of totality and universalization that makes Levinas's ethical ruminations valuable for cultural studies. Focusing on the lived experience of sentient beings, Levinas defines responsibility as the necessity of responding to the otherness of the other. As cultural studies has demonstrated, this response can take many forms – from the early anthropologists' objectification of the radicalized other to Cornel West's new cultural politics of difference (1999) or bell hooks's understanding of cultural diversity which must involve dissensus (1999).

There is no guarantee that otherness will elicit an ethical rather than violent response: but it is precisely this lack of a guarantee that gives cultural studies an ethical character.

Two important points emerge here. First, the ethical engagement of cultural studies has to be necessarily 'ceaseless': at no point will we able to arrive at the absolute knowingness of the other. Levinas warns us against the possession and objectification of the other in the following terms: 'The neutralization of the other who becomes a theme or an object ... is precisely his reduction to the same. ... To know amounts to grasping being out of nothing or reducing it to nothing, removing it from its alterity' (1969: 43–4). It seems to me that a cultural studies that defines and fixes its other in order to formulate its agendas and policies is founded upon the suppression of the ethical moment. Let me reiterate that the ethical moment in cultural studies arises out of an encounter with an incalculable difference. This inevitability of encountering difference – which can then be either acknowledged and respected, or suppressed and annihilated – explains the first assumption that organizes this chapter, i.e. that cultural studies has always been ethical, that it constantly finds itself – even positions itself – in ethical situations understood here in the Levinasian sense as an exposure to incalculable alterity. This alterity is always already singular and can be identified in the whole sequence of 'others' that cultural studies has traditionally been interested in – working classes, women, postcolonial/subaltern subjects or, more recently, cyborgs – but also in those for whom we do not yet have a name and whom we cannot grasp with a concept. And yet, at the same time, we have to acknowledge that cultural studies has not always *acted* ethically in the Levinasian sense – i.e. it has not always responded responsibly to the alterity with which it has been faced. Instead, it has at times attempted to reduce alterity to the knowable sequence of important 'others' and thus to prioritize its struggles in terms of bigger and lesser oppression. This allows me to claim that cultural studies has yet to become ethical; it has to adopt an attitude of unconditional openness which does not consume 'the other' in the name of cultural studies' politics.

The second important point that emerges from retracing cultural studies along the lines of Levinasian ethics concerns its pedagogical engagement. Levinas claims that the conversation with the other – for him the pinnacle of an ethical relation – 'inasmuch as it is welcomed ... is a teaching [*enseignement*]. Teaching ... comes from the exterior and brings me more than I contain' (1969: 51). If cultural studies is defined through its discursive engagements with the marginal, the subaltern and the dispossessed, if its project is focused on exploring the relationships of power that contribute to the process of 'othering', this engagement can be described – after Levinas – as pedagogy. Tom Steele confirms this embeddedness of pedagogy in the cultural studies project when he writes that 'interdisciplinary study in adult education was an important precursor of academic British cultural studies, the particular circumstances of which were focused by arguments over the role and status of the "literary" and the "sociological" in adult liberal studies' (1999: 9) But the pedagogic aspect of cultural studies has not been the sole prerogative of the 'British school': Henry Giroux's work on 'critical pedagogy', intended to turn students into active and critical citizens in a democratic society, approaches the question of education from a transatlantic perspective (see Giroux, 1992, 2000b). Significantly, for both Levinas and the cultural studies practitioners, pedagogy is not a separate discipline which can be easily distinguished from among a number of other projects characterizing an engagement with the other; it is its very 'essence'. Alan O'Shea claims that cultural studies' 'object of study, in a strong sense, is pedagogy itself' (1998: 514). However, O'Shea also expresses dissatisfaction with the fact that 'discussions of the institutional practices of cultural studies are underdeveloped, particularly the question of pedagogy' (514). The comprehension of cultural studies' engagement with the other in terms of teaching – not only as a classroom practice but as a wider project of the transmission and transformation of knowledge – prompts us to address the discourse of pedagogy from two sides. It makes us think not only about what cultural studies can teach us (what it can give to others, etc.) but also what cultural studies can learn from the alterity it addresses, embraces and studies. 'Cultural studies as a lesson' must be seen then as a project which is always open to the questioning of its own knowledge *and* self-knowledge, if we accept that 'to know amounts to ... reducing [being] to nothing, removing it from its alterity' (Levinas, 1969: 43–4).

WHAT IS CULTURAL STUDIES? A RESPONSIBLE RESPONSE

The ethical question of/in cultural studies is thus a foundational question: the act of responding to difference, to what calls for recognition and respect, to what is important enough to fight for, founds a discipline of cultural studies. We can turn here again to Levinas, for whom '*The Other produces the I* by putting it in question' (Chanter: 1995, 90). And yet it seems clear from the above that this 'foundational process' must be ongoing. Cultural studies understood as an ethical opening to the incalculable alterity *can never be properly founded*: instead, it can only be described as a project-in-the-making, on-its-way. If cultural studies is being constantly founded by the others it studies, protects, respects and celebrates, the responsibility of cultural studies thus seems twofold. Cultural studies has a duty not only towards the marginal and the dispossessed – towards its 'others' – but also towards itself, its own projects, responsibilities and boundaries. This realization has been evident in the simultaneous emergence of work in cultural studies that addresses such issues as homogenization of power or social injustice as well as investigating its own duties, tasks and responsibilities. And this double-vector decision in cultural studies – inherent, for example, in the title of the *What Is Cultural Studies?* anthology edited by John Storey (1996) – cannot be taken once and for all: it has to be constantly retaken. This does not mean that, rather than concentrate our political energy on resolving the 'real' issues concerning injustice, we will be wasting our time on theoretical investigations and hypothetical word-games. Jacques Derrida, whose work has been significantly 'marginal' in cultural studies (not in the sense of its relative unimportance but rather in the sense of bordering and infiltrating the more 'central' cultural studies debates, often without a direct acknowledgement, or even with a denial thereof), argues for this need for a certain 'undecidability' in any ethical or political project in the following way:

> Far from opposing undecidability to decision, I would argue that there would be no decision, in the strong sense of the word, in ethics, in politics, no decision, and thus no responsibility, without the experience of some undecidability. If you don't experience some undecidability, then the decision would simply be the application of a programme, the consequence of a premiss or of a matrix. So a decision has to go through some impossibility in order for it to be a decision. If we knew what to do, if I knew in terms of knowledge what I have to do before the decision, then the decision would not be a decision. It would simply be the application of a rule, the consequence of a premiss, and there would be no problem, there would be no decision. Ethics and politics, therefore, start with undecidability. (1999b: 66)

For the project of cultural studies to be truly political and ethical, it has to remain open to the possibility of its pervertibility,[7] collapse, annihilation and withering down. To give just one example from the 'cultural populism' debates of the late 1980s and early 1990s, in its exploration of popular culture and consumer pleasure cultural studies has to inhere the possibility of the absorption of its explicitly political dimension by the capitalist industry (something that was feared by, among others, Jim McGuigan and Nicholas Garnham). Any attempt to 'ban' the study of the popular as not political enough, or to accuse cultural critics of mindless celebrationism and 'headlong rush towards the pleasures and differences of postmodernism' (Garnham, 1997: 56), seems from this perspective to be an unethical, one might even say fundamentalist, act of trying to avoid the need for deciding by 'sealing-off' the decision in advance.

But how can such a politics of openness be practised? How does it situate itself in relation to the institutional formation of cultural studies already in place? Let me answer this question by looking at one of its recent institutionalizing projects, i.e. the agenda drawn by the proponents of the International Association for Cultural Studies. The primary aim of such an association is 'To help to promote and represent cultural studies as a legitimate scholarly and academic pursuit. The Association will promote public understanding of what cultural studies is and what it is not. When it is advisable, the Association can speak in defense of the cultural studies project or of particular programs or scholars who are under attack' (Pina, 2000).[8] Now while this project may perhaps seem more 'effective' than the constant deferral of a clearly defined cultural studies' politics (the term 'effective' itself featuring strongly in the proposal for the Association), its results can only be judged in relation to the previously defined criteria. In saying this I am not disputing the need for such an association but rather expressing a concern as to the processes of decision-making that have to be undertaken in order for such an association to be founded. Will there not be a price to be paid for acknowledging and then defending the academic legitimacy of cultural studies? I am concerned whether, defending its legitimacy and its essence ('what cultural studies is and is not'), an association of this kind will not have to establish in advance what belongs to cultural studies proper and what does not; i.e. whether it will not have to assume the predictability of the future and domesticate 'the order of things to come' in order to fulfil its self-appointed duty of evaluating the propriety of academic pursuits taking place within its limits. This is not to say that such an institution is not possible or even desirable: but perhaps its agenda could also include an indictment against what Derrida calls 'the crime of stopping to examine politics' (1997b: 9). Rather than determine in advance whether its activities are legitimate and whether they are political enough, is cultural studies not truly political and ethical only when it pays attention to every singular instance, practice and event, themselves constituting and founding cultural studies always anew? (Of course, for reasons of 'practicality' a number of strategic decisions will have to be made as to which events and occurrences are worth investigating and which can perhaps be left behind – but a decision regarding our choice and its justification cannot be made once and for all.) In this way, cultural studies has to take into account the whole spectrum of possibilities and occurrences, the horizon of which is always partially occluded by what we could describe as the 'spectre of the perhaps'. And yet, the possibility of the emergence of unforeseen intellectual or political tasks, alliances and connections, or even of the ultimate disavowal of the 'politicality' of cultural studies and its interventionist aspirations, also guarantees the openness of the political in cultural studies. The responsible cultural studies cannot avoid the indeterminacy of the perhaps, but it does *not* mean that cultural studies *is sentenced to indeterminacy*: 'If no decision (ethical, juridical, political) is possible without interrupting determination by engaging oneself in the *perhaps* ... the same decision must interrupt the very thing that is the condition of possibility: the *perhaps* itself' (Derrida, 1997b: 67).

These inevitable instances of interruption, legitimation and decision-making always bear the trace of hesitation and doubt, the memory of before-the-event of decision, the possibility of taking 'the other path'. And, while decisions have to be made – unless we can be satisfied with an academicism which believes it can refrain itself from 'arriving at any decision' by engaging in 'pure theorization' – it is precisely in the recognition of their instability that they become intrinsically ethical and political. Derrida acknowledges that this double bind – i.e. our need for knowing, predicting, programming and deciding in advance, coupled with the ultimate impossibility of predetermining what is going to happen and locking this prediction into a socio-political system, or a system of morals – constitutes the condition and the foundation of politics and ethics. He postulates that 'we have to do this, master the surprise, without, if possible, erasing the heterogeneity, the alterity of what is coming, and that is the political and the ethical challenge' (1997a: 7). In order to remain ethical and political, cultural studies does not need to replace its 'intervention into the relations between cultural practices and the social relations and organization of power' (Pina, 2000) with an abstract investigation of its aims and responsibilities: but it needs to allow itself to be constantly surprised by how power is structured and by what its interventions might bring. An attempt to master the surprise can thus be read as a 'call for action' – such as attending ecologist symposia, organizing anti-capitalist rallies, investigating the politics of the popular, listening to subaltern voices or setting up international academic associations – but this form of action, to remain truly political and ethical, has to be accompanied by a form of delay, or deferral. This deferral does not amount to stasis, a kind of theoretical impasse that over-intellectualized cultural studies has got itself into, but is rather a sign of the recognition that the surprise element of any action can never – 'perhaps' even *should* never – be mastered.

CULTURAL STUDIES AS A PROMISE

> The other, like the Messiah, must arrive whenever he or she wants. She may not even arrive.
>   Jacques Derrida, 'Hospitality, Justice and Responsibility'

In their Introduction to *Doing Science + Culture* Roddey Reid and Sharon Traweek declare that, rather than reflect on the history of cultural studies, i.e. its 'canons, traditions, and academic territories', they are more interested in focusing on cultural studies 'as a *promise*, a placeholder for a space of engaged experimentation with those we study and with our own research selves' (2000: 8). The notions of promise and experimentation highlight the open-ended nature of the cultural studies project, a project which is being constantly repositioned and rethought and whose 'outcome' can never be assured. However, contrarily to what Reid and Traweek propose, I do not want to conclude that the reorientation of the cultural studies project towards the future needs to depend on its disavowal of the past, as the extremely promising notion of a *'promise'* arises out of our past experience and current expectations. This is precisely the point at which for me the apparently exclusive trajectories of cultural studies as 'always already ethical' and as 'not yet ethical' come together. The notion of cultural studies as-a-promise describes a messianic project of awaiting the unknown and the not-yet, of opening ourselves not only to the differences we already know and can name but also to those that remain unnameable and unidentifiable, to what may yet surprise and scare us. It is in this very openness to the unknown, to the forms of political engagement that cannot yet perhaps be described in the discourse of cultural theory, sociology, ethnography or any other more established disciplinary discourses, that cultural studies becomes intrinsically ethical. We have nevertheless to move beyond the traditional concept of politics which is focused on the state, its achievements, plans and policies, towards what Derrida calls in his essay devoted to Levinas a 'messianic politics' (1999a). For Derrida messianic politics constitutes a viable political option arising out of the renunciation of a desire to rule, control and master; it is a politics which does not compromise its commitment even if it does leave a specific agenda behind. What we are left with are 'ways of respecting or greeting what remains to come – a future of which we know nothing. What comes will never belong to the order of knowledge or foreknowledge' (Derrida, 1999a: 77). A cultural studies which renounces the desire to know, to close off the dissensus, to erase incalculable alterity, but which does not at the same time sidestep its political commitment, presents itself as both an ethical possibility and a responsibility.

Notes

1   Even though predominantly targeted at the work of selected European philosophers (or, 'the Left Bank intellectuals', as the cover of *Intellectual Impostures* has it), Sokal's intentionally nonsensical article on physics and relativism published by *Social Text* in 1996, and his book *Intellectual Impostures* (1998), which he co-authored with Jean Bricmont, were quickly identified by the 'general public' as an attack on cultural studies. But it is precisely Sokal and Bricmont's lax, untheorized or, indeed, ignorant use of such concepts and terms as 'postmodernism', 'philosophy' and 'cultural studies' that has fostered this perception.

2   For an interesting discussion of cultural studies as an intervention and the meanings this concept has acquired in the work of different cultural studies theorists, as well as the coverage of the institutionalization processes in, and of, cultural studies, see Ted Striphas (1998: 454).

3   For the discussion of an inevitable relationship between politics and ethics – areas which should not be treated as identical but which cannot be entirely separated either – see Jacques Derrida (1999a) *Adieu to Emmanuel Levinas* and Simon Critchley (1999) *Ethics – Politics – Subjectivity.*

4   I take up bioethics as one possible paradigm for an ethics of alterity in the biotech age in the last chapter of this book.

5   Of course, Slack and Whitt were not alone at the time in associating postmodernism

with the 'devaluation of all values'. For a similar account see, for example, Dick Hebdige (1988) *Hiding in the Light*, a collection of essays which interprets postmodern life as 'life on another planet'. Hebdige hopes we will soon be able to return from this planet to recapture the certainties and truths that we have, in a moment of madness, left behind.

6   In this sense, Slack and Whitt's 'environmentalism' could be read as a form of what I term here 'politics after postmodernism' in the sense of a negotiation with the political and ethical discourses of both the past and the present. However, environmentalism is only one of a number of other projects that have evolved in recent years. Other projects include radical democratic movements, feminisms, Reclaim the Streets campaign in the UK, multinational anti-capitalist and anti-globalization movements, and hackerism.

7   The pervertibility of ethics is also its first and foremost condition. As Geoffrey Bennington explains, '[T]his pervertibility is the positive condition (to be affirmed, then) of all the "positive" values (the Good, the Just, and so on) ethics enjoins us to seek' (2000: 72).

8   Posting to the cultural studies mailing list, <cultstud-l@lists.acomp.usf.edu>, by Alvaro Pina on 15 November 2000. The Association for Cultural Studies was subsequently founded at the Fourth International 'Crossroads in Cultural Studies' Conference, held in Tampere, Finland, 29 June–2 July 2002. More information about the Association can be found on its website: http://www.cultstud.org.

3

Ethics and 'Moral Panics'

GUNS, YOUTHS AND HIP-HOP – A FEW FAMILIAR STORIES

The Wessex Scene, 23 January 2003[1]
It may sound absurd, but Birmingham is increasingly being compared to the worst parts of Los Angeles, while some areas of London are said to be more dangerous than Soweto. And while this street warfare has caused many deaths, there have been few convictions, as English gangs practise their own Mafia-inspired code of silence.

Organised crime is on the increase not only in Britain, but worldwide, particularly in Europe, and many argue that much of the so-called 'gun culture' is inspired by American gangsta-rap. Artists such as Snoop Dogg, NWA and the late Notorious B.I.G. are frequently condemned for espousing the values of violence, intolerance and the idealisation of guns in their music, with some US rap stars gaining greater prestige for their personal gun convictions. Closer to home, Ashley Wallace, aka Asher D of So Solid Crew, was jailed for 18 months last year for the possession of a revolver and live ammunition.

Following a dispute at a New Year party in a hairdresser's salon in Birmingham in the early hours of 2 January 2003, two teenage girls were shot dead and another two were injured. Charlene Ellis, 18, and 17-year-old Latisha Shakespeare, both died in the attack. Charlene's twin sister, Sophie, and another young woman, Cheryl Shaw, 17, were wounded. The four black teenagers were hit by a hail of bullets when, together with the other revellers, they stepped outside the salon for some air. They are considered to be innocent victims of the 'turf war' between local gangs.

The UK Home Secretary, David Blunkett, embraced a familiar line of reasoning in response to the Birmingham events – a reasoning which had previously associated the 1999 Columbine School massacre with the music of Marilyn Manson, and the murders carried out by the alleged Satanist Robert Steinhaeuser in a German school in April 2002 with the lyrics of the death metal, hardcore and hip-hop band, Slipknot. Blunkett announced that he was 'appalled' by some lyrics in rap and hip-hop music, and called on the record industry to stop glamorizing murder and black-on-black violence. In a similar vein, Culture Secretary Kim Howells suggested that rap groups, in particular London's garage collective So Solid Crew, were at least partly to blame. Fuming that 'Idiots like the So Solid Crew are glorifying gun culture and violence', Howells insisted

'people' should stand up to 'idiot macho rappers'. In a bizarre logical twist, the
argument that the two teenagers killed in Birmingham had been avid fans of rap
music was also frequently quoted in the media debates about their killing.

TIME *magazine Europe*, 20 January 2003[2]

[T]he Jan. 2 shootings and the gun-crime statistics don't surprise those who live
in Britain's inner cities, where drug gangs, particularly Jamaican dealers, protect
their multimillion pound profits with weapons ranging from replica pistols
and modified air guns to lethal Uzi submachine guns. [The race adviser to the
London mayor] Jasper says guns, many smuggled in from the Balkans, are easily
bought or rented, and that while the gangs are often homegrown, top killers, or
'shottas', are sometimes flown in from Jamaica to carry out assassinations.

Although Britain's inner cities are not nearly as violent as America's, the com-
bination of guns, drugs and gang culture makes for a volatile atmosphere. In
gangland interactions, perceived slights — over an inadequate display of 'respect',
say — can bring the guns out. One young Londoner says many of her friends have
stopped going to parties because even a spilled drink can lead to a shooting. Police
say some black inner-city youths use guns as fashion accessories. In London
last year, 20 of the city's 22 gun homicides were the result of black-on-black
crime. Simon Hughes, a Liberal Democrat frontbench MP for a South London
constituency, says 'the culture isn't limited to youngsters of Caribbean extrac-
tion but is spreading out into other black communities, and into Turkish and
Balkan ones'.

And thus the link between urban youth, gun crime, and rap and hip-hop music
was once again confirmed as fixed, as an undisputed object of police inquiry and
a problem that the government and other socio-political apparatuses needed to
'look into' and 'resolve'. Through constant comparisons with the United States,
through the evocation of its 'ghettos', and through the perception of urban crime
as a central symbol of tensions besetting Western social and political life in
general, race was established as a structuring element in the media and political
debates about 'gun crime'. This kind of rhetoric prepared the ground for a
moral panic – a term originally used by sociologists to describe the 'mounting of
a symbolic crusade' (Cohen, 2002: 3) against a perceived threat in a society at
a particular moment in time – connected with young black males. A number
of complex socio-economic problems have thus been subsumed under an all-
embracing label: 'black-on-black crime'. However, it was the very impossibility
of confining this 'crime-wave' to the black community, i.e. its penetration into
'mainstream society' through the rhythms of rap and hip-hop, that instigated
the panic involving guns, inner-city crime and So Solid Crew in Britain at the
beginning of the year 2003.

CULTURAL STUDIES AND 'MORAL PANICS'

The above story is symptomatic of the moral panics involving 'crime' and 'race' that I want to focus on in this chapter. However, I will not be conducting a sociological analysis of the phenomenon itself – which is not to say that detailed empirical studies of the causes and effects of gun violence, its racialization and its all too easy associations with rap, hip-hop and garage music are not necessary.[3] But I'm more interested here in the structuring of the *discourse of moral panics* in and by cultural studies, and in developing a cultural studies' response to such panics, in order to raise some broader questions about cultural studies' ethics and politics. 'Moral panics', I want to argue, constitute significant moments in society's self-affirmation as they simultaneously establish and legitimate its principles of social conduct and civic duty, i.e. its morality. My study of the principles of right conduct (*morality*) will nevertheless extend to the investigation of the 'lived moral philosophy' (*ethics*) which underlies – but which also, in some instances, contests and challenges – the established morals. This will lead me to ask whether cultural studies can *see ethics differently*; whether it can delineate a non-programmatic ethical response to ever-pervasive moral panics. In this respect, what interests me in particular here are the numerous passages from – or rather between – ethics and morality, but also between ethics and politics, that cultural studies has traversed.

My distinction between these various concepts derives from the thought of Emmanuel Levinas, who claims that 'while morality ... operates in the socio-political order of organizing and improving our human survival, it is ultimately founded on an ethical responsibility towards the other' (Levinas and Kearney, 1986: 29). For Levinas ethics is always already primary; it is an unconditional demand placed 'before-time' on conditioned beings that find themselves put in question and challenged by what is absolutely other to them. Thus the only passages that are both possible and necessary for a human society are those *from* ethics *to* morality, and *from* ethics *to* politics. Levinas argues:

> Ethics, as the extreme exposure and sensitivity of one subjectivity to another, becomes morality and hardens its skin as soon as we move into the political world of the impersonal 'third' – the world of government, institutions, tribunals, prison, schools, committees, and so on. But the norm that must continue to inspire and direct the moral order is the norm of the interhuman. If the moral–political order totally relinquishes its ethical foundation, it must accept all forms of society, including fascist and totalitarian, for it can no longer evaluate or discriminate between them. (Levinas and Kearney, 1986: 29–30)

While I remain in agreement with Levinas's diagnosis of ethics as *prima philosophia*, I want to trouble the directionality of the passages it is supposed to instantiate. The shift *from* ethics *to* politics seems somewhat problematic, as Jacques Derrida has demonstrated in his readings of Levinas. It will rather be the (irresolvable) tension, or aporia, between the two in the cultural studies project that will interest me here. But my reading *will* assert the Levinasian understanding of 'an excess of the ethical over the political, an "ethics *beyond* the political"' (Derrida, 1999a: 61).

Developing further some of the ideas raised in the previous two chapters, I will postulate that the cultural studies project, traditionally defined in more overtly political terms, has always been underpinned by an ethical injunction; that it has always been, *in the last* – but perhaps also *first* – *instance*, ethical (even if it has allowed its ethical vigilance to slip at times). Cultural studies has perhaps come closest to acknowledging this ethicality in its interrogation of morality in the 'moral panics' phenomenon, some- thing which has been a focus of a number of significant works. Drawing on two such 'classic' texts – Stanley Cohen's 1972 *Folk Devils and Moral Panics: The Creation of Mods and Rockers*, and Stuart Hall, Chas Critcher, Tony Jefferson, John Clarke and Brian Roberts's 1978 *Policing the Crisis: Mugging, the State, and Law and Order* – I want to explore some of the ways in which cultural studies has engaged with ethics and politics. Cohen's and Hall *et al.*'s texts are well worth revisiting because of the role they have played in shaping the discipline of cultural studies, in providing its 'foundation' and a justification for its political commitment. Significantly, for both Cohen and Hall *et al.*, moral panics are not really 'about' morality: the actual battle is seen to be taking place on the *political* front, where personal and group values and beliefs are being mobilized in the service of the dominant ideology. And it is on the political front that Cohen, Hall and a number of other cultural studies theorists often attempt to fight against 'moral panics', arguing that the panics are both a response and a control mechanism which arises in times of the loosening of the socio-political order. The discourse of panic is said to introduce or defend a set of concepts which are supposed to ensure the continued dominance of the leading class, with its institutions, ideologies and values. But in my reading of *Folk Devils and Moral Panics* and *Policing the Crisis* I hope to provide a different interpretation of those classic texts.

The inspiration for my reading comes from the thought of Jacques Derrida, whose work on deconstruction has been crucial for the reconsidera- tion of the law, legitimacy and justice in the ethico-political context. Indeed, it has enabled us to think about ethics and politics in a radically different way. Intervening into the field of oppositions, deconstruction results in a displacement of the system which relies on these oppositions; it consists in 'reversing and displacing a conceptual order as well as the nonconceptual order with which it is articulated' (Derrida, 1988: 21). We can thus speak about the revolutionary potential of the deconstruction, of its inherent promise of (socio-political) transformation which also entails a certain danger. And yet, due to Derrida's unwillingness to articulate a programme, manifesto or even a coherent theory and due to his insistence on the 'deferral of meaning' which always escapes ultimate fixing, deconstruction has been 'accused of encouraging procrastination, neutralisation, and resignation, and therefore of evading the pressing needs of the present, especially ethical and political ones' (Derrida, 1994: 31). In response to those criticisms, Derrida has explained that deconstruction, or *différance*, is a thought of 'a relation to what is other' which 'relates to what is to come, to that which will occur in ways which are inappropriable, unforeseen, and therefore urgent, before anticipation' (Derrida, 1994: 31). In its opening to the other deconstruction takes place 'ethically', if ethics is understood in Levinas's terms as an ordering 'towards the face of the other' contracted as a debt 'before any freedom' (Levinas, 1998: 10–11).[4] Set in motion by the idea of justice – an idea that for Derrida delimits an 'undeconstructible horizon' against which all 'concrete', political decisions take place – deconstruction becomes 'a thought of the pressing need' (Derrida, 1994: 31). The need in question is that of responding to the other, to the future, to 'the event' understood as something I can neither (ultimately) avoid nor appropriate. It is this pressing need to intervene in the systematic structures of authority and power that I take from Derrida's deconstruction of the law, and it is in this spirit that I propose to revisit the discussion of morality, politics and the law in *Folk Devils and Moral Panics* and *Policing the Crisis*. Deploying my own armoury of what I will call, somewhat tentatively, 'deconstructive manoeuvres', I will now turn to examining the assumptions regarding morality and ethics which organize Cohen's and Hall *et al*.'s studies.

BEWARE THE FOLK DEVILS!

On the whole, most sociologists and lay commentators have a fairly clear sense about what constitutes a moral panic. There are disagreements and difficulties over most social science concepts, but this is one that has been widely accepted and put to good use.

K. Thompson, *Moral Panics*

In *Folk Devils and Moral Panics*, Cohen uses the term 'moral panics' 'to characterise the reactions of the media, the public and agents of social control to the youth disturbances – the seaside fights between Mods and Rockers – in 1960s Britain' (Thompson, 1998: 7). He explains that a moral panic usually starts with a nomination of somebody (Rockers) or something (drugs) as a threat to dominant values or interests. This perception is then picked up and developed by the media – one of society's 'moral entrepreneurs' that both shape and guard the dominant values. Media reporting of the panic results in a rapid build-up of public concern and a response from a number of other 'moral entrepreneurs': figures of authority, experts and opinion-makers (see Thompson, 1998: 8). Significantly, the panics are never actually resolved, even though they might result in some social changes; instead, they tend to develop a 'spectral presence' which envelops the allegedly regained 'normality'.

Tracing the subsequent stages of the panic's development, Cohen does not look closely at its moral side – for him morality seems to take the form of what cultural studies will later describe as an 'ideology', a 'taken-for grantedness', a common-sense belief in ideas and values. In his constant emphasis on the 'sociological' approach of his work, his embracing of the 'labelling' theory, and in leaving the discussion of morality to the philosophers, Cohen constructs his argument on a foundation (i.e. the moral panic 'label') that he himself is in the process of elaborating. It is thus perhaps not surprising that Cohen *cannot* in fact engage with the morality that allegedly shapes these panics. His argument *points to, as if from outside*, and simultaneously *establishes*, the morality that causes the panic, even if this morality is firmly ascribed to the 'other': the news journalist, the social preacher, the 'law-and-order' guardian. I am not claiming here that, before Cohen, the British society of the 1960s and 1970s *did not have morality*; that it took a critical sociologist to *give it morals*. Rather I want to draw attention to the performative character of 'morality', to the fact that the critic's articulation of it participates in the process of drawing moral boundaries, of naming what belongs within their limits and what does not.

My understanding of performativity here is indebted to Derrida's deconstruction of the opposition between constative and performative utterances in Austin's speech-act theory, i.e. between statements perceived as true or false 'descriptions' of facts, which always involve a citation of a referent which is structural to them ('*The sky* is blue', '*The morality of British society* is like this'), and singular events which accomplish something through speech itself ('I pronounce you man and wife'). In *Limited Inc*, Derrida questions Austin's assertion that performatives need to be seen as 'special cases' in language due to the fact that they do not have their referent outside of themselves. Introducing the notion of iterability (1988: 13–19), Derrida argues that performatives cannot be perceived as structurally different from constative utterances because, for the former to succeed (i.e. to lead to a ship being named or a couple being married), their very formulation also needs to repeat a 'coded' or iterable formula, which has to be identified in some way as a 'citation'. If citation is at the core of *every* utterance, the distinction between speech acts that 'merely' name the status quo and those that actually produce it is revealed as untenable. And, further, if the production of reality is accomplished through a process of iteration, if iterability is creative rather than just repetitive – as was assumed by Austin in case of performatives – all speech acts which belong to the 'ordinary language' can be seen as productive, even if, in the speaker's intention, they are used *only* to describe reality. There is creation involved in every speech act, even if this creation remains obscured, unintentional. For Derrida, all utterances are thus performative, but performativity can be, perhaps to some extent must always be, unconscious. One of the most significant points in Derrida's reading of Austin comes for me in his taking issue with the logic of Austin's passing off 'as ordinary an ethical and teleological determination' of utterances (1988: 17). In this way Derrida links performatives (i.e. all forms of human communication) with an ethical and teleological determination, but he also points to the fact that this determination recedes into the unconscious, and is often presented as natural. (On the social level this process, which always involves operations of power, will be later described by Ernesto Laclau with the Gramscian term 'hegemony' – a point to which I will return later on in this chapter.)

Derrida's exposition of the ethical determination of articulation allows us to cast a different light on Cohen's engagement with moral panics. The overlooking of any thorough discussion of the question of morality in Cohen's book, his treatment of the process of the 'drawing and reinforcement of moral boundaries' (2002: xxxv) in the moral panic as transparent, obscures the very mechanisms involved in the production of 'society's' *ethos*, a process that involves both the observer and the observed, the critic and 'his' object of study. However, morality and ethics enter Cohen's argument 'through the back door' – even if he himself remains somewhat oblivious to the arrival of this unexpected guest. It is precisely in this 'ethical invasion', in this 'hospitality by stealth', that the promise of *Folk Devils and Moral Panics* lies for me. Cohen argues that most people in a society share common values and are able to recognize when the violation of these values occurs. In times of moral panic they are more open to this consensus than ever, but in order to maintain the sense of their own moral boundaries, to forge and confirm their morality, they need the figure of a deviant, a 'folk devil'. 'The deviant is seen as having stepped across a boundary which at other times is none too clear' (58). Two sets of boundaries (or oppositions) are being established in this pronouncement. On the one hand, we have the boundary separating 'society' from its 'deviants' – and this is the level that Cohen focuses on when describing the process. But there is also another level to this analysis – one that draws a boundary line between 'society' and the sociologist – although it remains unidentified in Cohen's argument. For me, these two levels of analysis imply the existence of two different forms of morality represented by the different groups or 'entities'. The first opposition, that between 'society' and its 'deviants', sets *morality understood as fear of losing an established way of life* (but also, in Cohen's implicit interpretation, as irrationality) against the *(a)morality of delinquency*, understood by Cohen as a 'reaction … to growing up in a class society' (lxvii). But it is in the second opposition – that between 'society' and the sociologist (society's critic) – that morality, understood as the 'hardened skin of ethics', to paraphrase Levinas, opens up to 'the norm that ... continue[s] to inspire and direct the moral order'. This norm reveals itself in the *commitment to exposing hegemony – i.e. the sedimentation of social identities and structures – and to rearranging (rearticulating) these identities and structures according to a principle of justice* (a principle that in itself requires a prior ethical investment). Cohen's book thus seems motivated by his own ethical investment; his commitment to a political intervention against the control of 'the means of cultural reproduction', his desire 'to identify and conceptualise lines of power' and the forms of manipulation used on 'us' by those in power (xxxv). The political and ethical significance of Cohen's sociological analysis of subcultural events that are perceived as criminal activities due to their nonconformity with the prevailing norms and values should not be underestimated. And yet at the same time there is something rather *un*ethical, I dare say, about his disavowal of ethics.

CULTURAL STUDIES' ETHICAL BLIND SPOT

The possibility of a more up-front ethical response to moral panics is something that is brought about by another 'key' cultural studies' text: *Policing the Crisis* by Stuart Hall, Chas Critcher, Tony Jefferson, John Clarke and Brian Roberts. Traditional interpretations of the book written both from 'within' and 'without' cultural studies have usually foregrounded its political aspects; i.e. its diagnosis of the crisis of capitalism and a consequent increase in state authoritarianism. Reflecting on these interpretations, Kenneth Thompson explains that Hall *et al.* saw the moral panic around mugging as manufactured by the ruling elite to divert attention from the crisis in British capitalism (Thompson, 1998: 10). For Thompson and a number of other critics, *Policing the Crisis* dealt primarily with structural tendencies in British political life, that is with the ways in which institutions tended to favour certain interpretations of events that had the effect of maintaining social order, because they were 'structured in dominance' (18–19). However, what I want to suggest here is that, as well as being a political intervention into the workings of hegemony, the book can be read as delineating an ethics that provides an alternative to the ethos of capitalist individualism and middle-class respectability. In this way, it develops further an ethical proposal which only remains a glimmering promise in Cohen's work. I thus want to revisit *Policing the Crisis* in order to look at the *foundations* of the moral panics Hall *et al.* analyse, and at their links with ethics. Drawing on the development of Gramsci's notion of 'hegemony' (which informs *Policing the Crisis*) in the work of Ernesto Laclau and Simon Critchley, but also on the 'deconstruction' of state laws and institutions performed by Jacques Derrida, I want to explore the ethical dimension of hegemony. My ongoing contention, however, is that the ethical dimension has been something of a blind spot when it comes to moral panics – overlooked not only by the so-called moral entrepreneurs who orchestrated those panics but also by many a cultural critic who diagnosed them.

POLICING THE (RACIAL) CRISIS

The moral panic that was of particular interest to the authors of *Policing the Crisis* concerned 'mugging' in Britain in 1972–3, a phenomenon that 'fits in almost every detail the process described by Cohen' (17). Hall *et al.* set out to investigate why society entered a state of moral panic about 'mugging' at that particular historical moment, which they define in terms of a 'crisis'; but also 'how the themes of *race, crime* and *youth* – condensed into the image of "mugging" – came to serve as the articulator of the crisis, its ideological conductor' (viii). The 'mugging label' itself arrived from the United States; it had an aura of sensationalism about it and carried anti-crime, anti-black and anti-liberal connotations. Acknowledging that it is impossible to explain the severity of the reaction to these crimes by using arguments based solely on the objective, statistical facts (as no *considerable* increase in these incidents had been recorded at the time), Hall *et al.* look at the 'progressive naturalisation' that the 'mugging' label played in the development of the moral panic about 'mugging', a term initially used to describe a *general* breakdown in 'law-and-order' (11, 23, 26). The adoption of this label indicates an exaggerated response, 'a reaction by the control agencies and the media to the *perceived* or *symbolic* threat to society' (29). This kind of response, representing an 'ideological displacement' performed by the 'control agencies' such as the media, the police and the courts, constitutes the fibre of a moral panic.

As indicated earlier by Cohen, the success of the 'control agencies' in orchestrating the panic depends on their appeal to the central value system shared by 'the whole society' (minus its 'deviant' elements). And yet the authors claim, after Gramsci (and this is where their argument regarding shared morality goes further than Cohen's), that the consensual nature of society which allows the formation of such a shared system of values is hegemonic, that the subordinate classes are won over – initially through persuasion, but also through coercion in the moment of crisis – to believe that it is *their* morality, *their* system of beliefs, that is the *only* possible, 'normal', set of values they might have. By drawing on Marx's conclusion that 'the media reproduce the definitions of the powerful' (57) and in this way exert control over 'mental resources', Hall *et al.* demonstrate how social and political definitions become objectified, thus 'providing the moral framework for the entire social system' (Parkin quoted in Hall *et al.*, 1978: 59). The authors argue that the media play a key role in reproducing the dominant ideology by the selectivity of its reports, by using the language of its readers and by relying on the 'consensus of values' which is deeply embedded in all forms of public discourse. The consensual value system is consolidated through an application of the principle of reflexivity – a difficult and, one might perhaps even say, 'illusionistic', philosophical concept which names 'the movement whereby that which has been used to generate a system is made, through a changed perspective, to become part of the system it generates' (Hayles, 1999: 8). Normative statements issued by the (predominantly tabloid) newspapers with a view to putting forward some new moral propositions – e.g. calls for moral discipline in a society in which the traditional family structure is disintegrating, appeals to the calculable rule of justice in which crime needs to be 'paid for' and in which 'no mercy to the victim' means that there should be 'no mercy to the offender' (Hall *et al.*, 1978: 133) – can only be articulated through an appeal to the existent value system of 'everyday decency, accepted morality, established values of living' (119). Significantly, it is the autopoietic *closure* of the traditional value system on a structural level, rather than its content, that plays a dominant role in its perpetuation. One can perhaps go so far as to say that the system itself needs to be content-free (even though it does temporarily get filled in with different contents) for it to accommodate the emerging new panics and folk devils. What binds it together is the 'ideology of common sense, known to all "normal" people as the right and proper way of life' (113).

But the authors of *Policing the Crisis* do not just explore the structuring of dominant social values; they also point to the structural discrepancies between different groups in society, discrepancies that need to be elimi-nated, forgotten or denied for the consensus to emerge. Looking at the role of print media in the production and affirmation of dominant values, Hall *et al.* explain that 'The contradictions of everyday social experience were suppressed by shifting the debate to the more abstract level of the law. ... Concrete social experience was dissolved by the editorial discourse into an abstraction – "society" – so that the morally totalising viewpoint aimed for in editorials was both generalised and mystifying' (92–3). However, the recognition of the underlying antagonism between different groups is extremely significant. It ensures the possibility of a socio-political change; it serves as a permanent guarantee of the breach of the consensus and the emergence of different, more just, value systems. *Policing the Crisis* does not thus only diagnose the status quo; it also *articulates a promise* inherent in consensual governmentality, while also *revealing its secret*. This 'secret' concerns the empty place of hegemony at the heart of the traditionalist consensus about values. Its perpetuation depends on the continued obfusca-tion of the system's foundations, on affirming the belief in its 'normality' and thus refraining from, or – to use another concept which is important in an ethical context – *sacrificing*, its investigation. But what is it exactly that needs to be sacrificed for the value system to hold? And what kind of sacrilege do the authors of *Policing the Crisis* perform in order to open up the political promise that has become one of the driving forces of cultural studies?

CULTURAL STUDIES BEFORE THE LAW

> *Telegraph,* 14 November 2003
> (reporting the trial of the four men accused of the Birmingham New Year party killings)[5]
> Before the men, who were all wearing trainers and casual clothes, were brought into court, district judge Rod Ross warned members of the public gallery to remain silent during the proceedings. He said: 'This is an emotional time for the relatives and stressful for the defendants. This court has draconian powers to deal with any outbursts. I will take the appropriate action to deal with any outbursts.'

To answer some of these questions raised in the previous paragraph, we should turn to the analysis of the legal system in 1970s Britain provided in *Policing the Crisis*. Drawing on press reports of 'mugging' cases which were themselves based on court proceedings and judges' comments, the authors argue:

> To understand fully the context of judicial action (and its relation to the 'mugging panic'), it is necessary ... to pass beyond the ideological inter-dependence between the media and the judiciary ... in order to look at those processes peculiar to the *internal* organisation of the judicial 'world': to look at the judicial apparatus itself, to go behind its routine practices and attempt to reconstruct the 'judicial mood' in the period leading up to 'mugging'. This task of reconstruction is not an easy one. The law stands, formally, outside of the political processes of the state, and above the ordinary citizen. Its rituals and conventions help to shield its operations from the full blaze of publicity and from the force of public criticism. The 'judicial fiction' is that all judges impartially embody and represent 'the Law' as an abstract and impartial force: individual differences of attitude and viewpoint between different judges, and the informal proc-esses by which common judicial perspectives come to be formed, and by which the judiciary orientates itself, in a general way, within the field of force provided by public opinion and official political or administrative operation, are normally shielded from public scrutiny .... The judiciary remains a closed institutional sphere within the state, relatively anony-mous, represented in its institutional rather than its individual person, and protected, in the last resort, by the threat of contempt. (33–4)

Significantly, this paragraph does much more than point to the 'bias' of individual judges or even the institutions within which they function. It questions the 'judicial fiction', which involves the interrogation of the very structure of 'the Law' and what Derrida calls the 'mystical foundation' of its authority (1990: 939). The interpretation takes place on two levels here. As well as investigating the concrete material institutions of the British judiciary, the authors span the bridge to the level of the 'universal', or, one might even be tempted to say, 'spiritual' or 'mythical' – the level at which the belief in the authority of the law is consolidated. It is precisely the embodiment of the law in the minds and hearts of different judges as a closely kept secret that leads to its consolidation – but it also works towards the development of a 'judicial mood'. Elevated to the sublime heights, 'above the ordinary citizen' (just as it was envisaged in Kant's third *Critique*), the law is nevertheless subject to the 'judicial mood'. A number of questions arise out of Hall *et al.*'s reading. Guarding the judicial fiction which in turn sustains it, is the law itself not in danger of seeming somewhat 'moody', of revealing its capriciousness? If it is held together by the exclusion of contempt, as the authors indicate, does it not also mean that it is *worthy of contempt* (otherwise, why impose an injunction against it?), or indeed that it is founded on contempt *as its condition of being and its limit*? Does it not make the law a usurper, acquiring its authority through violence and force? That would in turn allow us to see violence as the very condition and principle of the law's functioning. Speaking of the 'enforceability of the law', Derrida indeed points out that

> there is no such thing as law (*droit*) that doesn't imply *in itself, a priori, in the analytic structure of its concept*, the possibility of being 'enforced', applied by force. There are, to be sure, laws that are not enforced, but there is no law without enforceability, and no applicability or enforceability of the law without force, whether this force be direct or indirect, physical or symbolic, exterior or interior .... (1990: 925–7)

And yet, for the authority of the law to hold, its foundational violence has to be veiled, it has to be re-coded as legitimate and justified in terms of the common good – of the nation state and its citizens. This does not of course mean that the law's authority remains unthreatened – Hall *et al.* claim that, when society becomes more 'lax and permissive', 'the boundaries between sanctioned and illegitimate activity become progressively blurred'. This leads to a 'feeling amongst some social groups that the erosion of moral constraints, even if not directly challenging the law, would in the end precipitate a weakening in the authority of the law itself' (1978: 34). Morality is perceived here as being in the service of the law – as its protector and a guarantee of its untouchability. But a certain threat is recognized at the same time. If the erosion of the established moral rules were to result in the weakening of the law, the law itself needs to be hardened; it needs to appeal for the 'toughening' of moral standards. The law is thus positioned as both external to morality (legislating and protecting it from outside as its constitutive limit) and internal to it: its own 'mysticism' or 'spirituality' is nourished on the concrete moral rules and regulations.[6] Consequently, it seems that so much has been invested on a socio-historical level in the idea of the law – the idea that in popular imagination connects with the notions of decency and respectability[7] – that its defence comes to be seen as a 'natural' duty. (One could draw a comparison here with the protection of other ideas whose sanctity and the 'mystical foundation' of whose authority has led to enhanced moral vigilantism in the last few decades: the idea of God, of the family unit, of compulsive heterosexuality, etc.)

The foundational violence of the law, of its 'mystical authority', is thus silenced by the moral discourse whose alleged transparency obscures the performative processes at the heart of the juridical system. But, as Derrida argues, the role of violence in the law is more complex than that; for even though it serves as the law's condition and its foundation, violence also threatens the juridical order. This is the reason why British, and more broadly, European law prohibits and condemns individual violence. The reduction of violence outside of the law, the preservation of violence as solely the prerogative of the legal system, is in fact the driving force of the law (Derrida, 1990: 985). In a similar vein, Hall *at al.* argue: 'The state, and the state only, has the monopoly of *legitimate* violence, and thus "violence" is used to safeguard society against "illegitimate" uses' (1978: 68). Violence itself, which is 'on the side of the law', establishes the very boundary between the legitimate and the illegitimate, it draws the social boundaries. According to the authors of *Policing the Crisis*, the consequence of this drawing of boundaries in a capitalist society, based on the protection of capital and private property, is the consolidation of the class system, with the poor and propertyless being '*always* in some sense on "the wrong side of the law", whether they actually transgress it or not' (190). We can conclude that poverty comes to be seen as a form of 'crime' in a society whose dominant morality is rooted in the Protestant ethos which embraces what Max Weber described as 'the spirit of capitalism': 'thrift, self-discipline, living the decent life' but also self-help, self-reliance and competitive success (Hall *et al.*, 1978: 140). The moral panic about crime, the possibility that someone might be 'on the wrong side of the law', can therefore be understood as the anxiety about the social divisions that the law establishes and then passes off as natural. Of course, this boundary is very tenuous due to what Derrida describes as the 'essentially inaccessible character of the law' (1992a: 196): we are all, in some sense, on its 'wrong side'. This is why the fear is embraced by both the powerful and the subordinate – the former having more interest in perpetuating the status quo, i.e. the illusion of their proximity to the law, the latter internalizing the dominant ideas and making them their own. Significantly, Derrida argues that the state ('being law in its greatest force') is not so much afraid of crime as such, but rather 'of fundamental, founding violence, that is, violence able to justify, to legitimate ... or to transform the relations of law ... and so to present itself as having a right to law' (1990: 989).

If what the state fears more than the singular 'criminal activities' (that it itself defines and then punishes) is the transformation of the relations of law, and a right to law, then the 'mugging panic' of 1970s Britain – but also the 'guns and rap panic' of 2003 – can be seen as strategies elaborated for the protection of the law and its authority. This is not to deny the existence of individual cases of street crime, or the increased participation in them of young black youths (and Hall *et al.* do not deny that). But it is to draw attention to the vulnerability of the British state at those times, a state in the process of working through its relationship to its colonial past and its ex-colonial 'new citizens'. Threatened by its own spectres, the state (with all its supporting institutions) needs to elaborate a number of strategies that will maintain the law in its authoritarian position, that will permanently keep some members of society both *before* and *outside* the law, convinced that the law has nothing to do with them but also unlikely to question its structure. The moral panic is thus one way of ensuring that some 'unwanted' social elements – young black youths, teenage mothers, drug addicts – will not attempt to approach the law too closely, that they will stay away from it.

HEGEMONY AND ETHICAL STRATEGY

However, the investigation of the hegemonic process of the British state in the 1960s and 1970s conducted by Hall *et al.* is not just a simple description of social and political life, or what Simon Critchley calls a value-neutral power analytics (Critchley: 2002, unpag.). This investigation contains an inherent ethical injunction (by which I mean something more than their commitment to 'left-wing' values). I want to suggest that *Policing the Crisis* can be seen as an ethical proposal, as entailing an ethical promise which is linked to its politics. Let me try to explain what I mean by referring to Critchley's work, which has played an important role in situating debates on hegemony in an ethical context. Although his engagement has been mainly with the notion of hegemony that has been proposed by Ernesto Laclau – which is a somewhat refined version of the Gramscian-Althusserian framework that *Policing the Crisis* also draws on[8] – I believe that Critchley's interrogation of the ethical foundations of hegemony is also relevant[9] to Hall *et al.*'s work. Drawing on Laclau's theories, Critchley describes hegemony as the process of the formation of social identities and relations (Critchley, 2003: 64). He explains: 'Hegemony reveals politics to be the realm of contingent decisions by virtue of which subjects (understood here as persons, parties or social movements) attempt to articulate and propagate meanings of the social. At its deepest level, the category of hegemony discloses the political logic of the social' (Critchley, 2002: unpag.).

And yet Critchley is not content with leaving politics 'to itself'. Drawing on Derrida's deconstructive thinking and Levinas's ethics 'before philosophy', he argues that the category of hegemony is and has to be 'a normative critique of much that passes for politics insofar as that politics attempts to deny or render invisible its contingency, operations of power and force' (2002: unpag.). If the theory of hegemony is not going to risk collapsing into the arbitrariness of a thoroughgoing decisionism, if – in other words – it is not to assign equal 'value' to fascism and democracy, for example, it requires a normative presupposition: an ethical dimension of infinite responsibility to the other. Taking a cue from Critchley, I want to ask: what drives the analysis of hegemonic social structures in *Policing the Crisis*? The category of hegemony that Hall *et al.* employ in their study allows them to trace the meanings and origins of social relations in the British society in the 1960s and 1970s – its power structures, the social actors involved in consolidating them, its beliefs and morals. In other words, it allows the authors to reactivate 'sedimented social strata'. Although Hall *et al.* do not articulate any specific proposal, any manifesto – and indeed insist that the book is not 'a practical manual' (1978: vii) – I want to postulate that this exposure of the sedimented social structures as unjustified and unjust occurs against a certain (undeconstructible) horizon.

To explain this further, I would like to return to Levinas's discussion of the relationship between ethics and politics. He argues: 'The state is usually better than anarchy – but not always. In some instances – fascism or totalitarianism, for example – the political order of the state may have to be challenged in the name of our ethical responsibility to the other. This is why ethics must remain the first philosophy' (Levinas and Kearney, 1986: 30). It is in this ethical responsibility to the other – which moves the authors of *Policing the Crisis* to attempt to do things otherwise (i.e. to shift the boundaries and limits of the law, to think about the possibility of a different race politics) – that the ethical injunction of their book, and, more broadly, of the emergent cultural studies project developed in the Birmingham Centre by Hall and his colleagues, lies for me. By pointing to the possibility of transforming the relation to law (although not in an overly optimistic or uncritical way), Hall *et al.* sketch an alternative to what they diagnose as the dominant moral paradigm of the day – a petty-bourgeois ethic (1978: 161–4) which is still very much with us today. In exposing the hegemonic invisibility of politics in Britain, they allow for a rethinking of the accepted notions that are consolidated by it: work, family, decency and respect. To use Gramsci's words, they demonstrate that 'hegemony is ethical-political', as well as economic (quoted in Hall *et al.*, 1978: 227).

The possibility of the transformation of the relations of law, of the right to law, which *Policing the Crisis* implies, inevitably entails violence, but this does not mean that such an intervention will be unjust, that it will be unethical. Perhaps we can go so far as to postulate that it belongs to the regime of what Levinas terms 'justifiable violence',[10] which entails the possibility of a different justice beyond capitalist calculation that brings about 'some different good'.[11] (I develop the notion of 'good violence' in the next chapter.) The debates about 'muggings' in 1970s Britain,[12] about black youths and crime, but also, to draw on more recent examples, about the panics concerning guns in British and American inner-cities, about 'black-on-black crime', about gang warfare, can only ever, *will* only ever, be conducted from a position of violence, because, as Derrida has it, 'violence appears with articulation' (quoted in de Vries, 1997: 26). So even 'the denunciation of violence must engage in an intricate negotiation with violence itself' (de Vries, 1997: 25). This is not to suggest that black culture, which constitutes the background of Hall's analysis (or the background of the recent moral panic involving guns and So Solid Crew), is 'intrinsically violent', but rather to point to violence as foundational to any sense of identity. Of course, there is no absolute and prior guarantee that this particular moment of intervention (revolution, 'crime' or 'mugging') will be good, that it will be just. But it may inaugurate discursive transformation; it may loosen up the boundaries of the law and allow for their redrafting. Following Levinas, we may conclude that the very idea that the state might need to be (perhaps violently) challenged in the name of our responsibility to the other, that its totalitarianism may need to be interrupted, is founded upon an ethics of the interhuman. A 'pure', non-violent analytical position, on the other hand, could only ever be an autarchic fantasy that would be both transcendental and totalitarian in its origin.[13]

Indeed, it is *Policing the Crisis*'s engagement with violence, rather than a naive distancing from it, that is the source of its ethical promise. And it is in its interrogation of who the victims of crime are (is it only ordinary hard-working citizens remaining on 'the right side of the law', or is it also 'muggers' themselves?) that its ethicality is revealed. This interrogation does not amount to 'promoting moral relativism' but it does allow us to turn an ear to the story of those whom the more traditionally racialized moral and political discourses have already sentenced 'as if in advance'; it does allow us to see them as *victims of discourse*. It is here that the lesson of *Policing the Crisis* becomes extremely important for cultural studies' engagement with the current 'guns and rap' panic. By saying this I do not intend to impose an identification between two sets of socio-political circumstances – those of the 'mugging' panic in 1970s Britain and those of the 'guns and rap' panic emerging at the beginning of the twenty-first century. In fact, I remain convinced that even to begin to engage *responsibly* with the latter we need a more thorough sociological analysis that takes its specificity and difference into account. We need to deal patiently with its context, in the way that Cohen and Hall *et al.* did in the case of the respective panics they dealt with. But I want to postulate that *Policing the Crisis* carries an important lesson for cultural studies practitioners today.[14] Even though the actual socio-political context of the 'guns and rap' panic is different – the issues of racism have changed today; the division between 'mainstream culture' and the 'the black (sub)culture' is less evident in the case of rap, hip-hop and garage; the 'hedonist' consumer morality that Hall *et al.* only diagnosed as emerging in the early 1970s today underwrites most transactions in the music industry – some of the mechanisms that Hall *et al.* identified in 1970s Britain are still embryonic in our current 'global' media culture. Simplistic analogies between events and acts are still being violently imposed; moral rhetoric is still used as a controlling and repressive mechanism; victimhood is all too often pre-decided, while violence frequently remains ascribed only to 'the other', the social 'folk devil'. *Policing the Crisis* does not thus provide us with a ready-made formula for investigating the current media culture, but it does indicate that any *responsible* forms of social critique need to be underpinned by ethical thinking.

Policing the Crisis also shows that certain discursive concepts that bear the marks of criminality and exclusion can in fact instantiate ethics, as they enable the transformation of the relations of law, order and justice. The authors offer an example of how this 'discursive revolution' can work by engaging with the concept of 'hustling'. Described in *Policing the Crisis* as a sub-cultural activity in the West Indian 'colony community' in 1960s Britain 'on the border of the law', the notion of 'hustling' contains the seed of this transformation, of enabling the redefinition of what belongs on the side of the law and what does not. Identified in the traditional police discourse as criminal activity in the black community – mainly consisting of brothel-keeping, living off immoral earnings and drug-pushing – in Hall *et al.* hustling is conceptualized as an alternative mode of survival. They explain:

> Hustling is quite different from professional or organised crime. It certainly takes place on the far or blind side of the law. Hustlers live by their wits. So they are obliged to move around from one terrain to another, to desert old hustlers and set up new ones in order to stay in the game. ... They work the system; they also make it work. (1978: 352)

The ethical alternative that arises out of the pages of *Policing the Crisis* does not translate itself into a set of rules and regulations. The authors do not naively suggest that we should all move to the interstices of the law, that we should dis-respect it, that we should give up 'legal' or 'legitimate' ways of earning our living and create new urban colonies. But they indicate that a decision about 'crime' – be it hustling, joyriding or drugs (as crimes often associated with 'the black community') – cannot be innocently and thus 'justly' taken once and for all. To be an act of justice rather than an implementation of a programme, every decision has to look at the law always anew – appealing to the law's authority, reinstating it, but also 'inventing the law' by reinterpreting it, and thus simultaneously conserving and destroying it.[15] Of course, this is not to suggest the total abandonment of the law (were such a thing at all possible), but rather to indicate that any just decision which is not to be merely a (thoughtless, and thus irresponsible) application of a legal paragraph has to exist in a tension between establishment and innovation, between the old and the (radically) new. It is precisely this possibility of thinking anew about crime that *Policing the Crisis* inaugurates, and it is in its rethinking that the transformation of the relations of law, and a right to law, lies. In this way, the authors sketch the possibility of a different economic order in which values of propriety and property are redefined beyond the traditional lines of power. Their consistent use of the word 'mugging' in inverted commas is a graphic indication of the term's unstable status – but it is also a call for thought, for a response and responsibility to those who have been interpellated by it. Hall *et al.* can thus enable us to re-evaluate moral panics and to think differently – ethically, responsibly – about the Birmingham shootings, So Solid Crew and street crime. Any such response would need to involve a suspension of *prior* judgement, a decontextualization of the 'crime' from the panic rhetoric in which any such debates have so far been rooted, a search for a new language and a new understanding.

BBC News website, 13 November 2003[16]

For starters, So Solid aren't a neatly-moulded group like the Spice Girls or Westlife. They are a self-made collective of men, women, children – oh, and there's even a dog in there somewhere.

But as I talk to DJ Swiss, one of the massive's more vocal members, it's clear that So Solid's roots lie at the heart of everything they do.

'We come from a different environment from where you grew up,' says Swiss, scrutinising my clipped tones.

'We're segregated there, and people don't really want to know about it.'

This sense of alienation is the message behind the Crew's new single You Don't Know, which has given them another top three smash.

'It's a tune from the heart,' explains Swiss. 'It's says that as much as people want to speculate about who we are and what we do, they don't really know.'

But doesn't mainstream pop success pull you further away from your roots? My question causes a rumble of disapproval amongst the Crew.

This does not mean reiterating the stereotypical distinction between 'us' and 'them', between society and its folk devils, no matter if we were to ascribe their 'intrinsic' difference to their race or their ethnicity, to 'nature' or 'culture'. Instead, this kind of ethics – which, to be ethical, has to go through a suspension of judgement and morality – could perhaps turn to what Levinas describes as 'the listening eye' (1998: 38). 'The listening eye' does not attempt to fix the essence of being but rather 'regards', i.e. is concerned about and listens to the other's story which always has to remain, to some extent, theirs. This kind of ethics would, for example, advise vigilance to a BBC journalist 'with clipped tones' who interviewed So Solid Crew before he ventured to ask the 'massive' 'from a different environment': *'But doesn't mainstream pop success pull you further away from your roots?'* 'The listening eye' would hear the traces of imperial history and its consequences in this sentence, it would pick up the signals about the distribution of capital according to the lines of power established and protected by the colonial institutions – by the schools in which one gains 'clipped tones', by Oxbridge and the BBC. Revealing the desire to keep the capital away from the ghetto, not to allow 'the likes of' So Solid Crew to get the share of it, and thus to keep them *in* the ghetto, the listening eye would also grasp inner-city divisions in which some 'subcultures' are established along racial as well as financial lines. And it would attempt to avert the gaze in order to stop the (well-meaning, perhaps) journalist (but also the cultural studies practitioner) from fixing, i.e. totalizing, the other's otherness in an account that speaks of 'cultural difference' without reflecting on its socio-historical structuring. But 'the ethics of the listening eye' would also create problems for some forms of ethnographic cultural studies research which engages with 'groups' of people ('young black youths', 'hip-hop fans', 'teenagers') that it actually produces as its object of study. This is by no means to say that cultural studies would have to renounce its engagement with 'people' – but rather to suggest something we might call ethico-graphy, in which 'the extreme exposure and sensitivity of one subjectivity to another' is not *superseded* by one subject's totalizing theorization.

PERMANENT VIGILANCE

Policing the Crisis can thus be read as instantiating an ethics of cultural studies which offers a passage to the political, while also keeping a check on it. It is an ethics that calls for judgement *always anew*; that explores 'the contingencies involved in specific, historically situated encounters' (Campbell and Shapiro, 1999a: ix). That it may seem suspiciously 'like' the Levinasian-Derridean ethics of alterity should not be seen as an attempt on my part just to transplant a set of ready-made ideas 'from' philosophy 'into' cultural studies, and then call them something else. Although inspired by Levinas's and Derrida's questioning of ethics, justice and the law, the ethics of cultural studies I speculate about here does not *have* an essence; it is rather an idea and an intervention which is always already rooted in the material, specific and 'concrete' reality (all the terms beloved by cultural studies!) of its texts and contexts, its practices and people. So, even though this ethics of cultural studies may look like 'the stuff that Levinas and Derrida talk about', it would not have been possible without Hall and the Birmingham School, without Gramsci and *Policing the Crisis*. What is most significant about it is that, in posing questions (about morality, politics and justice) to both cultural studies theorists and their 'objects of study', it enables the performance of one of cultural studies' most important tasks – a task on which its idea of itself as a politically committed field rests: the overcoming of the distinction between 'academia' and its 'outside'.

This kind of ethics will allow us a way out of the social scientist's impasse, which Cohen perceives in terms of a dilemma between moral absolutism and moral relativism – when 'The same values of racism, sexism, chauvinism, compulsive masculinity and anti-intellectualism, the slightest traces of which are condemned in bourgeois culture, are treated with a deferential care, an exaggerated contextualization, when they appear in the subculture' (2002: lxviii). Cohen admits he shares the horror of 'peering into abyss which yawns in front of us' when faced with different values for 'different cultures'. I am not going to state here what kind of exit to the dilemma between, for example, the absolutist condemnation of racism and sexism and the subcultural celebration of terms such as 'nigga' and 'bitch' in rap, will be offered to us by this new, tentatively called 'ethics of cultural studies'. It is not possible to respond to this dilemma without looking in detail at the particularities of a given subculture, its modes of protest and its cultural productions, but also at the relationship between the history of colonialism and women's movement and the linguistic reappropriation of some of its terms at a given moment in time, as well as the actual process of the delineation of cultural and subcultural boundaries. But I would not like my readers to see this refusal to provide an up-front resolution to this dilemma as a retreat to incessant 'theorization' and thus as 'procrastination, neutralisation, and resignation ... evading the pressing needs of the present, especially ethical and political ones'. (These accusations, as we know, have frequently been levied at any 'deconstructive' modes of thinking.) The ethics of cultural studies will (carefully, slowly and deliberately) engage with 'moral panics', its folk devils and 'moral entrepreneurs' but it will not provide a corrected version of morality in advance, even if it was to come disguised as political intervention. Instead, motivated by the relation 'in which our responsibility to the other is the basis for reflection' (Campbell and Shapiro, 1999: x), it will call for a permanent vigilance – towards the injustice and power games committed by the third party but also towards our own prejudices.

So let me round off by employing one of Derrida's favourite mottoes as a justification for this foundation-less and content-free ethics of infinite responsibility which calls on both cultural studies theorists and 'the people in the outside world': 'Those who want to simplify at all costs and who raise a hue and cry about obscurity because they do not recognize the unclarity of their good old *Aufklärung* are in my mind dangerous dogmatists and tedious obscurantists. No less dangerous (for instance, in politics) are those who wish to purify at all cost' (1988: 199). Should these words seem aggressive and violent, and thus inappropriate to justify any ethical project, I hope the hard work (Derrida's, Hall and his colleagues', mine) that has gone into the argument that precedes them, and that is not yet at all finished, will soften the blow of an ethical sword.

A POSTSCRIPT

'Young and loaded – It's not just about having a gun but the right kind of gun'.
('Guns and Rap', BBC2, 9 December 2003)

Just as I was finishing writing this chapter, BBC2 broadcast a programme titled 'Guns and Rap' (9 December 2003, dir. Fatima Salaria). Composed out of a collection of clips from the rap music scene, it was interspersed with 'sound-bite' interviews with music journalists, rappers and 'black teenagers from a council estate', and accompanied by a voiceover. The message transmitted through the programme was clear. Presented with a close-up of a selection of hand guns, we were told: 'These weapons aren't in the hands of contract killers. They are stylish accessories in the hands of Britain's new generation.' And then: 'Black youths are dying and the rappers are glorifying the gun but the industry says it is not to blame.' With rap and hip-hop playing in the background, the voices were punctuated by the regular beat, drumming a message home. 'It seems nobody can believe how young this gun generation is.' 'Rap has never been cited in court as a reason for anyone picking up a gun but it does promote a luxury lifestyle. Guns and extravagant excess – a must-have culture.'

Notes

1   Sarah Bennett, 'Gangster Culture'. http://www.wessexscene.co.uk/article.php?sid=399 accessed on 18 November 2003. Online Scene is the Internet website of *The Wessex Scene*, a paper which is written and produced by and for students at the University of Southampton in the UK.

2   Helen Gibson, 'Bullets over Britain', *TIME Magazine Europe*, 20 January 2003, http://www.time.com/time/europe/magazine/article/0,13005,901030120–407298,00.html, accessed on 18 November 2003.

3   See Thompson (1998) for an extensive list of sociological works on moral panics.

4   For a detailed discussion of deconstruction in an ethical context see Critchley, Simon (1992) *The Ethics of Deconstruction*.

5   Nick Britten, 'Mothers face four accused of New Year party killings', *Telegraph*, 14 November 2003, http://www.telegraph.co.uk/news/main.jhtml?xml=/news/2003/11/14/nshoot14.xml, accessed on November 2003.

6   Hall *et al.* argue: 'The law thus comes to represent all that is most impartial, independent, above the play of party interests, within the state. It is the most formal representation of universal consent. Its "rule" comes to stand for the social order – for

"society" itself. Hence a challenge to it is a token of social disintegration. In such conjunctures "law" and "order" become identical and indivisible' (1978: 208).

7   Hall *et al.* claim that 'respectability' became a 'universal social value' in late 1960s and 1970s Britain, although it had different inflections in middle and working classes. Strongly connected with the ideas of self-help and self-reliance, and with conformity to established social standards, for the middle classes it was translated into an ethos of competitive success, keeping up appearances and affording things which supposedly befitted their social standing. For the working classes, in turn, respectability meant hard work, thrift and making-do in the face of adversity. The authors of *Policing the Crisis* emphasize the role of respectability in disciplining society, in 'holding the nation together from the inside when it is under stress'. They argue: 'Respectability is the collective internalisation, by the lower orders, of an image of the "ideal life" held for them by those who stand higher in the scheme of things; it disciplines society from end to end, rank by rank. Respectability is therefore one of the key values which dovetails and inserts one social class into the social image of another class. It is part of what Gramsci called the "cement" of society' (1978: 141). See also 1978: 140–6.

8   I am grateful to Jeremy Gilbert for raising some of these points in an email conversation.

9   This 'relevance' works nevertheless in a somehow anachronistic way, as it is only in Laclau and Mouffe's *Hegemony and Socialist Strategy*, published in 1985, that the concept of hegemony is developed into a theory of society.

10 In 'Who Shall Not Prophesy?' Levinas says: '[T]he origin of the meaningful in the face of the other nevertheless calls – before the factical plurality of humans – to justice and knowledge; the exercise of justice demands tribunals and political institutions and even, paradoxically, a certain violence which all justice implies. Violence is originally justified as the defense of the other, of the neighbor (if he be my parent or my people!), but it is violence *for* someone' (Robbins, 2001: 220–1).

11 Another example of a challenge to the older Protestant ethics and to the economic order it supported came in the form of 'new hedonism', an ethos of narcissism and spending, which emerged in the early 1970s together with the arrival of the Rolling Stones and the development of the mods' subculture. However, this form of the loosening of traditional morality was not politically significant from the point of view of the cultural studies project, as it was quickly co-opted by the neo-liberal ethos of consumerism which allowed the conservation or even strengthening of the traditional economic structures. See Hall *et al.* (1978: 234–40).

12 I'm using 'mugging' in inverted commas just as Hall *et al.* did in order to draw attention to the discursive nature of this term, to its ideological sedimentation, as opposed to it being an objective description of what happened.

13 If violence is everywhere, if it is at the foundation of every identity (of humans, states, institutions), then any debate on violence, any ethico-political intervention into the legal system (whose foundations are inevitably, even if not explicitly, violent) 'takes place under the submission to – or negotiation with – the general economy of violence' (de Vries, 1997: 27).

14 Significantly, the fifth 'Crossroads' conference – the biggest and most prestigious event in the international cultural studies calendar, which was held at the University of Illinois, Urbana-Champaign from 25 to 28 June 2004, focused on 'Policing the Crisis' (as both a key text and a concept). Indeed, the conference Call for Papers stipulated further that 'In light of these uncertain and violent times, *cultural studies scholars have a moral obligation to police this crisis*, to speak to the death of people, culture and truth, and to undo the official pedagogies that circulate in the media' (emphasis added).

15 I discuss the notion of 'decision' in cultural studies in an ethical context in the previous chapter. See also Derrida (1990: 961).

16 'So Solid Crew's "heartfelt" tunes', BBC News website, 13 November 2003, http://news.bbc.co.uk/1/hi/entertainment/music/1652598.stm, accessed on 17 November 2003.

4

Ethics, Violence and the Media

INTRODUCTION: AN IM*MEDIA*TE RESPONSE TO *MEDIA*TED MURDER

How does one do justice to parents who have lost their child in street violence? Can the 'crimes' of the Oklahoma bomber or the 9/11 'terrorists' *really* be avenged? Is an ethical response to murder possible? What kind of principle of calculation would be applicable here? In posing these questions, I want to raise the issue of ethics, accountability and accountancy in late capitalist societies, in the face of what I describe as 'mediated violence'. This investigation is rooted in the assumption that capitalist economy both engenders and is informed by (in a performative, self-reflexive way) the logic of calculation that attempts to balance all gains and losses. As Jacques Derrida puts is, 'the law of economy is the circular – return to the point of departure, to the origin', which he traces through the etymology of *nomos* (law) and *oikos* (home, property, family) (1992b: 6–7). Thus, capitalism ensures that there is no remainder in the economic exchange and that any returns have been calculated and accounted for. I propose that this structure of equivalence, controlled profit and 'good use' informs the dominant moral paradigms in capitalist societies – from the utilitarian perspectives that try to achieve 'the greatest surplus of happiness' for the greatest number of people to less philosophically grounded, more 'instinctive' moral positions which recommend the 'settling of accounts' as a fair response to crime. All these lead to the development of a system of retributive justice, in which punishment is expected to 'fit' the deed, and where any behavioural excess can be controlled by the judiciary and penitentiary apparatuses. This does not mean that society's 'moral entrepreneurs' are consciously applying the laissez-faire capitalist logic to morality; sometimes it is the fear of capitalism and the greed it causes (see Hall *et al.*, 1978: 35), as well as a nostalgic desire for control and order, that leads to the adoption of calculation as a model for justice. Morality based on economics is supposed to serve as a guarantee of a return to the 'centre', the lost 'home' of yesteryear.

According to Stuart Hall and the other authors of *Policing the Crisis* – the study of the emergence of 'moral panics' as responses to the changed sociopolitical order – it is precisely this logic of accountancy and calculation that underpinned the hegemonic morality in 1970s Britain. Looking at the way in which cases of 'mugging' were portrayed in the British newspapers, Hall *et al.* argue that 'the ideas of "cost and "payment" were used to organise the definition of crime and punishment, which was interpreted through a notion of "equal exchange": no mercy to the victim, therefore no mercy to the offender; violence to one, violence to the other' (1978: 131). I suggest that this 'mathematical' attitude is still predominant in conservative, or what Hall *et al.* term 'traditionalist', responses to crime and violence, delivered by the media and other 'ideological apparatuses'. My aim in what follows is to pick up some of the threads from the previous chapter in order to look at the issues of crime and violence in the context of 'mediated murder' (by which I predominantly mean representations of murder *in the media*, although I will also speak about some other processes of mediation) in late capitalist societies. This will allow me to question the foundations of what I term 'the mathematical moral paradigm' but also to consider the possibility of developing a different *ethical* response to violence, one that goes beyond the capitalist logic of calculation. Although I acknowledge here, after Derrida, that the processes of *mediation* between an actual act of violence and its representations – be it in the media or academic discourses – are 'numerous, complicated, and difficult to interpret', and although they call for patience and caution on our part, 'I shall not use [these difficulties] as a pretext to wait and remain silent before that which demands *immediate* response and responsibility' (Derrida, 1991: 39). On the contrary, a responsible response to mediated murder will be my theme.

Instances of mediated murder – some of them, such as 'Oklahoma bombing' or '9/11', more 'global' in their scale and representational scope, others, like the 'Jamie Bulger killing',[1] more 'local' – occupy a significant position in contemporary news media. Although each of them is unique and singular, they are nevertheless universalized through, on the one hand, the staple rhetoric of moral panic and, on the other, the media conventions of the representation of terror, catastrophe and violent death. One might thus say that individual events of violence and murder are always already enveloped in a certain ambiguity, or aporia, between singularity and universality, an aporia that for many contemporary thinkers[2] corresponds to the ambiguous relationship between ethics and politics. The reason for this analogy is that such events span two spatio-temporal orders, or schemas. On the one hand, they can be seen as singular, irreplaceable occurrences that speak to every one of us in a most direct, perhaps even *aggressively* direct, way, appealing to our *ethical* sensibilities while also demanding a *response* from us. (We can think here of the intrusion of the images of 9/11 or Columbine high school massacre into our singular field of vision, and the way it disturbed our sense of the mundane, our situatedness in time and place.) On the other, such events are framed by communal acts and responses that draw on, test and reformulate the notions of *politics* and *justice* which we as members of the Western democratic public sphere are all supposed to share to some extent. The media images of violence and murder thus both call for and provide a mediation between these two different orders – the singular and the universal, the ethical and the political. I should perhaps point out that we are dealing with a few analytical levels here: the 'event' itself, which only ever functions as an idea, and its different mediations – from those provided by the news media, which is how these events become known to most of us, to those enacted by our cognitive and emotional mechanisms, no matter if we are experiencing these events 'directly' or 'indirectly'. (I will elaborate this notion of multiple mediation further on.)[3]

The tabloid reaction of 'moral panic' – where a moral panic describes a situation in which '[a] condition, episode, person or group of persons emerges to become defined as a threat to societal values and interests' (Cohen, 2002: 1) – can be seen as one possible outcome of such a process of mediation, in which the singularity of the ethical is superseded by the ideological practice of consensual governmentality. Thus, in case of 'moral panics', this process of mediation can eventually give way to hegemonic domination, leading to the outright politicization, but also the 'overcoming' of the ethical. As Angela McRobbie explains, 'Moral panics remain one of the most effective strategies of the right for securing popular support for its values and policies' (1994: 198). However, what I want to do in this chapter is propose an ethical way of addressing such events of mediated violence and murder that goes beyond such moralistic perspectives.

Even though a certain universalizing tone is inevitable in academic analyses of this kind, in order not to obscure the singularity of such events, I propose to root my analysis in one specific instance of mediated violence: '9/11'. Its uniqueness has been strongly emphasized, but this particular event has also been inscribed in a network of political discourses around the international world order, globalization and terrorism. Jean Baudrillard conveys the an-archic, a-temporal and thus paradoxically all-embracing singularity of 9/11 by describing it as 'the absolute event, the "mother" of all events, the pure event uniting within itself all the events that have never taken place' (2002: 4). Arundhati Roy gives a somewhat different account of this paradox of 'pluralised singularity' represented by 9/11: before being associated with the attack on the Twin Towers, 11 September stood for the proclamation by the British government of a mandate in Palestine in 1922, for General Pinochet's violent overthrowing of the democratic government of Salvador Allende in Chile in 1973, and for a day in 1990 when George W. Bush Sr, then President of the US, made a speech to a joint session of Congress announcing his government's decision to go to war against Iraq (Roy, 2002: 283–9). Roy thus argues that, contrary to what the 'global' media have attempted to make us believe, the significance this date carries for American media audiences is not universal. But what is significant about this process of the universalization of 9/11/2001 by the (American) broadcast media is that the attacks on the Twin Towers radically changed the perception of ordinary Americans 'that "it can't happen here": namely, that organized, mass destruction was something that was exclusively limited to the nightly news' (Weber, 2002: 450). Samuel Weber acknowledges that 'The bombing of the Murrah Building in Oklahoma City ... marked a first breach in this widely held belief', but emphasizes the singularity of 9/11 which prepared the ground for a new concept of universality by adding, 'This rule ... collapsed altogether with the imploding towers on September 11' (2002: 450).

THE SUBLIME: BETWEEN ETHICAL CALCULATION AND INFINITE SPENDING

Focusing on '9/11' – of which, like most people, I have only 'mediated' knowledge generated by TV news and images, together with the emergent political commentaries – will allow me to speculate on the broader, more 'universal' question of violence, ethics and repayment, and the related issues of debt and justice. It is this exploration of the intertwinings between ethics and economics, between ethical spending and a capitalist calculation of gains and losses, that is of particular interest to me here.

The relationship between ethics and capitalization is in fact well established in our political culture and can be traced back at least to the eighteenth century, a period traditionally associated in the humanities and social sciences literature with the 'rise of the modern subject' (see de Bolla, 1989: 7). 'It has long been held ... that the period witnessed the emergence of "bourgeois individualism", the capitalist entrepreneur, and the dissenting businessman' (de Bolla, 1989: 7). For Peter de Bolla, author of the monumental study, *The Discourse of the Sublime*, the autonomous 'capitalist' subject is one of the outcomes of the discourses on debt and the sublime, which both described and prescribed the aesthetico-political landscape of eighteenth-century Europe.[4] It is precisely in this period that 'the capitalist description of the subject – still very much with us and under which we are represented' (1989: 14) today, brought together sublimity – a discourse of production to excess, of the experience of breaking through a boundary (12) – with ethics, seen as an attempt to regulate and control 'the degeneration of morals brought about by selfish profiteering' (134). As a result of this transformation, an ethos of collective individualism – what Arundhati Roy calls 'the algebra of infinite justice' (2002) – under which twenty-first-century capitalist economies still operate, becomes an ethics.[5] The question I raise in this chapter is whether this ethics of debt and repayment, of justice based on economic calculation, can be challenged by another, more just and more politically responsive/responsible notion of ethics. To do this, I want to explore further the notion of the sublime, which, in articulating the contradictory feelings of fascination and horror as well as the tension between excessive spending and calculated gain, seems to me a propitious metaphor for the technocapitalism of the twenty-first century. As Jean-François Lyotard points out:

There is something of the sublime in capitalist economy. ... It is, in a sense, an economy regulated by an Idea – infinite wealth or power. It does not manage to present any example from reality to verify this Idea. In making science subordinate to itself through technologies, especially those of language, it only succeeds, on the contrary, in making reality increasingly ungraspable, subject to doubt, unsteady. (1991: 105)

Defined, post-Burke and Kant, as a feeling of negative pleasure which mixes fear with delight, the sublime seems to have undergone something of a renaissance in contemporary debates on culture and media (see Zylinska, 2001).[6] Writers can resort to it when describing the hopes, fascinations, anxieties and horrors associated with capitalism, with its spending to excess on the one hand, and its insistence on the regulation of gains and losses on the other.[7] Spanning the realms of aesthetics, ethics and politics, the sublime inheres a societal contradiction between a desire to overspend and a need not to go beyond the limit – a contradiction that has at times been *temporarily* resolved by the critique of the hyperspace of postmodern architecture (Jameson, 1991), by the postulation of a religiously inflected ethics of calculation in response to socio-political disturbance (see Hall *et al.*, 1978), and by supporting politics driven by the regulatory mechanisms of the market (from Thatcherite and Reaganite politics to their various neo-liberal mutations in early twenty-first-century Britain and the US). Used as a response to social, political or natural upheavals, the discourse of the sublime foregrounds the impossibility of representation and the failure of imagination in the face of the tumultuous events that both constitute and pulverize a self that is exposed to, entrapped, or even violated by them. This unexpected event can turn out to be a violent attack, an earthquake, a stock exchange crash or an amorous encounter (there are no guarantees here). Yet it is precisely this unknowability of what is going to happen that suspends the self's self-sufficiency and safety. In Kant, imagination exposed to the infinitely dangerous and infinitely great collapses, only to be followed by an achievement of a higher goal – 'the awakening of a feeling of a super-sensible faculty within us' (1952: 97). And thus reason triumphs because it has managed to make order out of disorder, to grasp the ungraspable, an achievement that allows it to rise towards moral consciousness. In this way, the Kantian sublime offers a passage to ethics.

Due to its ability to overcome the conceptual contradictions between excess and regulation, between the impossibility of representing the event and a need to give it a name, the discourse of the sublime is frequently applied in descriptions of *events of terror and trauma,* and accounts of the emergent relationship between victims and persecutors in pogroms, wars and other acts of genocide. Indeed, Thomas Elsaesser argues that 'traumatic events for contemporary culture turn around the question of how to represent the unrepresentable, or how ... to name the unnameable' (2001: 195).

One might point out here that the sublime and trauma belong to two different registers: the first is an aesthetic (or better, aesthetico-ethico-political) concept, the second – a psychological or psychoanalytic one. However, in Burke's *A Philosophical Enquiry into the Origin of our Ideas of the Sublime and the Beautiful* – one of the key texts on sublimity – the sublime in fact names the *psychological effect* of a terrible but fascinating phenomenon on the human body and mind. Meanwhile, Shoshana Felman points out in *Testimony: Crises of Witnessing in Literature, Psychoanalysis, and History* that testimony to a trauma, apart from its more obvious clinical associations, encompasses 'the *political dimension* of oppression and the *ethical dimension* of resistance which proceed from, and inscribe within the testimony, the historical occurrence' (Felman and Laub, 1992: 12; emphasis added).[8] The discourses of trauma and the sublime thus come together in their attempt to describe the difficulty of, or struggle with, representation – a struggle that, as I will demonstrate below, profoundly transforms the self's experience of itself and opens it to ethics. It is this link between the sublime and trauma – two 'mediating discourses' in our political culture[9] used to describe transformative, revolutionary but also devastating events – that will allow me to develop an ethical response to the issue of mediated violence and murder.

THE SECULAR SACRED: MASS MURDER, MEDIATION AND *RAUSCH*

Dominick LaCapra is someone who has applied the sublime framework to the analysis of mass murders, and the mediation of these events in subsequent literary and cinematic accounts. In *History and Memory after Auschwitz* he focuses on the mass execution of the Jews during the Holocaust – an event that for many is seen as absolutely singular and defying any comparison. I want to emphasize here that by referring to LaCapra's work I am not asserting the unproblematic 'applicability' of narratives about the Holocaust to 9/11 or other events of mediated murder, nor am I pursuing a highly problematic analogy between 'the Nazis' and 'the terrorists'. And yet, even though I acknowledge the absolute singularity of the Holocaust, I am also aware of the processes of mediation that are activated in any attempt to think about, address and respond to any event, no matter how unique it may be. And it is the notion of 'trauma' that serves as a bridge between these different events. Cathy Caruth defines trauma as 'the response to an unexpected or overwhelming violent event or events that are not fully grasped as they occur, but return later in repeated flashbacks, nightmares, and other repetitive phenomena' (1997: 208). The development of 'trauma studies' in recent years – inspired by the work of Shoshana Felman and Dori Laub, Cathy Caruth and Susannah Radstone – has provided a framework for the study of the experience of Holocaust survivors, of the more recent wars, massacres and other 'apocalyptic events' (described by some as 'holocausts'), of the clinical case stories around post-traumatic stress disorders, and of the dramas and melodramas exposed by 'reality TV'. I am interested in these unexpected and overwhelming violent events – and, in particular, in the mediation and ethicization of responses to them – but this does not amount to imposing an analogy between different events of horror and trauma.

Let me make two further qualifications. First, as I explained earlier, my recognition of the singularity of every event, every occurrence, is not an attempt to inscribe them in an economy of calculation (in the sense that the Holocaust's singularity and horror would 'equal' that of 9/11 or the Oklahoma bombing). On the contrary, thinking in terms of singularities will prevent us from applying a capitalist logic of calculation, which carefully regulates all overspending and excess, to the analysis of these events. Second, even though I am focusing here on media representations of murder events, I claim that every 'event' of violence and murder is always already mediated – through language, our sensory and cognitive apparatus, our notion of what eventality and murder involve, etc. – no matter whether it is occurring on the TV screen or before our very own eyes. (This of course is not to state that all these processes of mediation are the same, and that there are no issues of power involved in them; only to point to their multiplicity, which would then require a painstakingly careful analysis of their operation.) Caruth points to a paradox involved in traumatic experience – that 'the most direct seeing of a violent event may occur as an absolute inability to know it, that immediacy, paradoxically, may take the form of belatedness' (1997: 208). The processes of mediation are activated in any event in which our cognitive faculties are at a loss to grasp what defies them, to articulate what defies articulation. (Again, the sublime provides us here with a set of discursive terms for describing these processes.) The mediating processes can be both external and self-imposed, unconscious and conscious – as the example of the latter we can mention the distance advocated by Kant, which acts as a protective screen in the apprehension of sublimity. (I will return to this point a little later.) Therefore, when LaCapra is speaking about the sublime in the context of the Holocaust (to some the most singular, atrocious, unthinkable event in Western history), he is also activating a series of intermediations that stretch out to German pre-war history, Kant's idealism, the discursive mechanisms involved in the construction of testimonies, the politics of record-keeping, conscious and unconscious knowledge about the extermination of the Jews, and so on. And it is precisely because of this *passage between* the immediate and the mediated, between the singular and the universal, that I find his work interesting and useful for my own engagement with mediated violence and murder, and, in particular, 9/11.

MASTERING THE SUBLIME: THE 'PROSTHETIC TRAUMA' OF
9/11

The events of 9/11 were introduced to our living rooms through global
satellite networks; yet at the same time they were presented as alien, unfath-
omable, as if 'out of this world'. It is this 'eventality'[10] which rips open the
everyday with the arrival of the extraordinary, its simultaneous proximity
and strangeness, that inscribes it for me in the discourse of the sublime (a
discourse which will allow me to think about ethics, retribution and justice
'otherwise'). Indeed, sublime rhetoric dominates aesthetic descriptions of
the grandeur of One World Center and of its collapse – an event whose full
traumatic impact could only be felt and registered through an act of repetition, through the destruction of the second tower.[11] For example, Baudrillard
claims that 'These architectural monsters ... have always exerted an ambiguous fascination, as have the extreme forms of modern technology in general
– *a contradictory feeling of attraction and repulsion*, and hence, somewhere,
a secret desire to see them disappear' (2002, pp. 45–6; emphasis added).
The Twin Towers seemed to be a perfect incarnation of what Kant terms
'the mathematically sublime' – that 'in comparison with which everything
else is small' (1952: 97): even though they were comparable *as buildings*, the
Idea of financial and political might behind them brought imagination to a
halt. The difficulty of the representation of the 'event' of their downfall can
be conveyed by pointing to the fact that 'the two enormous towers' – symbolic not only of the almost incomprehensible grandeur of global capital
but also of the everyday impoverishment and misery of many standing at
their feet – were not 'just collapsing, but imploding and disappearing into
themselves, producing a huge cloud of dust and rubble, racing toward the
camera, and implicitly, toward the millions of viewers all over the world
who sat in disbelief riveted to their screens' (Morgan Wortham and Hall,
2002: 703). Threatened by the horror happening before their very own eyes,
by the 'billowing clouds' so reminiscent of Kant's 'thunderclouds piled up
the vault of heaven, borne along with flashes and peal' (1952: 110), viewers
could nevertheless rejoice in their own protection from *too near a closeness*,
and could thus, ultimately, celebrate their own survival. Significantly, for
Kant, '*provided our own position is secure*', sublime landscapes 'raise the forces
of the soul above the height of vulgar commonplace, and discover within
us a power of resistance of quite another kind, which gives us courage to be
able to measure ourselves against the seeming omnipotence of nature' (1952:
110, emphasis added).[12] Perhaps it was this sort of courage that encouraged
US leaders to publicly articulate[13] a call to arms post-9/11, intended to hunt
down and defeat the barbaric enemy, who was to be found on the side of the
'seemingly omnipotent' nature (cf. references to al-Qaida's primitive trib-
alism, their dwelling in caves, etc.). And yet the media audiences' sense of
security and togetherness was disturbed by the very act of *witnessing* the 9/11
event, whose sacrifice-beyond-calculation undermined the economic logic

in which politico-ethical transactions are conducted in Western democracies. It is precisely the sacrificial aspect of the 9/11 attacks that shattered the protective screen which had separated Burke and Kant's spectator from the pulverizing sublime event. The power of resistance that Kant hoped for, and which was supposed to elevate the soul towards moral law, foundered when the protective screen turned out to be a mirror for the violence forbidden by and yet wished for by the system that was undergoing implosion (see also Baudrillard, 2002: 18).

LaCapra hints at precisely such a possibility of double-mirroring in his account of the sublime, in which the protective screen initially seems to separate the source of horror from its witnesses/victims. He associates the sublime with the perpetrators' (i.e. the Nazis') elation at the moment of persecution of their victims: it is the moment when inexpressible horror leads to *Rausch*, delight, or, better, fascination. He notes further that in Kant 'the sublime is evoked by the *near-death* experience, by coming to the brink of the abyss or of annihilation while escaping death and destruction oneself' (1998: 35). It is important to point out that *Rausch* here arises precisely out of survival – at the cost of the sacrifice of the 'other'. Thus the 'Nazi formula' of killing and jubilation cannot be easily applied to 9/11, even though there are some structural elements common to both (killing on an immense scale; repetition compulsion; ceremonial framework). But it is the *self*-sacrificial aspect of the 9/11 attacks that disallows this moral parallelism. What is more, this act of self-sacrifice can open up a debate about new forms of 'the justice of infinite spending'. (I will come back to this point later.)

In the Kantian sublime, the very process of mediation and distancing can be a source of negative pleasure, mixing pain with joy, or fear with delight. Mediation functions as a safety mechanism: the physicality of a TV screen (in the case of 9/11), but also the numerous projection screens put up by our unconscious, allow us to observe and simultaneously consolidate the 'polluting or contaminating other', seen as 'an impurity or stain', from a distance. LaCapra interprets such images as 'a phantasmatic projection of one's own anxieties onto the other that wasn't so wholly other' (1998: 187–9). If we follow his interpretation of the sublime as a secular sacred, we can read the media rituals of sacrificialism and victimization (191) – from the designation of 9/11 actors as beasts, monsters and subhuman creatures in the tabloid press to the exposure of terrorism suspects in spectacularized places like Camp X-Ray – as a reflection of a desire to seek purification through the enclosure of alterity in a ceremonial framework which prevents the sublime from overspilling. By drawing strictly delineated boundaries between the source of horror and the selves exposed to it, the integrity and moral superiority of the media producers *and* audiences is firmly established.

Quoting from Saul Friedlander's *Memory, History, and the Extermination of the Jews in Europe*, LaCapra describes one of the components of *Rausch* (delight) felt by perpetrators as the effect of 'a growing *elation stemming from repetition*' (33; emphasis added); it is an instance in which perpetrators are seized by a compelling, interminable lust for killing on an immense scale. Significantly, the broadcast media are able to enhance the sense of the massification of murder and the accompanying conflicting feelings of fear and delight through their constant relay of images and headlines. This is not to impose a naive identification between the Nazis and the media, but rather to point to a mechanism of differentiation (supporting a clear distinction between good and evil, between victims and perpetrators, 'society' and its 'folk devils', embraced by traditional discourses of moral panic) that is at work in such footage. However, these assertions are threatened by the media participation in the performativity of the event, in its staging before our very own eyes. This repetition feature of the media has been particularly exploited in reporting the attack on the Twin Towers. We can perhaps argue that on 11 September the pain aspect of the sublime sprang from the repetition compulsion, from the need to show, and the *im*possibility of *not* seeing, the relay image of the Towers collapsing. According to Thomas Elsaesser (2001), repetition serves the function of creating in the viewer 'prosthetic trauma' by establishing a gap between the sensory impact of an event or image and the media's ability to make sense of it.[14] The accompanying pleasure, or, better, relief, would in turn result from survival, from surmounting the near-death experience. This is connected with the sidestepping of this gap between image and context, between perception and cognition – which, because it is phantasmatic, does not make trauma disappear. By providing us with an illusion of a linear narrative and thus allowing us to 'take it all in', by creating communal, ready-made traumatic 'flashbacks', television helps us master the sublime; it holds trauma at bay.

WHOSE TRAUMA IS IT ANYWAY? ETHICS AND SACRIFICE

Of course, there is something rather sinister about the *Rausch*, or delight, that LaCapra talks about since the act of one's own survival comes at the expense of someone else's death. Using the Nazi example, he goes so far as to argue that their very lust for killing, for the other's death, is a source of fascination and delight, and that the other's death in this instance is absolutely gratuitous, rather than necessary to the survival of the self and the self's revaluation of its own relation to mortality. And yet, as psychiatrist Robert Jay Lifton asserts in an interview with Cathy Caruth, 'my view is that you cannot kill large numbers of people except with a claim to virtue, so that killing on a large scale is always an attempt at affirming the life power of one's group' (Caruth, 1995: 140). For LaCapra the sublime ultimately forecloses on ethics – what emerges in its place is a form of perverse morality. Indeed, he points to the strengthening of Nazi moral principles as a result of their actions, which were supposed to lead to the purification of their 'Aryan nature'. As I mentioned earlier, LaCapra describes the sublime as a secular displacement of the sacred, involving the attempt to transvalue trauma into a disconcerting source of elation and transcendence. The sublime is thus for him based on sacrifice, on the degradation of the unpresentable radical alterity (identified with the Jew, but also, we might add, with the Muslim, the terrorist, or the asylum seeker) for the sake of the erection of morality. Through a disavowal of the ultimate trauma of death (which belongs *to the other*), the self emerges victorious and strengthened.[15] As Lifton points out, 'the Nazi movement saw itself as conquering death and never dying' (Caruth, 1995: 140).

As a result of this 'faithful' reading of Kant, LaCapra disallows the sublime its politico-ethical role and only links it with Nazi morality. Perceiving the sublime in the Kantian way as an overcoming of the sensual and the rise of practical reason, he confines it to the negativity of history: to its horrors, atrocities and deaths. It is not even that LaCapra *denies* the sublime an ethical side; he just follows Kant's interpretation of ethics as conscious reflection – only to point out what happens when this reflection is misapplied. But he also speaks of the need for 'vigilance and *the mounting of conscious resistance* to deadly tendencies that are fostered but never simply determined by certain historical conditions whose genesis should be controverted in every legitimate manner' (LaCapra, 1998: 34-55; emphasis added). LaCapra thus understands ethical judgement as something that a self – exposed to a traumatic event that defies representation and imagination – can nevertheless make uncompromisingly. Rather than consider some possible ways of working through the trauma of the unspeakable, he demands that now and again we 'step outside' our situatedness in the everyday to make an ethical statement. Ethics thus seems to be situated in some pre- or extra-discursive realm – but it is not the pre-ontological of the Levinasian kind, which interrupts, and makes demands on, being. The realm of the ethical is for LaCapra both separable and accessible to the conscious self, which will be able to make a rational decision about value and thus rise above the animalistic and the deadly. Continuing along the lines of the Kantian sacrificial sublime, LaCapra proposes the erection of barriers between the other in me, who – even if not denied, 'to the extent it is desirable' (1998: 34) – can nevertheless be isolated at the right moment for ethics to take place. However, philosophers such as Nietzsche, Levinas and Derrida have argued that 'violence is not necessarily the exclusive characteristic of the other but rather, and perhaps even above all, a means through which the self, whether individual or collective, is constituted and maintained' (de Vries and Weber, 1997: 2). Thus violence, as an act of making a decision at the expense of all other decisions, is foundational to human existence. This allows me to suggest that LaCapra's proposition for a conscious ethical reflection in fact sidesteps the problem of trauma and violence, as the latter is only seen as something that the self sets itself *against*. But is it possible to think of an ethical response which embraces violence as a 'good', and which turns it into a responsibility?

GOOD AND BAD VIOLENCE

In their introduction to the collection, *Violence, Identity and Self-Determination*, Hent de Vries and Samuel Weber argue that, if violence as an 'object' of analysis

> seems inextricably bound up with the structurally ambivalent relation of self and other, then this relationship cannot but affect the nature of the knowledge that takes violence as its object. Indeed, the Nietzschean suspicion that violence is never just the object, but always also the medium of all cognitive discourse suggests that its structural ambivalence may call for new kinds of discourses prepared to take into account the ambiguous relationship between conceptualization and violence. (de Vries and Weber, 1997: 13)

Violence is thus never something we can talk *about*; any discourse on violence is always unavoidably violent – and thus a positive discourse of ethics must necessarily entail, and account for, the negativity of violence. This intrinsic violence of ethical discourse – of any human discourse, in fact – springs from the fact that discourse (speech, writing) is always an attempt at self-constitution, an attempt to claim or establish a position which would be different from that of the other. The demarcation of discursive boundaries – of speech, of writing, of art – is an act of self-constitution at the origin of which lies the exclusion and denial of that which cannot be incorporated, of that which has to be left out, cut off, severed.[16]

The debate on violence and murder in the media – one of the staple topics of daytime TV talk shows hosted by 'life pundits' and 'moral entrepreneurs' – can therefore only ever be conducted from a position of violence itself, as violence is intrinsic to the process of self-constitution, of taking a stand, of making a choice (be it on the individual or communal level). Even if an ethical self might want to strive to avoid violence, even if absolute nonviolence might be our ethical goal, it can only ever exist as a goal, a horizon. As Hent de Vries argues, 'Critiques of violence are not without violence. They are successful only if they turn violence inside out, if they are somehow violent *in turn*, turning good violence against bad or the worst violence' (1997: 27).[17] But how exactly can this 'bad violence' be turned into a 'good one'? What can allow us to read the violence of mediated murders as potentially ethical?

For Emmanuel Levinas, violence constitutes subjectivity; it is intrinsic to the formation of the subject, which can only emerge in responding to the intrusion of alterity. Levinas describes violence as 'the shock with which the infinite enters my consciousness and makes it responsible' (de Vries and Weber, 1997: 29, see also Levinas, 1969: 194–7). Violence corresponds here to the 'welcoming [of] a being to which [consciousness] is inadequate' (Levinas, 1969: 25). This kind of violence is not identical with the violations of identity associated with terror and war. Instead, it is 'good violence' because it brings in some good: the responsibility of the subject which is established in this violent act, and which is made *ethical* – i.e. *responding*, exposed to the alterity of the other – in its foundation. For Levinas, trauma (as a violent intrusion and wounding) is a foundational moment of consciousness (see Levinas, 1998: 12, 15, 48, 50, 56). Our subjectivity is thus always already born in violence, it is a response to what we cannot comprehend, master, grasp, to what escapes our conceptual powers. But it is also a response to the instance of death, of the other's death. In the case of 9/11, the trauma is 'prosthetic'; it is permanently suspended in the feedback loops of the collapsing Twin Towers, and yet it still makes a demand on us, disturbing our self-complacency and togetherness, and pushing us to respond.

By repeating the trauma and theatricalizing it through the feedback play of selected, quickly-to-become-familiar clips, the broadcast media make trauma liveable, bearable. Size is not insignificant here – the miniaturization of the trauma on the 10, 14 or 21-inch TV screen allows for the theatrical staging of the psychic drama which accompanies the emergence of consciousness and its opening itself up to the other, yet also encourages a proximity, even intimacy with it. Weber talks about our tendency to 'recognise violence only when it is televisible, televisual' (Weber, 1997: 82). The media, with its violent rituals of victimization and sacrifice, can thus perhaps at the same time be seen as lending us all a helping hand in recognizing our own foundational violence and in coming to terms with it. And also, if it is true that 'we can only think of death as a spectacle, representation – and a death of the other' (Weber, 1997: 97), the media events of murder and violence provide us with a set-up in which death can be watched, enclosed and temporarily mastered. By experiencing trauma resulting from the enforced repetition of the violent image we form a relationship to death through relegating it to others. In this sense we can argue that television and video help us 'survive'; they teach us a more mature relationship to death, while also keeping it at bay for us (Weber, 1997: 99–102). And yet this intrinsically violent response of every self – unconsciously rejoicing at the fact that it is not *me* that has perished in the plane attacks of 9/11 and that it is not *my* child that was snatched by Thompson and Venables from that shopping centre in Liverpool[18] – simultaneously establishes the self as ethical. Exposed to trauma, the self emerges as taking responsibility, as responding to what is happening before his/her eyes. This response can take a number of forms and is not always ethical – we can try to decide to be better people and not hurt others in the future, we can start working in a hospice as volunteers, but we can also become physically violent towards our family in an attempt to master the trauma, or switch off the TV and try not to think about the images we have seen. However, a response is already occurring in all these instances; the self has to respond to the images seen and the intrusion of alterity. Furthermore, this response is also accompanied by the realization that I have survived the screen trauma, that this time I am not part of the traumatic event I have witnessed. As Lifton explains:

> When one witnesses the death of people, that really is the process of becoming a survivor, and the witness is crucial to the entire survivor experience. The witness is crucial to start with because it's at the center of what one very quickly perceives to be one's responsibility as a survivor. And it's involved in the transformation from guilt to responsibility. ... carrying through the witness is a way of transmuting pain and guilt into responsibility, and carrying through responsibility has enormous thera-peutic value. (Caruth, 1995: 38)

Of course, there is a danger that the self will try to dis-identify with these images of death for good, and that s/he will pursue the dream of his/her own immortality, intactness. The phantasy of permanent survival would represent a foreclosure of ethics – and there is no guarantee that some viewers will not respond precisely in this way to the media images of murder and violence. But there is always something that resists, returns or remains (see Morgan Wortham and Hall, 2002: 713) – what psychoanalysts call 'the real' – and this 'real' will always disturb the ultimate foreclosure of the autonomous self, of the immortal survivor of the traumatic event. By placing alterity at the very core of being, the real that returns, that makes a demand on us beyond the relief of overcoming the trauma of witnessing the painful images, is also a guarantee of the possibility of ethics. The self – threatened by the intrusion of the infinity it cannot master – will always have to respond, and to take responsibility for the otherness it is not able to grasp fully (Levinas, 1998: 12, 15). (The paradox of the Levinasian ethics consists precisely in this *need to respond* to alterity even if one chooses to disavow it and to remain ir*respons*ible towards it.)

AN(OTHER) ETHICS OF THE SUBLIME

Can the sublime provide us with a different model of ethical thinking from the one delineated along Kantian lines? Unlike LaCapra, I do not want to claim that an ethics of the sublime is impossible, or that the Kantian sublime ultimately forecloses on ethics. Working through the mechanisms involved in establishing the separateness and inviolability of the self and its elevation towards conscious reflection, I want to suggest in the final part of this chapter that it is possible to view the sublime as a politico-ethical option in a different sense (even if it means reading Kant 'against Kant', through the writings of Derrida, Levinas and Lyotard), and that the sublime can help us conceptualize a different form of justice. In *The Truth in Painting* Derrida points out that the sublime 'exists only by overspilling' (1987: 122), i.e. that there is always an excess in every encounter with alterity and horror that cannot ensure an equivalent moral exchange between viewer and event. This allows me to postulate that it is *only* when exposed to the possibility of trauma, sacrifice and death that the sublime becomes intrinsically ethical. The ethics of the sublime I propose[19] does not therefore celebrate the inviolability of the self in the sublime experience, or the self's rational side – but rather springs from seeing ourselves in the symbolic mirror of our own violence held up by the murderers, alleged terrorists and 'Saddams'. It arises out of the recognition of the other in me, of the consequences this recognition may yield.

Interestingly, it is precisely the uncertain positioning of the other – who has 'all the traits of the *Is it happening?*' (Lyotard, 1988: 15) – that allows Jean-François Lyotard to interpret Levinas's ethics in the context of the sublime. For Lyotard, sublimity does not have an essence. Instead, it consists in acknowledging that something is taking place, almost against all odds. Here, the withdrawal of knowledge about both the other who will be arriving and the character of this encounter deprives the self of conceptual mastery. Wounded and bare, it can only await the uncertain arrival of the other, who puts the self in question. But, to develop this Levinasian thread further, when I open myself to the infinite alterity of the other, 'the proximity of the neighbour in its *trauma* does not only *strike up against me* but *exalts and elevates me*, and, in the literal sense of the term, inspires me' (Levinas, 1989b: 113–14; emphasis added). Levinas's description of this encounter is embedded in the rhetoric of the sublime, emphasizing pain mixed with pleasure, elevation and greatness. The ethical relation with the other transforms the everyday into the most significant event, whose importance is stressed by the upward movement the self experiences when confronted with the other's alterity. And it is precisely in its eventality – in its uncertain, deferred and yet awaited (what Derrida would call 'messianic') arrival and its interruption of the ordinary – that the sublime is revealed as ethical, provided that ethics is understood here in the Levinasian sense as 'responsibility for the alterity of the other', as intrusion, wounding and taking-hostage (see Levinas, 1969: 43, 47; 1998: 11-15). While we can thus conclude that the subject is *constituted* in and through the sublime event, through an encounter with infinite alterity, it is also simultaneously *ripped open, wounded, traumatized* and made to face 'the presence of the other in oneself'. Alterity does not have to come from outside – in the form of a 'terrorist', a street mugger or a genomic intervention. Instead, alterity is *originary* (even if it remains forgotten, suppressed or denied), which means that it *founds* and *conditions* our sense of selfhood and our relations with exteriority.

Being faced by the death of the other which is reported, narrated and televised by the media, I am held in captivity, taken hostage, made to realize not only that it is him/her and not me that has died, but also that his/her death constitutes part of my mortality. Seeing images of the dead I am also made aware of the fact that I have not died in their place and that *I should have* perhaps *died* in place of them. Elated at my own survival, I am also made to feel responsible for the death which is not mine, and exposed to the ultimate suffering of the other. (On 9/11, this would not only have been the suffering of the victims of the plane attacks and their families but also the prior suffering of the non-televisable dispersed victims of the economic power of *One World Center*.) The other's death thus puts me in question and challenges my singularity and solipsism, my comfort and 'place under the sun'.

Significantly, the processes of *photographic and cinematic mediation* through which such deaths are conveyed to me entail protective mechanisms similar to those involved in the production of the sublime (see Kant, 1952: 110-11). One can be tempted to perceive the body of journalists and news reporters as neo-Kantian moralists, attempting to shock us with their footage and thus – through a distantiation involved – eventually lead us to rational, *moral* reflection. (After the initial shock, the recovered self would thus be able to conceptualize the infinite violence and terror but also to position itself on its other side – a line of reasoning that would lead to supporting the 'clash of civilizations' argument evoked in the context of 9/11.)

But even if the sublime experience of survival leads to an *economic morality* of retributive justice rather than *ethics*, it also brings about an *ethical experience* of being exposed, in one's vulnerability and sensibility, to the alterity of the other – to his/her suffering and death. It thus breaks with the algebra of justice by introducing the possibility of the justice of infinite spending, which I mentioned earlier. And if the sublime works only by overspilling, and if it is characterized by an encounter with incalculable and undescribable alterity, the ethics it calls for, the justice it promises, is always already inscribed in the horizon of the undecidable. This does not mean that the questions of justice, punishment, guilt and repayment should not be raised in relation to the Oklahoma bomber, the perpetrators of the attacks on New York and Washington DC, or the killers of Jamie Bulger, merely that the decision as to their outcome cannot be taken in advance, by means of an application of a rule – be it common sense, mathematical logic or a legal paragraph. But also, if justice stands for the affirmation – rather than denial – of the 'experience of the other as other',[20] it also displaces the equivalence of guilt and punishment. Indeed, the balance sheet needs to be redrawn, with the question of justice extended beyond its perception of a 'debt' that the other (the 'terrorist', Osama bin Laden) needs to repay 'us'. And thus,

even if the sublime in its elevation toward morality always inheres the possibility of the 'pervertibility of justice' (as we saw in the case of the Kantian
sublime as 'applied to' the Nazi perpetrators), it also radically questions the
established legal and moral discourses in which we speak about such acts.

RESPONSIBILITY AND THE GIFT OF DEATH

The problem, then, is not only how to repay ethically for the crimes that
leave us speechless – as positing the problem in these terms would mean
confirming the moral position in which justice has been pre-calculated and
decided upon in advance – but what can we learn, what kind of (perhaps
undesirable, abject or offensive) gift can we accept from Timothy McVeigh,
Thompson and Venables, Osama bin Laden or Saddam Hussein. Even
though it may be a scandalous, unwanted and unthanked-for gift – because
it disturbs our sense of Western socio-economic comfort, justice and right-
fulness – it does perhaps approach the ideality of the Derridean *Gift*, which
secretly makes its way into the organism, distributing both poison and cure.
In this way, it disturbs our 'being at home with ourselves' and makes us
responsible in the face of a horror that we do not maybe even comprehend.
(In case of the 9/11 attacks, perhaps the real horror – displaced by the media
images of the destroyed towers and lost lives – involved the possibility of
the Western economic hegemony crumbling beyond recovery, returning
to a 'ground zero' point?) This does not of course mean that on being presented with such instances of 'mediated murder' we will necessarily actively
answer to this responsibility instead of, for instance, ignoring, silencing or
displacing it. But we will be placed in the transformed economic network in
which the call for justice comes from behind the mediating screen – from
the death of the other and the ongoing life of the third party (i.e. somebody
else beyond 'me' and 'the victim'), who, *like me*, has also survived. It is the
presence of the third that opens up the ethical realm to the political, thus
allowing us to commence the process of the sublimation of the trauma. And
thus it is through non-programmatic, open-ended and ethically motivated
political acts that the work of reparation can be undertaken. The ethics of
the sublime – with its (no matter how temporary) elevation towards the
infinitely great – will save us from a lifetime of trauma, from a political
paralysis and an abyss of the ethical night, but also from the algebraic politics of injustice.[21]

Levinas explains the political responsibility posed by the presence of the
third person as follows: 'I pass from the relation in which I am obligated
and responsible to a relation where I ask myself who is the first. I pose the
question of justice: within this plurality, which one is the other par excellence? How to judge? How to compare unique and incomparable others?'
(Robbins, 2001: 214). We have thus returned to the problem of calculation,

which is played out in the ambiguity between singularity and universality – but it does not mean I am advocating here a necessary return to the mathematical moral paradigm. Even if Levinas makes us aware that calculation is sometimes inevitable, and that politics involves making decisions at the *cost* and *expense* of other decisions, these decisions need to be made within the horizon of the justice of infinite spending, to which politics needs to appeal if it is not to become 'a purely political calculation – to the point of totalitarian abuse' (Levinas in Robbins, 2001: 220).

Notes

1 In 1993 in Liverpool a two-year-old, Jamie Bulger, was abducted, assaulted and killed by two ten-year-olds: Robert Thompson and Jon Venables. Subsequently, the killers were treated as adults, tried in an adult court and sentenced to a mandatory 'tariff' sentence of eight years, later extended to fifteen years. The case has since been revisited by human rights organizations. Having been given new identities, the two boys were released in 2001, at the age of eighteen – an event which led to a public outcry for retribution and 'justice'.

2 Theorists such as Jacques Derrida, Ernesto Laclau and Judith Butler all emphasize the importance of this aporia, or 'passage without crossing' which we nevertheless need to attempt to traverse, between universality and particularity in their writings on politics and ethics.

3 By proposing the notion of 'multiple mediation' I attempt to avoid the linear perspective implicated by the currently fashionable term 'remediation', a term that seems to rely on the belief in the possibility of a recuperation of a direct, unmediated experience.

4 De Bolla is focusing here on the Seven Years War of 1756–63.

5 This ethos of collective individualism has its religious (e.g. Puritanism in the US) and secular (industrialism or entrepreneurialism in Western Europe) incarnations.

6 I discuss the significance of the sublime as a trope through which we can think about the fears, desires and fascinations associated with 'the technological age' in *On Spiders, Cyborgs and Being Scared: the Feminine and the Sublime* (2001).

7 The notion of the sublime has been most famously introduced into debates on capitalism by Fredric Jameson, who has connected sublimity with our inability to create an orderly cognitive map under late capitalism. This inability results from the increasingly complex technological and media forms we are surrounded by. Jameson writes: 'The technology of contemporary society is … mesmerizing and fascinating not so much in its own right but because it seems to offer some privileged representational shorthand for grasping a network of power and control even more difficult for our minds and imaginations to grasp: the whole new decentered global network of the third stage of capital itself' (1991: 37–8). However, I am more inclined to follow Lyotard's position on the sublime, as – unlike Jameson – he is able to see it as a 'positive negativity' which offers a certain promise for the future. Lyotard believes that aesthetic innovation – which he traces back to the avant-garde arts – can lead to political transformation, while for Jameson aesthetics cannot achieve anything any more as it remains under the domination of the all-pervasive and menacing world economic system.

8 Significantly, it is the discourse of the sublime that is traditionally analysed in politico-ethical categories. See Andrew Ashfield and Peter de Bolla (eds), *The Sublime: A Reader in British Eighteenth-Century Aesthetic Theory* (1996) and Paul Crowther, *The Kantian Sublime: From Morality to Art* (1989).

9   This is not to assert that it is possible to have an *un*mediated engagement with such events, only to point to a particular usefulness of the discourses of trauma and the sublime for dealing with them.

10 The notion of the event plays an important role in the work of a number of contemporary philosophers – one can mention here Jean-François Lyotard (who, significantly, links the event with sublimity), Jacques Derrida and Alain Badiou. For all of them, the event inscribes itself in politico-ethical trajectories. However, while Derrida and Lyotard would probably be more inclined to recognize the eventality of the everyday, i.e. the *constant* possibility of an eruption of the extraordinary in the ordinary, for Badiou events are far more rare. They are also universalizable and clearly connected with the political imaginary which can transform the world.

Samuel Weber provides an interesting justification for his use of the term 'event' in relation to 9/11:

> Take … the events of September 11. I call them 'events' because the word seems best to condense and to complicate the two meanings of the term with which I am familiar. First, the usual use of the term in English, to designate a spatiotemporally localizable occurrence. And second, the Heideggerian meaning of *Ereignis*, designating an unpredictable, uncontrollable outbreak that disrupts spatial and temporal continuities and dislocates and transforms frames of reference. What happened on September 11 was an event in both senses. (Morgan Wortham and Hall, 2002: 716–17)

11 'After the first, one could still believe it was an accident. Only the second impact confirmed the terrorist attack' (Baudrillard, 2002: 46).

12 In his discussion of the sublime in *A Philosophical Enquiry into the Origin of our Ideas of the Sublime and the Beautiful* Burke focuses on one's *self-preservation* in the face of the threatening event; i.e. on the instance of *overcoming* the threat or *mastering* it.

13 There were many attempts to issue this call to arms earlier on, in the case of both Afghanistan and Iraq, but 9/11 seems to have provided the politicians with a propitious moment for its public voicing through the media channels.

14 As Samuel Weber observes, 'The separability of image from context, of vision and audition from the organs of an individual body, of perception from reception – all this is intensified with the media in general, and with television in particular' (1997: 101).

15 Even though trauma is seen as belonging to the persecuted other, one might perhaps argue that the Nazi perpetrators – the authors of the singular traumatic event of torture or murder – also found themselves inhabiting the 'larger' traumatic event of the Second World War. This is by no means to impose a 'moral equivalence' between the perpetrators and their victims but rather to point to the multi-layered working of the trauma in the shaping of every self – a self, that is, in its potentiality, always already ethical. Thus an attempt to reassert a denial of death, to sidestep its trauma, paradoxically leads to a trauma of disavowal, 'a form of numbing' (Caruth, 1997: 140).

16 The self thus always emerges as fragmented, wounded, lacking.

17 The previous chapter analyses the relationship between subjectivity, violence and the law in more detail.

18 The rejoicing at one's own survival is less a psychological description of an emotion and more a transposition of the Kantian relief at the confirmation of the intactness of one's own cognitive faculties and one's 'bodily schema' in the sublime experience. Of course, this survival can trigger off other unconscious responses: pleasure at the annihilation of the repudiated other, desire to occupy its fantasized place, guilt – but the jubilatory aspect is important here because through it the reparation of trauma (through an ethical response) can begin, although the structural ambivalence of this 'rejoicing' should not be ignored.

19 For a more detailed discussion of the ethics of the sublime which arises out of the exploration of the 'forgetting' of sexual difference in the traditional discourse of sublimity, see Zylinska (2001).

20 See 'The Deconstruction of Actuality: An Interview with Jacques Derrida' (1994), especially 36-7 and Jacques Derrida, 'Force of Law: the "Mystical Foundation of Authority"' (1990).

21 I am not trying to assert an unproblematic analogy between the sublime and sublimation here, although certain parallelisms between these two concepts have been traced by thinkers such as Jacques Lacan, Slavoj Žižek and Joan Copjec. Instead, I want to point to the need for sublimation (i.e. transformation to a higher, or psychoanalytically 'better', plane) in trauma – a process that should save one from remaining permanently entrapped in one's incapacity to respond adequately to the horrific event. Both the sublime and sublimation provide a passage to ethics – the former, in the form of the mind's elevation above the natural towards the supersensual and the moral (as explained by Kant), the latter, in the form of the transformation of sexual instincts into a creative activity demanded by society. The difference, of course, is that while the Kantian sublime, and Kantian ethics, originate in the self, it is the outside influences, or the Superego, that condition the emergence of morality and productivity in/through sublimation. However, my re-reading of the sublime via Levinas opens up a possibility, I believe, for an ethics of the sublime that does not originate in the self but rather arrives as an outside demand on the self, posed by the infinite alterity of the other. Perhaps sublimation could thus be re-read not as a violent attempt to satisfy a Superego but rather as a responsible response to the demand of the Other.

5

Ethics and the Body

THE PEOPLE YOU NEVER SEE

In one of the final scenes of Stephen Frears's film, *Dirty Pretty Things* (UK, 2002), 'legitimate' London meets its 'constitutive outside': an illegal immigrant from Nigeria, a Turkish asylum seeker and a black prostitute.

> *'How come I've never seen you before?'*, asks a 'native' Briton when facing this alien crowd that has gathered to meet him at an underground hotel car park.
> *'We are the people you never see. We're the ones who drive your cabs, clean your rooms and suck your cocks,'* replies the Nigerian immigrant.

What exposes this network of interdependency, woven out of multiple see-through threads, is a thwarted business transaction, in which Señor Juan, a head porter and a trade *courier* between the two worlds, becomes himself the *object* of a business exchange. The goods in question are human kidneys, which are surgically removed from the bodies of illegal immigrants and asylum seekers for the price of a forged Western passport and then smuggled to 'the other side'. Señor Juan's 'health network' falters when Okwe, a Nigerian doctor turned hotel porter, manages to anaesthetize Juan and remove one of his own kidneys – thus saving Juan's next imminent victim, a Turkish girl desperate to buy an EU passport and move to New York, from unnecessary surgery. Accompanied by his 'assistants', Okwe quickly delivers the promised 'goods' to the client waiting in the hotel car park – and hence the client's surprise: 'How come I've never seen you before?'

Frears's film is interesting in its metaphorization of the issue of asylum seekers' bodies. Frequently represented as contaminating agents, always on the verge of penetrating the healthy body politic of the community or nation,[1] the asylum seekers in *Dirty Pretty Things* are positioned as a secret source of life, which sustains and nourishes the body proper. And it is the issue of asylum seekers' bodies, or even of asylum seekers *as bodies*, that will concern me in this chapter. Drawing on official acts of Western multicultural democracies – predominantly the UK Nationality, Immigration and Asylum Act (2002) and its accompanying documents and actions – I will investigate, via an engagement with Judith Butler, the constitution of what I will term the biopolitics of immigration.[2] Butler's work on the performativity of cultural identities, including notions of gender, kinship and the body, has been influential on my thinking about asylum, immigration and nationality. But it is in particular her investigation of *which bodies come to matter* – addressed most explicitly in her 1993 book, *Bodies That Matter*, but also developed further in her later writings – that has inspired my analysis of the issues of asylum and immigration in the context of biopolitics.

THE UNIVERSAL ACTS AND THE BIOPOLITICS OF IMMIGRATION

The notion of biopolitics comes from Michel Foucault, who in the final section of *The History of Sexuality* puts forward a claim that, in modernity, ancient sovereign power exerted over life and death has been replaced by bio-power: 'a power to *foster* life or *disallow* it to the point of death' (1984: 138). Biopolitics describes the processes through which Western democracies, with all their regulatory and corrective mechanisms, administer life by exercising power over the species body (139). What is now at issue, according to Foucault, is not so much 'bringing death into play in the field of sovereignty' as instantiating the idea and sense of the norm, which is supposed to regulate society and ensure the intactness of its sovereign authority. The biopolitics of immigration – one of the forms through which bio-power is enacted in Western democracies and through which life is 'managed' – thus contributes to the development of the idea of normative universality, against which particular acts of political (mis)practice can be judged.

And yet, as Judith Butler, Jacques Derrida and Ernesto Laclau have demonstrated in numerous works, the notion of universality proposed in official political discourses always entails (or is contaminated by, as Laclau has it) a certain particularity. Indeed, the universal juridico-political acts acquire their 'universal' value only if they draw on the particularity of the official and non-official regulatory mechanisms that are supposed to exclude whatever may pose a threat to this idea of universality. This is to say, they rely on state legislation already in place, on the concept of citizenship embraced by the democratic community, but also on 'public opinion' that has to be taken into account and responded to.

Judith Butler in particular has gone to great lengths to expose the productive ambiguity entailed in the notion of an act – an ambiguity that the heading of this section is intended to convey.[3] The noun group 'the universal acts' (no matter whether we are speaking more generally about constitutive acts of Western democracies, or, more specifically, about legal acts regulating issues of nationality and immigration) is also a clause, pointing to the transition process in which the timelessness of universality is put in question. If the universal *acts*, it is then taken out of the frozenness of an instant and undergoes a certain transformation, maybe even a deformation. The acting out of universality simultaneously establishes this very idea of universality through the sequence of acts, through their citation, or repetition. I thus want to argue here that the alleged universality of the acts and actions directed at, or involving, asylum seekers, is in fact only established through the working of the performative, i.e. through the reiterative performance of these acts. But I will also claim that this biopolitics of immigration both *presupposes* – in the form of an injunction – and *produces* a certain ethics: what I will call, drawing on Butler's work, 'an ethics of bodies that matter'. And it is precisely this *ethics of bodies that matter* that I will see as a source of political hope, as well as a guarantee of the possibility of *enacting differently* the political acts which regulate the issues of asylum, immigration and nationality.

The double-movement of presupposition and production inherent in the phrase 'the universal acts' indicates that an ethics of bodies that matter will not be a mere 'correction' to the official politics of immigration. Rather than work as an addition produced by work of reflection, this ethics will be shown to underlie, but also expose, or even explode, the official political discourses producing and legitimating the issues of immigration, nationality and citizenship. As the reader will hopefully realize by now, ethics is not understood here in a normative sense; it does not refer to a collection of morals. The notion of ethics I draw on in this book is based on the work of Emmanuel Levinas, for whom ethics is the 'first philosophy', situated 'even before ontology', and thus 'before politics' – not in the temporal sense, bur rather in the form of an unconditional demand on the conditioned universe, with its particular places, customs and political acts. Levinasian ethics[4] – defined as concern about the alterity of the other, but also as response and responsibility – is most pertinent for my investigation as it seems to tally with the multiculturalist position of 'respect for cultural difference' that might be easily, perhaps *too* easily, applied to 'the issue of asylum seekers'. But it is the rigour of Levinas's philosophy and its deployment by a number of post-structuralist and post-Marxist thinkers that allows me to question what is actually meant by this idea of 'respecting the other'. However, I would like to defer talking about ethics as response and responsibility and dwell for a little while on notions of *ethos* (understood as 'custom') and *ethnos* ('place') that underlie certain ethical conceptions but which also provide a bridge to the political. It is the customs, norms and regulations of the democratic public sphere that will be of particular interest to me.

PERFORMATIVITY OF THE PUBLIC SPHERE

The 'issue' of asylum seekers lies at the very heart of the broader issue concerning the constitution of the public sphere. According to Butler, democratic participation in the public sphere is enabled by the preservation of its boundaries, and by the simultaneous establishment of its 'constitutive outside'.[5] She argues that in contemporary Western democracies numerous singular lives are being barred from the life of the legitimate community, in which standards of recognition allow one access to the category of 'the human'. In order to develop a set of norms intended to regulate the state organism, biopolitics needs to establish a certain *exclusion* from these norms, to protect the constitution of the *polis* and distinguish it from what does not 'properly' belong to it. Significantly, Giorgio Agamben goes so far as to suggest that the inclusion of bare life in the political realm constitutes *the original* – if concealed – nucleus of power, or even that the production of a biopolitical body is the original activity of sovereign power (1998: 6). But it is not only the host population that is subjected to – and simultaneously constituted through – the regulatory controls such as population censuses, vaccination programmes and the politicization of sexual health. The 'healthy' body politic needs to be maintained in its vitality by preventing contamination from 'outside' – through viruses and plagues of all sorts. The biopolitics of immigration looks after the bodies of the host community and protects it against parasites that might want to invade it. In order to be able to do this, the sovereign state needs to equip itself with technologies and tools that will allow it to trace, detect and eliminate these parasites. Technology is mobilized to probe and scan the bare life of those wanting to penetrate the healthy body politic: through the use of fingerprinting, iris recognition and scanners in lorries travelling, for example, across the English Channel, the presence and legitimacy of 'asylum seekers' can be determined, confirmed and fixed.[6] The biopolitics of immigration is thus performative in the sense of the term used by Butler: through probing the bodies of the population a boundary between legitimate and illegitimate members of the community is established. This process depends on a truth regime already in place, a regime which classifies some bodies as 'genuine' and others (be it emaciated bodies of refugees arriving in Dover, squashed in lorries in which they have been smuggled to the 'West', or confined to the Norwegian *Tampa* ship hopelessly hovering off the shores of Australia) as 'bogus'.

The bare life of the host community thus needs to be properly managed and regulated, with its unmanageable aspects placed in a relation of exception, 'an extreme form of relation by which something is included solely through its exclusion' (Agamben, 1998: 18). The inclusion of bare life in the juridico-political order depends on a regulatory ban, on the constitution of bandits whose bare life is exposed to harm and wounding (see Agamben, 1998: 104–5). This allows for a different treatment of 'illegal' immigrants from that of 'legitimate asylum seekers', which goes some way towards explaining why, for example, the US federal government could have passed welfare legislation in 1996 which specifically denied Medicaid-funded prenatal care to illegal immigrants, or why the UK Home Secretary could have proposed in 2002 to cut off benefits of those refugees who do not declare their 'status' on entering the country and are thus not considered 'genuine'. But the question that remains occluded in these processes of 'life management' is '[w]hich bodies come to matter – and why?' (Butler, 1993: xii).

Butler demonstrates the regulatory mechanisms involved in the production and simultaneous exclusion of 'bare life' in a number of her works, referring to such excluded groups as transsexuals and transgender people (1990, 1993), non-traditional family units (1990, 1993), racial minorities (1997) or even cyborgs (1993). But it is the literary heroine Antigone, analysed in *Antigone's Claim: Kinship Between Life and Death*, that I want to turn to for my discussion of the issue of asylum seekers in Western democracies. Butler's reading of Antigone, who, '[p]rohibited from action, ... nevertheless acts', and whose 'act is hardly a simple assimilation to an existing norm' (2002: 82), will allow me to think about the working of the performative in different political discourses, and about the possibility of their resignification entailed in the act of repetition. To approach the issue of the public sphere through Antigone is an attempt on my part to situate the debate around its constitution at the crossroads between singularity and universality,[7] between the singular event of public exclusion – be it Antigone's debarment from burying her brother inside the city walls in Sophocles's play, or the attempted deportations of Somalis from Minnesota and other North American states to their war-ridden homeland post-9/11 – and the 'universal' performative of belonging, legitimacy and exclusion that has informed, or even conditioned, the democratic tradition since the Greeks. But I hope it will be more in the form of a close encounter than an illustration or even a reappropriation that the parallel reading of these different narratives will take place.

Towards the end of *Antigone's Claim* Butler asks:

How are we to understand this realm ... which is precluded from the public constitution of the human, but which is human in an apparently catachrestic sense of that term? Indeed, how are we to grasp this dilemma of language that emerges when 'human' takes on that double sense, the normative one based on radical exclusion and the one that emerges in the sphere of the excluded, not negated, not dead, perhaps slowly dying, yes, surely dying from a lack of recognition, dying, indeed, from the premature circumscription of the norms by which recognition as human can be conferred, a recognition without which the human cannot come into being but must remain on the far side of being, as what does not quite qualify as that which is and can be? Is this not a melancholy of the public sphere? (2002: 81)

It could be argued perhaps that any attempt merely to designate the bodies of asylum seekers as the constitutive outside of the body politic, an allegedly pure body which nevertheless parasitically nourishes itself on the diseased bodies of those that, in a virus-like fashion, are trying to penetrate it from outside, would amount to performing an intellectual exercise. But Butler does not seem interested in such exercises. Her thinking always involves an enactment of a certain political practice. In the above quote she poses questions regarding the political force of this constitutive outside and its ability to transform the alleged universality of the norms that regulate the public sphere, with its constitutive concepts of identity, citizenship and belonging.[8] Significantly, Butler does not just dismiss these norms straight away and then propose to replace them with a set of fairer norms that she herself would devise and impose. Instead, she looks at the process of the development of these norms, and, more precisely, at the speed of their circumscription, which she deems 'premature'. Occurring against the horizon of universal justice, and of the idea of the human that, since the Enlightenment, has organized but also produced this sense of justice, this process seems to arrive at too abrupt an end. *It just comes too quickly.* It happens *so* quickly that we do not even have the time to mourn the loss of life that this 'biopolitical normativity' brings about. Instead, we experience the 'melancholy of the public sphere', a political impasse linked to our narcissistic fantasies of the ('pre-catachrestic') past in which our cultural and political identifications were allegedly fixed and secure, and which allowed for more efficient political mobilization. And yet the norms regarding the humanness of different humans, and the mechanisms of recognition that regulate this humanness, are not just considered obsolete by Butler. But the question that her argument provokes is whether we could perhaps take a little more time with these norms. She encourages us to procrastinate over the question of legitimacy, to dwell on this aporetic tension, or dilemma, of language that both positions a certain normativity and rips it apart. And it is this moment of 'ripping normativity apart', of an intrusion which is also an invitation and an injunction, that I now want to focus on.

For Butler, Antigone 'is not of the human but speaks in its language', thus upsetting 'the vocabulary of kinship that is the precondition of the human', but also enacting a possibility 'for a new field of the human ... the one that happens when the less than human speaks as human, when gender is displaced, and kinship founders on its own founding laws' (2002: 82). Antigone indicates the political possibility 'that emerges when the limits to representation and representability are exposed' (2002: 2). Butler thus takes issue with Hegel's perception of Antigone, whom he does not see as a political figure but rather as 'one who articulates a prepolitical opposition to politics' (2002: 2). Hegel introduces a strict caesura between the law of the household gods, which Antigone both represents and dissolves, and the emergent ethical order and state authority based on principles of universality. The ethical as the realm of articulated norms, habits and customs (i.e. *ethos*), and the political as the realm of participation, together constitute the public sphere, which is opposed in Hegel to the sphere of kinship. Yet Butler points out that this idealized separation does not in fact work, as even though she is situated outside the terms of the *polis*, Antigone enables its very functioning by being its 'constitutive outside', i.e. she confirms and actively contributes to its constitutive exclusions. Instead of accepting Hegel's reading of Antigone as the story of the superseding of the order of kinship by the ethical order belonging to the state, Butler looks at the process of disruption that kinship (understood broadly as 'family' but not in any normative sense) poses to the idea of the state as we know it. Her Antigone is not confined to the order of the pre-political but rather incarnates 'a politics ... of the scandalously impure' (2002: 5). The daughter of Oedipus, in a compulsive desire to bury her brother against all state interdictions, acts against the incest taboo for which her father stands. This raises for Butler the question of what is going to happen to the inheritance of Oedipus when the rules that he blindly defies and institutes no longer carry the stability accorded to them by anthropology and structural psychoanalysis, but also what consequences such a destabilization will have for our public sphere, with numerous constitutive prohibitions embedded in its gender norms.

ON THE STATE'S THRESHOLD

Before I consider the consequences of this de-Oedipalization of the family structure for contemporary socio-political alliances and formations, let me just remark in passing that one might perhaps question the legitimacy of resorting to classical literary or philosophical texts to provide 'examples' or 'explanations' for current political events. And yet, in his own reading of Antigone and Oedipus in the context of hospitality towards the alien and the foreign, Jacques Derrida justifies such a cross-cultural translation by arguing that these 'urgent contemporary matters' 'do not only bring the classical structures into the present. They interest us and we take a look at them at the points where they seem, as though of themselves, to deconstruct these inheritances or the prevailing interpretations of these inheritances' (2000: 139). Derrida often indicates that we have never really left the Greek legacy behind in our political life, and that our current institutions are an extended gloss on the classical structures whose 'proper name' may have receded into the collective unconscious of many politicians and legislators of the public sphere. But it is the moment of betraying the Greeks, of being unfaithful to some of their democratic institutions, laws and regulations, that Derrida sees as vital in this process of cross-cultural translation, 'a crossing of languages or codes'.⁹ This of course does not just mean abandoning these inheritances, but rather thinking them differently, or allowing them to reveal, 'as though of themselves', certain ambiguities inherent in them, ambiguities that will in turn allow us to interpret and enact our democratic laws in a new, maybe even unexpected, way.

This idea of (im)proper inheritances goes some way towards helping us understand why the liminal position of asylum seekers in Western democracies on the threshold of the state – both in a literal and figurative sense

– provokes similar discourses around issues of legitimacy, belonging, ethics and kinship to those developed around Antigone's deed. Even though it is the consolidated state units that are seen as laying down the law for the definition of their own politicality and its ethics, and for making decisions regarding the possible inclusion of outsiders into them, the border position of asylum seekers throws up questions regarding state and blood affiliations, gender norms and roles, and ethical positions. Butler herself accounts for her interest in the 'de-Oedipalization' of the kinship structure underlying the symbolic order in which we participate in the following way:

> I ask this [question] … during a time in which children, because of divorce and remarriage, because of migration, exile, and refugee status, because of global displacements of various kinds, move from one family to another, move from a family to no family, move from no family to a family, or in which they live, psychically, at the crossroads of the family, or in multiply layered situations, in which they may well have more than one woman who operates as the mother, more than one man who operates as the father, or no mother or no father, with half-brothers who are also friends – this is a time in which kinship has become fragile, porous, and expansive. (2000: 22)

But it is not only the porosity and fragmentation of kinship but also its permeation of the body politic that creates possibilities for thinking immigration politics otherwise, and for delineating – perhaps even detecting – an ethics that goes beyond the Hegelian *Sittligkeit*, i.e. an ethics of the community which is already in place. This ethics of permeation and intrusion, an *ethics of bodies that matter*, as I want to call it, both constitutes and challenges the established political discourses of the host community. Before I move on to look at some specific examples of its enactment, I want to propose one more deferral, or detour, via these 'classical structures' – structures that both underlie and are destabilized by the 'urgent contemporary matters' – and look at the figure of Tiresias.

The blind prophet Tiresias, another borderline character in Sophocles's *Antigone*, seems to have returned to the British *polis* at the dawn of the 'third millennium' in the figure of UK Home Secretary, David Blunkett, proponent of the new immigration regime and author of the White Paper, 'Secure Borders, Safe Haven: Integration with Diversity in Modern Britain' (February 2002), a document which paved the way for the subsequent Nationality, Immigration and Asylum Act. What is it that links Tiresias with Blunkett, apart from their physical blindness? In Sophocles's play Tiresias appears before Creon to warn him that Thebes is on the 'edge of peril' and that Creon should 'listen to the voice of reason' and withdraw his prohibition against the burial of Antigone's brother, Polynices. On hearing Creon's refusal to open the city gates, Tiresias accuses Creon of suffering from 'the disease of wealth' and predicts the impending wrath of gods which will descend upon Creon and his family (see Sophocles, 2000). The figure of Tiresias as a blind seer on the border of the *polis* is therefore particularly relevant for me in the context of current legislation regarding asylum and immigration in our democracies. But one might perhaps say that it is too facile a gesture to propose an analogy between a modern Western politician and an ancient prophet of doom and gloom on the basis of their shared 'disability', or even that it is inappropriate to draw attention to Blunkett's actual blindness. Aware of such possible reservations, I am nevertheless prepared to risk accusations of impropriety and pursue the Tiresian (dis)inheritance, and its accompanying blind spots, in the discourse on immigration and asylum as developed in the UK government's White Paper,[10] 'Secure Borders, Safe Haven'.

THE POLITICS OF BLINDNESS

'Secure Borders, Safe Haven' opens with a foreword, which has been authored and signed by the Home Secretary himself. Blunkett adopts here a somewhat paternalistic, sermon-like tone in order to explain to the British public that 'There is nothing more controversial, and yet more natural, than men and women from across the world seeking a better life for themselves and their families'.[11] In his apparent attempt to win over 'the British public', he establishes a sequence of (il)logical equivalences (e.g. between a 'natural' desire for migration and a 'natural' feeling of apprehension felt by those whose territory the migrants enter) which are supposed to embrace and convey how 'the nation' feels about the issue of immigration. In the tone reminiscent of the Greek prophet, Blunkett speaks about the need to offer 'a safe haven' to 'those arriving on our often wet and windy shores'. Just as Tiresias takes it upon himself to point out that Creon speaks unwisely, the Home Secretary addresses and unravels the anxieties of all those self-appointed guardians of the national shores, from editors of tabloid newspapers to 'my home is my castle' John Bulls, who want to turn Britain into a fortress. Blunkett's discussion of the problems connected with migration and asylum is supposed to rebuke accusations that Britain is out of line with other European nations when it comes to the way in which it deals with illegal immigration and asylum seekers, and that 'people coming through the Channel Tunnel, or crossing in container lorries, constitutes an invasion'. Blunkett's Foreword is thus aimed 'against false perception', which he attempts to overcome with 'clarity' and reason. Blunkett lays out his argument carefully, indicating errors in the public perception and correcting them with his own argument. But it is not only the correction of errors that interests the Home Secretary. Blunkett's primary aim is the development of an immigration and asylum policy that 'looks forward'. As if repeating the instruction given to Creon by

Tiresias, Blunkett warns the people not to act unwisely; he explains carefully that migration brings significant benefits and that it can advance the prosperity of the nation – provided it is properly managed. This last reservation makes Blunkett a thrifty prophet, resorting to the discourse of economics and management to explain his vision. As we know from Foucault, the biopolitics of modern democracies works precisely through 'the administration of bodies and the calculated management of life' (1984: 140). And, as if to illustrate this, it is by means of proposing 'rational controlled routes' of immigration (rather than 'the international "free for all", the so-called "asylum shopping" throughout Europe, and the "it is not our problem" attitude which is too often displayed') that Blunkett hopes to promote his policy. But the calculated rationality of his outlook seems permanently threatened by the irrational – coming not only from the opponents of his policy but also from the author of the White Paper himself. After laying out his proposal for a 'rational' and 'controlled' economic migration and asylum system, Blunkett adds: 'It is possible to square the circle'. At this instant the voice of reason founders, and immigration policy reveals that it is only a very rough sketch, one that allows the draughtsman to resort to illicit geometrical moves in order to complete the picture.

Indeed, Blunkett's prophetic vision for Britain as a 'safe haven' depends on a number of exclusions firmly in place. First of all, the Home Secretary affirms that this new vision will only work if we are 'secure within our sense of belonging and identity'. Significantly, Butler makes it clear that 'This exclusionary matrix by which subjects are formed thus requires a simultaneous production of a domain of abject beings, those who are not yet "subjects", but who form the constitutive outside to the domain of the subject' (1993: 3).[12] At best a utopian fantasy of homeliness, at worst a conscious foreclosure of an ethics of openness to the alterity of the other – an alterity that *always* poses a challenge to our own security and self-knowledge[13] – Blunkett's politics of migration therefore seems premised on a logical impossibility. It is a hospitality which is in fact based on the originary closure, on foreseeing the foreign threat and trying to avert it. This is the moment when the classical heritage gives way to bizarre miscegenation. Blunkett-Tiresias stops instructing Creon to actually *become Creon* – a protector of the public sphere whose law both produces and excludes the unlawful, those without the integrity and belonging shared by the members of the *polis*. For it is this when he goes on to announce: 'We have fundamental moral obligations which we will always honour', only to counterbalance this claim with the following reservation: 'At the same time, those coming into our country have duties that they need to understand and which facilitate their acceptance and integration.' His paradoxical immigration policy of 'squaring the circle' is also described as 'a "two-way street" requiring commitment and action from the host community, asylum seekers and long-term migrants alike'. It is perhaps not surprising (which does not mean it is intentional on Blunkett's part) that a linguistic paradox is used when outlining *our* moral obligations and *their* duties, since the asylum seekers' position 'before the law' itself entails a paradox – even though they are *outside* it, they are supposedly *subject to* its power. Constituted as threshold political beings, migrants and 'asylum seekers' are defined precisely through their liminal status that places them on the outskirts of the community. Then how can they be expected to 'have duties' imposed on them by the host community and manifest commitment to these duties if this very community needs a prior definition of itself, a definition which confirms identity and belonging in relation, or even opposition, to what might threaten it? We also need to consider how the political status of asylum seekers and migrants is actually established. Who legislates the duties that they will be expected to follow? What is the source of the moral obligation that will help Britons 'manage' the asylum issue? Agamben explains that 'The sovereign decides not the licit and the illicit but the originary inclusion of the living in the sphere of law' (1998: 26).[14] To what extent, then, is the sovereign entitled to impose the law on those whose identity he defines as being situated 'before' the law, both in the spatial and temporal sense? In particular, given that in the years 2001–3 the majority of all asylum seekers in the UK were Iraqi, is this conditional openness in the context of 'Gulf War II' not a certain blind spot in the rhetoric and politics of the sovereign government which does not see a connection between the Iraqi *refugees from* their own country, whose lives are threatened by Western bombs, and the Iraqi *asylum seekers trying to come into* Britain? This form of politics, with its underlying moral obligations, seems to be based on a certain occluded but inevitable and thus constitutive violence, where 'the sovereign is the point of indistinction between violence and law, the threshold on which violence passes over into law and law passes into violence' (Agamben, 1998: 32).

Indeed, even the very process of naming an Iraqi, Albanian or Kurdish refugee an 'asylum seeker',[15] towards whom the hospitality of the host nation is to be extended, is inevitably violent. Butler explains that 'The naming is at once the setting of a boundary, and also the repeated inculcation of a norm' (1993: 8). Taking account of the performativity of the hegemonic political discourses can enable us to shift the borders that delineate and establish the contours of the human within these discourses. This in turn can create a possibility for a new politics of immigration, a politics which is informed by an ethics of response and responsibility that goes beyond the set of moral obligations. Looking at excluded, abject, non-human bodies positioned at the threshold of the legitimate political community, Butler declares:

> The task is to refigure this necessary 'outside' as a future horizon, one in which the violence of exclusion is perpetually in the process of being overcome. But of equal importance is the preservation of the outside, the site where discourse meets its limits, where the opacity of what is not

included in a given regime of truth acts as a disruptive site of linguistic impropriety and unrepresentability, illuminating the violent and contingent boundaries of that normative regime precisely through the inability of that regime to represent that which might pose a fundamental threat to its continuity. (1993: 53)

Taking a cue from Butler we might thus argue that a responsible immigration policy should not be based on the idea of integration and immersion but rather on the preservation of the outside as 'the site where discourse meets its limits'. This does not of course mean that all asylum seekers should be permanently kept on the threshold of the country or community they want to enter, and that we should naively celebrate them as an irreducible alterity that resists incorporation. But it is to suggest that the biopolitics of devouring the other, of digesting and disseminating him or her across the body politic, in fact forecloses on the examination of the normative regime that establishes and legitimates the discourse of national identity. The 'asylum seeker' – itself a product of the regime to which s/he is subsequently opposed – can only function on the outside of that regime as its limitation and a guarantee of its constitution. (Once the community truly opens itself up to what it does not know, both its knowledge of alterity and self-knowledge are placed under scrutiny, a state of events that leads to the inevitable shifting of the boundaries between the host as the possessor of goods and the newcomer as their 'seeker'.) The idea of liberal multiculturalism in which all alterity is welcomed and then quickly incorporated into the host community risks occluding the violence at the heart of the constitution of this very community, even if this community defines itself in terms of diversity or pluralism, and not necessarily national or ethnic unity. The task of refiguring the 'outside' as a future horizon, without attempting to annul and absorb this outside altogether, presents itself as a more responsible response to the 'asylum question'.

AN ETHICS OF BODIES THAT MATTER

[Asylum seekers] don't have three heads. They are people with legs and arms, who live and breathe and bleed like everyone else.
(Stephen Frears, director of *Dirty Pretty Things*, in the *Independent on Sunday*, 23 February 2003)

It is through Butler's engagement with 'bodies that matter' that I now want to sketch an ethical response to the biopolitics of immigration practised by the UK and many other 'sovereign democracies'. Of course, Butler's own argument develops out of the investigation of the 'heterosexual matrix' which legislates genders through the reiterated acting of accepted gender roles.

Nevertheless, it also enables us to think through the regulatory mechanisms that are involved in producing, or performing, legitimate citizenship. Butler suggests that in our investigation of juridical acts that legislate different forms of political subjectivity we should turn to the notion of matter, 'not as a site or surface, but as *a process of materialization that stabilizes over time to produce the effect of boundary, fixity, and surface we call matter*' (1993: 9, emphasis in original). She is interested in investigating how the materialization of the norm in bodily formation produces a domain of abjected bodies, a field of deformation which, in failing to qualify as the fully human, fortifies those regulatory norms (1993: 16). But, as I mentioned earlier, Butler does not just want to highlight the 'inside/outside' opposition that separates, however temporarily, the healthy body politic from the parasites that threaten its well-being. The main thrust of her investigation is to find out what this contamination means for the 'universal acts' of Western democracies, and for the political actions embarked upon to guarantee the survival of these acts. And, further, if there is a certain ambivalence already inherent in these acts, can we think them otherwise? Butler thus formulates the following question: 'What challenge does that excluded and abjected realm produce to a symbolic hegemony that might force a radical rearticulation of what qualifies as bodies that matter, ways of living that count as "life", lives worth protecting, lives worth saving, lives worth grieving?' (1993: 16).

I want to suggest that the challenge that the excluded and abjected realm produces to a symbolic hegemony comes in the form of an ethical injunction, in revealing the originary ethicality of the 'universal political acts' already in place. For these acts – such as the 2002 Nationality, Immigration and Asylum Act – can only be formulated *in response to* the other, an other whose being *precedes* the political and *makes a demand on it*. Knocking on the door of Western democracies, 'bodies that matter' are ethical in the originary Levinasian sense; they are already taken account of, even if they are to be later found not to matter so much to these sovereign regimes. Butler's argument thus poses a blow to the alleged sovereignty of the democratic subject, whose response to the needs of the 'other' has to be properly managed through the application of utilitarian principles intermixed with a dose of human-rights rhetoric. Though in *Excitable Speech* she does not arrive at her questioning of political subjectivity via Levinas but rather via a parallel reading of Austin and Althusser, to me her account of 'how the subject constituted through the address of the Other becomes then a subject capable of addressing others' (1997: 26) sounds positively Levinasian.[16] In *Totality and Infinity* Levinas describes this relationship between self and other in the following way:

The alleged scandal of alterity presupposes the tranquil identity of the same, a freedom sure of itself which is exercised without scruples, and to whom the foreigner brings only constraint and limitation. This flawless identity freed from all participation, independent in the I, can nonetheless lose its tranquillity if the other, rather than countering it by upsurging on the same plane as it, speaks to it, that is, shows himself in expression, in the face, and comes from on high. Freedom then is inhibited, not as countered by a resistance, but as arbitrary, guilty, and timid; but in its guilt it rises to responsibility. … The relation with the Other as a relation with his transcendence – the relation with the Other who puts into question the brutal spontaneity of one's imminent destiny – introduces into me what was not in me. (1969: 103)

Levinas understands this inevitability of responsibility and ethics as a need to respond to what precedes me and challenges my self-sufficiency and oneness, to what calls on me to justify 'my place under the sun'. This realization is crucial for developing our notion of citizenship and political justice. To actively become a citizen, a host, a member of the public sphere – instead of just passively finding oneself inhabiting it as a result of an alleged privilege that occludes what it excludes – I need the other not in a negative sense, as an outside to my own positive identity, but to put me in question and make me aware of my responsibility. This is the only way in which mature political participation can take place; otherwise we will only be 'running a software', as Derrida describes it, i.e. applying a ready-made programme to an allegedly predictable situation in which a need for a decision gives way to a technicized manoeuvre. It is the other that makes me aware of the idea of infinity in me, an idea which, according to Levinas, 'establishes ethics' (1969: 204). Through an encounter with the other I realize that the political subjectivity I inhabit is always already temporarily stabilized, that it can be changed, redrafted, or – to use Butler's term – recited. And it is biopolitics that establishes the sense of normativity through managing and regulating 'bare life', a life which is subject to this ethical injunction, to intrusion and wounding, to a call to response and responsibility.

Levinas writes, '*To be a body* is on the one hand *to stand* [*se tenir*], to be master of oneself, and, on the other hand, to stand on the earth, to be in the *other*, and thus to be encumbered by one's body. But – we repeat – this encumberment is not produced as a pure dependence; it forms the happiness of him who enjoys it' (1969: 164, emphasis in original). One might perhaps conclude that the situation the self finds itself in is indeed tragic, and that the need to bear the weight of corporeality which is not all mine does not easily lead to 'happiness'. But Levinas does not propose a naive celebration of difference; he only suggests the openness to (or the enjoyment of) what befalls us may be, in the long term, an easier and *better* response to our corporeal existence. It is precisely this openness and enjoyment that my term 'an ethics of bodies that matter' refers to.

The problem of openness which is to be extended to our current and prospective guests – even, or perhaps *especially*, unwanted ones – is, according to

Derrida, coextensive with the ethical problem. 'It is always about *answering for* a dwelling place, for one's identity, one's space, one's limits, for the *ethos* as abode, habitation, house, hearth, family, home' (Derrida, 2000: 149-51, emphasis added). Of course, this absolute and unlimited hospitality can be seen as crazy, self-harming or even impossible. But ethics in fact spans two different realms – it is always suspended between this unconditional hyperbolic order of the demand to answer for my place under the sun and open to the alterity of the other that precedes me, and the conditional order of *ethnos*, of singular customs, norms, rules, places and political acts. (The latter can only *refer to* the universal without becoming universal itself.) Derrida argues that there is a distinction but also an indissociability between these two ethical orders or 'regimes'. If we see ethics as situated between these two different regimes it becomes clearer why we always remain in a relationship to ethics, why we must respond to it, or, in fact, why we will be responding to it *no matter what*. Even if we respond 'non-ethically' to our guest by imposing on him a norm or political legislation *as if it came from us*; even if we decide to close the door in the face of the other, make him wait outside for an extended period of time, send him back, cut off his benefits or place him in a detention centre, we must already respond to an ethical call. In this sense, our politics is preceded by an ethical injunction, which does not of course mean that we will 'respond ethically' to it (by offering him/her unlimited hospitality or welcome). But, and here lies the paradox, we *will* respond ethically to it (in the sense that the injunction coming from the other will make us take a stand, even if we choose to do nothing whatsoever and pretend that we may carry on as if nothing has happened).

The ethics of bodies that matter is not only a paradox though. It also entails the possibility of changing the laws and acts of the *polis* and delineating some new forms of political identification and belonging. Indeed, in their respective readings of Antigone, Butler and Derrida show us not only that the paternal law towards the foreigner that regulates the idea of kinship in Western democracies can be altered but also that we can think community and kinship otherwise, that the *Sittlichkeit* of the community already in place is just one possible enactment of an ethics of response and responsibility. If traditional hospitality is based on what Derrida calls 'a conjugal model, paternal and phallocentric', in which '[i]t's the familial despot, the father, the spouse, and the boss, the master of the house who lays down the laws of hospitality' (2000: 149), openness towards the alien and the foreign changes the very nature of the *polis*, with its Oedipal kinship structures and gender laws. Since, as Butler shows us, due to new family affiliations developed by queer communities but also as a result of developments in genomics it is no longer clear who my brother is, the logic of national identity and kinship that protects state boundaries against the 'influx' of asylum seekers is to be left wanting. This is not necessarily to advise a carnivalesque political strategy of abandoning all laws, burning all passports and opening all borders (although such actions should at least be *considered*), but to point to the possibility of resignifying these laws through their (improper) reiteration. Enacted by political subjects whose own embodiment remains in the state of tension with the normative assumptions regarding propriety, gender and kinship that underlie these laws, the laws of hospitality are never carried out according to the idea/l they are supposed to entail (see Butler, 1993: 231).

And it is precisely Butler's account of corporeality and matter, of political subjectivity and kinship, that makes Levinas's ethics (and Derrida's reworking of it) particularly relevant to this project. Although the concepts of the body and materiality are not absent from Levinas's writings – indeed, he was one of the first philosophers to identify embodiment as a philosophical blind spot – Butler allows us to redraw the boundaries of the bodies that matter and question the mechanisms of their constitution. Her 'others' are not limited to 'the stranger', 'the orphan' and the 'widow' of the Judaeo-Christian tradition, the more acceptable others who evoke sympathy and generate pity.[17] It is also the AIDS sufferer, the transsexual and the drag queen – people whose bodies and relationships violate traditional gender and kinship structures – that *matter* to her. By investigating the contingent limits of universalization Butler mobilizes us against naturalizing exclusion from the democratic *polis* and thus creates an opportunity for its radicalization (1997: 90). The ethics of bodies that matter does not thus amount to waiting at the door for a needy and humble asylum seeker to knock, and extending a helping hand to him or her. It also involves realizing that s/he may intrude, invade and change my life to the extent that it will never be the same again, and that I may even become a stranger in the skin of my own home.

Notes

1　Anthony Browne argues in *The Spectator* that, by promoting mass immigration from the Third World, New Labour has been importing killer diseases. He writes, 'The thousands of infected immigrants who are arriving in Britain each year are doubling the rate of HIV, trebling the rate of TB, and increasing twentyfold the rate of hepatitis B. All of these are life-threatening diseases which could be, and in some cases have been, passed on to the host community' ('The Government Endangers British Lives', *The Spectator*, 25 January 2003: 12). A similar argument concerning the US is made on the website of FAIR: The Federation for American Immigration Reform:

> The impact of international migration on our public health is often overlooked. Although millions of visitors for tourism and business come every year, the foreign populations of special concern are immigrants – one million arriving as permanent residents each year – and illegal residents, most often from countries with endemic health problems and less developed health care. These populations are of greatest consequence because they are living among us and often are using US health care services. ... As serious as these problems are, they are secondary to the threat of reintroducing serious contagious diseases into our society. 'Contagious diseases that

are generally considered to have been controlled in the United States are readily evident along the border ... The incidence of tuberculosis in El Paso County is twice that of the US rate. [Director of the El Paso health district] Dr Laurence Nickey also reports that leprosy, which is considered by most Americans to be a disease of the Third World, is readily evident along the US–Mexico border and that dysentery is several times the US rate.... People have come to the border for economic opportunities, but the necessary sewage treatment facilities, public water systems, environmental enforcement, and medical care have not been made available to them, causing a severe risk to health and well being of people on both sides of the border.' ... Contrary to common belief, tuberculosis (TB) has not been wiped out in the United States, mostly due to migration. In 1995, there was an outbreak of TB in an Alexandria high school, when 36 high-schoolers caught the disease from an immigrant student. The four greatest immigrant magnet states have over half the TB cases in the US. In 1992, 27 per cent of the TB cases in the United States were among the foreign-born; in California, it was 61 per cent of the cases; in Hawaii, 83 per cent; and in Washington state, 46 per cent. Disease within the immigrant community can be particularly difficult to combat. 'Immigrants present a special challenge, as health officials struggle with language and cultural barriers to find active TB cases and cure them before they spread to the general population.' 'When the migrants develop TB they often remain untreated, as health systems tend to overlook mobile individuals. They can then spread TB to others in crowded housing and can infect otherwise healthy populations as they move through new towns and countries ... And as many as half the world's refugees may be infected with TB' (source: http://www.fairus.org/html/04149711.htm, accessed on 15 May 2003).

2   The current media and political debates on asylum and immigration frequently inscribe themselves in the 'moral panic' schema, which I outlined in the previous two chapters (see Cohen, 2002: i–xxxv). I hope the reader will be able to trace a continuity between this and the preceding two chapters and identify some of the mechanisms I discussed in relation to the panics connected with 'guns and rap', street crime, violence and terrorism in the dominant discourses through which issues of immigration and asylum are being structured.

3   See in particular her *Excitable Speech* (1997: 1–41, 72, 141–59).

4   This ethical position has subsequently been taken up by a number of contemporary thinkers, including Jacques Derrida, Luce Irigaray, Ernesto Laclau and Chantal Mouffe. Butler's own work engages with similar ethical discourses. This is most explicitly articulated in her *Excitable Speech* (which to me has a quasi-Levinasian feel, although Butler develops her argument regarding response, responsibility and speech via Althusser's work on interpellation), her article 'Ethical Ambivalnce' (2000) and *Antigone's Claim* (2002). But I would argue that a certain sense of ethical normativity which underpins any political practice – a normativity of the kind she discusses with Ernesto Laclau and Slavoj Žižek in their collaborative project *Contingency, Universality, Hegemony* – can already be traced in her *Gender Trouble* and *Bodies That Matter*.

5   The notion of the 'constitutive outside' plays an important role in the work of a number of philosophers and cultural critics whose work is informed by deconstructive modes of thinking. In her book *The Democratic Paradox* Chantal Mouffe provides a useful explanation of the significance of this notion, and the need to understand it first of all as a structuring device and not a negatively marked opposite of a certain positivity (i.e. it is an 'outside' because it is 'not inside'). Mouffe points to the fact that the binary oppositions between 'inside' and 'outside', 'us' and 'them' or, in the case of this chapter, 'legitimate citizens' and 'asylum seekers', are put into question by the deconstructive logic that regulates the working of the 'constitutive outside', a concept that both breaks through these oppositions by exposing the constitutive *formal* and

structural dependence of the first set of terms on its 'others' (i.e. on what they exclude but also what they are defined 'against'). Mouffe writes:

> In order to be a true outside, the outside has to be incommensurate with the inside, and at the same time, the condition of emergence of the latter. This is only possible if what is 'outside' is not simply the outside of a concrete content but something which puts into question 'concreteness' as such. This is what is involved in the Derridean notion of the 'constitutive outside': not a content which would be asserted/negated by another content which would just be its dialectical opposite – which would be the case if we were simply saying that there is no 'us' without 'them' – but a content which, by showing the radical undecidability of the tension of its constitution, makes its very positivity a function of the symbol of something exceeding it: the possibility/impossibility of positivity as such. ... [T]he 'them' is not the constitutive opposite of a concrete 'us' but the symbol of what makes *any* 'us' impossible. (2000: 12–13)

6   This is how the UK Home Office explains its asylum procedures: 'When an asylum application has been made, the applicant is screened, during which his or her personal details are recorded, and his or her fingerprints and a photograph are taken. These details are put on an Application Registration Card (ARC) which is issued to the applicant'. It then informs the public that 'a package of measures to increase security at the Fréthun rail freight yard has been agreed. This package includes a double fence, lighting and video surveillance equipment, a vehicle track inside the perimeter, alarm systems, infrared barriers, and the deployment of additional gendarmes and private security personnel'. It also adds, 'Early in 2003 it is planned to activate an EU-wide fingerprint database of asylum applicants and certain other third-country nationals, known as "Eurodac". This will allow for the computerised exchange of fingerprints in order to identify those applicants already known to other participating states.' 'The asylum reforms, which are set out in the Nationality, Immigration and Asylum Bill currently proceeding through Parliament, include introducing a managed process of induction, accommodation, reporting and removal centres to support and track asylum seekers through the system, leading to fast-track removal or integration. Application Registration Cards (ARCs) are now being issued to asylum seekers to provide more secure evidence of identity and better protection against forgery' (source: 'Fairer, faster and firmer – an introduction to the UK asylum system', http://www.homeoffice.org. uk, accessed on 15 May 2003).

7   The figure of Antigone appears in numerous Greek myths and tragedies. There is not thus one 'authoritative' narrative of, or on, Antigone. Antigone's 'act' can nevertheless be summarized as follows: a daughter of the former king of Thebes, Oedipus, and his mother/wife, Jocasta, Antigone returns to Thebes after a long period away. Her brothers, Eteocles and Polynices, have lost power in a battle with Creon. One of Creon's first edicts is to forbid the burial of any of the invaders, especially Polynices – whom he considers a traitor – within the city walls. Antigone commits an act of civil disobedience by sprinkling dust over her brother's body and thus performing a burial ceremony. She is caught and sentenced by Creon to be buried alive – even though she is betrothed to his son Haemon. On listening to the prophet Tiresias Creon changes his mind but it is too late – Antigone has already hanged herself.

8   Giorgio Agamben's argument on the biopolitics of the modern sovereign state can also be useful here. He writes in *Homo Sacer*: 'Only within a political horizon will it be possible to decide whether the categories whose opposition founded modern politics (right/left, private/public, absolutism/democracy, etc.) – and which have been steadily dissolving, to the point of entering today into a real zone of indistinction – will have to be abandoned or will, instead, eventually regain the meaning they lost in that very

horizon. And only a reflection that, taking up Foucault's and Benjamin's suggestion, thematically interrogates the link between bare life and politics, a link that secretly governs the modern ideologies seemingly most distant from one another, will be able to bring the political out of its concealment and, at the same time, return thought to its practical calling' (1998: 4–5).

9   For an account of Butler's position on cultural translation as a way to rearticulate established political formations and idea(l)s see *Contingency, Universality, Hegemony* (Butler, Laclau, Žižek, 2000: 35–41).

10 The White Paper is the last-stage pre-legislation document before the official Act is published.

11 This and all the subsequent quotes from 'Secure Borders, Safe Haven' have been taken from an Internet version of the document, available at http://www.asylumsupport. info/law/act.htm, accessed on 15 May 2003.

12 Butler explains further: 'The abject designates here precisely those "unlivable" and "uninhabitable" zones of social life which are nevertheless densely populated by those who do not enjoy the status of the subject, but whose living under the sign of the "unlivable" is required to circumscribe the domain of the subject' (1993: 5).

13 A Western politician, just as any other citizen or 'political subject', does not need to be well versed in Levinas's or other writings in continental philosophy to find him- or herself called upon by the ethics of openness that demands a response and responsibility. Of course, this call can be ignored or even violently silenced but it has to be responded to in some way.

14 For a detailed discussion of the question of the law and the significance of being placed 'before the law' see Jacques Derrida, 'Before the Law' (1992a) and Giorgio Agamben, 'The Logic of Sovereignty' in *Homo Sacer: Sovereign Power and Bare Life* (1998). See also Chapter 3, 'Ethics and "Moral Panics"', in this book.

15 This is the definition of the asylum seeker used in the 2002 Nationality, Immigration and Asylum Act:

> 18 Asylum-seeker: definition
> (1) For the purposes of this Part a person is an 'asylum-seeker' if –
> (a) he is at least 18 years old,
> (b) he is in the United Kingdom,
> (c) a claim for asylum has been made by him at a place designated by the Secretary of State,
> (d) the Secretary of State has recorded the claim, and
> (e) the claim has not been determined.
> (Source: http://www.hmso.gov.uk/acts/acts2002/20020041.htm, accessed on 15 May 2003)

16 The following part of the quotation from *Excitable Speech* is also significant for tracing a parallel between Butler and Levinas: 'the subject is neither a sovereign agent with a purely instrumental relation to language, nor a mere effect whose agency is pure complicity with prior operations of power. The vulnerability to the other constituted by that prior address is never overcome in the assumption of agency (one reason that "agency" is not the same as "mastery")' (1997: 26). In my response to a paper on her work, which constituted an early draft of this chapter, and which I presented at the 'Close Encounter with Judith Butler' panel organized by Ewa Ziarek at the 27th annual conference of the International Association for Philosophy and Literature in Leeds on 26–31 May 2003, Butler acknowledged the lack of her explicit engagement with the Levinasian themes in her earlier work but also commented on her more recent 'turn to Levinas'. Significantly, in her keynote address 'Precarious Life' presented at the same conference, Butler adopted a Levinasian framework in an attempt to develop

what she termed 'a possible Jewish ethic of non-violence', as a response to the Israeli-Palestinian conflict and the 2003 war on Iraq. See also Butler's *Precarious Life* (2002: 128–51).

17   Shannon Bell raises similar questions regarding Levinas's ethics in her paper, 'Fast Feminism: A Levinasian Pragmatics' available at http://www.hichumanities.org/AHProceedings/Shannon%20Bell.pdf.

6

Ethics and National Identity

THE NATION AT WAR (WITH ITSELF)

On 10 July 1941 in the little town of Jedwabne in the north-east of Poland some 1600 Jews were murdered by their Polish neighbours. After the initial outbreak of violence, the majority of the Jews had been gathered in a barn and burnt to death. There were seven survivors of the Jedwabne pogrom, all saved by a Polish woman.

This event has been reported in Jan Tomasz Gross's book *Sąsiedzi* (2000), subsequently released in English as *Neighbors: The Destruction of the Jewish Community in Jedwabne, Poland* (2001). The disclosure of the story in Poland erupted in a national debate, which, in its scope and intensity, became a Polish version of 'the Dreyfus affair' (Michnik, 2001: unpag.). The debate was predominantly situated at the intersections of a religious and juridical discourse, and – perhaps unsurprisingly – concerned issues of guilt, forgiveness and responsibility. The highlighting of the legal and methodological aspects of the matter, represented by the 'Who did it?' and 'Is Gross a credible historian?' lines of enquiry, gave the debate an aura of seriousness. It demonstrated Poles' willingness to 'face the facts' while also, to some extent, diverting attention from examining the cracks and wounds in national identity that were suddenly found gaping. As journalist Dawid Warszawski put it, 'The Jedwabne affair has made it impossible for us to go on rejecting the possibility that Poles may have committed the mass murder of Jews in some other places, as well', concluding further that 'posing such a thesis is, in the light of the facts, both a scholarly and a moral imperative' (2000: unpag.). While the main thrust of the discussions was on the 'Who did it?' aspect of the story – could the Poles have really committed such an atrocious crime? How do we know it wasn't the Nazis? And even if the Poles did 'technically' commit the deed, surely the Nazis must have been its main orchestrators? – this does not mean that the book only resulted in the displacement of guilt or denial. Gross's disclosure of the Jedwabne massacre indeed met with some fierce rejections from the extreme right, but it also led to interventions and calls for 'an account of conscience' from the nation's President, the Catholic Church and representatives of Poland's intelligentsia.[1]

What are the consequences of facing – even if not yet accepting – the emergent 'truth' about Jedwabne? How does one deal with this knowledge that defies all knowledge in order to respond to the unimaginable? My engagement with the Jedwabne murders in this chapter, while springing from personal investment in a singular event, is also an attempt to ask broader – one could even perhaps risk saying 'universal' – questions about the conditions of ethics 'under duress', and about the associated issues of response, responsibility and forgiveness. There are numerous reasons why the language I am adopting here – with its rhetoric of 'forgiveness' and 'guilt' – belongs to a religious heritage (let us call it, after Derrida, 'Abrahamic, in order to bring together Judaism, the Christianities, and the Islams' (2001: 28)). Religious tropes permeate multiple debates on national memory and history – predominantly articulated in and through the discourses of law, politics, economy and diplomacy – which are currently taking place in the postcolonial world. Thus my focusing on the Jedwabne tragedy, and on the wider question of 'Polish anti-Semitism', should be seen as 'at once singular and on the way to universalisation through that which *a certain theatre of forgiveness* puts in place or brings to light' (Derrida, 2001: 28; emphasis added). This engagement is also an attempt to face and comprehend what is making me – a Pole living in Britain and working at an English university within the methodological framework of 'cultural studies' – churn inside, and to adjust my back under the burden of responsibility which the majority of Poles are not able to cast away or forget.

'THEY'RE ALL ANTI-SEMITIC THERE'

Is it true that the Poles are anti-Semitic?'
Jerzy flushed. 'No.'
'People say they are. I read somewhere that Begin had said he'd never set foot on Polish soil again.'
'In the Middle Ages,' said Jerzy coldly, 'under a liberal king, Poland was the refuge for every Jew in Europe. It was the one safe country.'
'Why do you sound so angry?'
He flushed again. 'I don't feel angry. Not exactly. I just can hardly talk about it without churning inside.'

(Sue Gee, *Spring Will Be Ours*)

'What died in him at Chelmno?'
'Everything died. But he's only human, and he wants to live. So he must forget. He thanks God for what remains, and that he can forget. And let's not talk about that.'

(Michael Podchlebnik in *Shoah*, quoted in Carroll)

I am aware of the danger, or even inappropriateness, of juxtaposing in the epigraph above two such different instances of a call to silence, and of adapting the silence of 'that' which is related to the memories of the Shoah, to the question of Polish anti-Semitism (a question that for many will be situated at the other end of the victims/perpetrators spectrum). However, these two narratives are not unconnected: not only do they both deal with witnessing and responsibility, as well as a desire to forget and 'move on', they also arise out of the extremely complicated and conflict-riven landscape of interwar Europe. Michael Podchlebnik's reluctance to speak about his camp experience is seen by David Carroll as paradigmatic of the difficulties shared by other victims of the Nazi terror. In the Foreword to Jean-François Lyotard's *Heidegger and the 'jews'*, Carroll writes that

> in almost all of the narratives of survivors of the Nazi concentration camps, especially of those who survived the death camps, one finds state-ments of this kind, which both command and plead at the same time. They are the pleas of a reluctant narrator not to be made to talk, at least not yet, not here, not with these listeners and in this situation ... pleas to be left alone, to be allowed to go on with his or her life. ... Such pleas/ commands, however, inevitably open the way for 'talk' and narration and thus constitute a way of talking about the Shoah in the mode of refusing to talk about it. (1990: vii)

Undoubtedly, in the context of the silence referred to by Jerzy from the first epigraph quoted above, the plea 'to be left alone', combined with the compulsion to speak about the past which one is trying to forget, springs for many Poles from different historical experiences and different motiva-tions. This plea is in fact a painful cry to be allowed to forget, cast away, *talk themselves out of,* the 'burden' they feel has been imposed upon them. Poland's most recent attempts at neo-cosmopolitanism, successfully realized through joining NATO in 1999 and becoming members of the European Union in 2004, have been continually haunted by the spectre of anti-Semitism. Seen by some as an unsavoury part of the nation's identity and by others as an unjust accusation which threatens to tarnish and disrupt Poland's efforts to 'rejoin Europe', Polish anti-Semitism is something the majority of Poles can hardly talk about. It is precisely its uncertain, denied, ghostly status and the difficulty of giving 'it' a name that for me situate the debates on anti-Semitism in Poland in the trope of screaming silence. So, even if the juxtaposition of the two silences in the stories evoked here will be interpreted as violence, it should also be seen as an act of self-wounding, of probing beneath the scabs of national identity and national self-image that cover up the unnameable. Meandering between discomfort, guilt, shame and a push to give 'it' a name, I am myself looking for ways of releasing 'Polish anti-Semitism' and the debates surrounding it from its still somewhat innocent 'it-ness' in which the aforementioned silence envelope the layers of Polish national history and memory. If this reads like an apology, it is already a displaced one – it is easier to apologize for one's stylistic vacilla-tions than to respond to what defies comprehension. And yet comprehend it I must, but let me repeat here after Hannah Arendt that

[c]omprehension ... does not mean denying the outrageous, deducing the unprecedented from precedents, or explaining phenomena by such analogies and generalities that the impact of reality and the shock of experience are no longer felt. It means, rather, examining and bearing consciously the burden that events have placed upon us – neither denying their existence nor submitting meekly to their weight as though everything that in fact happened could not have happened otherwise. Comprehension, in short, means the unpremeditated, attentive facing up to, and resisting of – reality – whatever it may or might have been. (1973: xiv)

Trying to comprehend the crime of Jedwabne should not be seen here as a veiled attempt to justify or understand *why* it happened, but it is a refusal to confine it to the realm of the unspeakable, or to see it *only* as the incomprehensible. I note with interest that Arendt's definition of comprehension situates itself at the crossroads of psychoanalysis and ethics, even if she is not interested in positioning the events of the Shoah 'between good and evil', or in applying a ready-made moral paradigm to examine and judge the crime's perpetrators. Instead, she perceives the process of comprehension as an act of opening ourselves to what we have always been exposed to anyway; of 'active facing up' to the burden of history and memory that challenges and unhinges our self-sufficiency and oneness. We are not talking here about 'submitting passively' to the burden we have been carrying – where passivity would stand for an *impossibility to refuse* engagement; for an inability to feel absolved of responsibility for the event which had already taken place and which we cannot undo. What Arendt seems to be saying is that, even though we do recognize that the event did indeed happen, we must still actively respond to it; that an act of accepting responsibility out of weariness, helplessness or lack of argument simply will not do.

In this sense, the demonstration of 'guilty conscience' by the Poles facing the story of Jedwabne could be interpreted as a refusal to comprehend, as a passive situation of 'finding oneself burdened' without actually feeling the need to face up to this burden. In *Remnants of Auschwitz: The Witness and the Archive* Giorgio Agamben suggests that a tendency to assume a collective guilt arises 'whenever an ethical problem cannot be mastered' (1999: 94–5). He also comments, after Arendt, on the fact that the 'surprising willingness of post-war Germans of all ages to assume collective guilt for Nazism ... betrayed an equally surprising ill will as to the assessment of individual responsibilities and the punishment of particular crimes' (95). Agamben points to instances when the German Protestant Church declared itself 'complicit before the God of mercy for the evil that our people did to the Jews' while simultaneously refusing to call for the punishment of those preachers guilty of having justified anti-Semitism. By relegating the operations of justice to the celestial level the crimes were collectively passed on to the economy of mercy which sidesteps the stately law. Agamben also reminds us of the expression of collective guilt towards the Jews by the Catholic Church, which was never accompanied by the thorough and open investigation of the activities of Pope Pius XII during the Second World War.[2] In the aftermath of the 'Jedwabne revelation' the head of the Catholic Church in Poland, Archbishop Józef Glemp, did not even go that far: his collective apology for the Polish 'sins' was addressed not at the Jews but only at God, thus firmly situating the debate about the economy of forgiveness and the channels of its circulation that had been instantiated by the publication of *Neighbors* on a vertical axis. All this does not mean that 'collective guilt' is morally wrong, rather that it is not enough. Comprehension, as Arendt points out, should not thus be reduced to 'explaining phenomena by such analogies and generalities that the impact of reality and the shock of experience are no longer felt' or to resorting to collective demonstrations of guilt and sorrow: it must also involve facing up to the horror that haunts every one of us, of allowing ourselves to be disturbed, shaken and terrified, of hearing the other scream.

But instead, the debate on Jedwabne, and on alleged Polish anti-Semitism, became predominantly a question of accountancy; it was frequently reduced to establishing the 'facts and figures': the exact number of Jews who had perished in Jedwabne on that day, the exact proximity of the Germans stationed in the area. In this way, many Poles found a way of talking about Jedwabne and not talking about it at the same time, reenacting the trauma of the repressed memory without yet being ready to connect with it. Even the call for 'an account of conscience' was quickly linked to debates about mutuality, and thus absorbed into an economy of exchange in which guilt and forgiveness were prevented from circulating freely by being inscribed in the regulatory discourses of political sermons and historical analyses.[3] And yet the Catholic rhetoric of accountability, rooted in the idea of God as both merciful and just, not only opens up a gap between generosity and equal measurement – which perhaps can also be seen as 'a hiatus between ethics and politics'[4] – but it also involves a certain impossibility of mixing two different mathematical orders. And it is precisely between these two orders – one regulated by an ethics of infinity, the other by the politics of justice – that conflicting ideologies of the nation state find themselves wedged.

UNVEILING THE TRUTH

It is thus perhaps understandable that, when posed with both the proximity and enormity of 'the Jedwabne tragedy', many Poles have reacted to it with shock, disbelief or even anger. The author of *Neighbors* himself recounts how he experienced exactly the same sense of disbelief and inertia when coming across the witnesses' testimonies, especially the transcript of the report presented by Szmul Wasersztajn before the Jewish Historical Commission in Białystok in April 1945. As Gross puts it, 'it's hard to understand at first the full meaning of this testimony' (2000: 15),[5] a sense of bemusement he reiterates when stating: 'It also took me four years to understand what Wasersztajn had said. It's only when watching raw footage for the documentary film *Where Is My Older Brother Cain?* made by Agnieszka Arnold (or, specifically, when suddenly seeing the daughter of the owner of the barn in which the Polish neighbours had burnt the Jews of Jedwabne in July 1941, being interviewed in front of a camera) that I grasped what had really happened there' (2000: 15). But, as if he had not reassured us enough about the difficulty of comprehending the full story of Jedwabne, Gross feels compelled to recount once again, *now for the third time*, in a footnote attached to the above confession, this moment of delayed revelation he had experienced. He writes: 'A few months after submitting the commissioned manuscript [an earlier essay on the Polish-Jewish relations in Jedwabne] I was watching Agnieszka Arnold's film and then I grasped what had really happened' (2000: 15).

This is a significant moment in the history of *Neighbors* – it is a moment when, to quote Gross, 'the veil finally falls from our eyes and we realise that what has so far been unimaginable is precisely what happened' (2000: 15–16).[6] Afterwards, it turns out that the actual event has already been well documented, that many witnesses of the tragedy are still alive and that the memory of the pogrom has survived in Jedwabne through generations. Indeed, in 1949 twenty-two inhabitants of Jedwabne had been arrested and put on trial, indicted with 'the murder of Jewish people, as stated in the testimony of Szmul Wasersztajn who witnessed the pogrom of the Jews' (2001: 15). One defendant was sentenced to death, eleven others to imprisonment of between eight and fifteen years (although, due to amnesty, none served the full sentence), while the remaining twelve were found innocent. Gross ascribes this leniency of approach to the relative lack of significance given to the case by the Polish communist authorities. However, he also considers it significant that the trial resulted in the construction of numerous written reports, documents and testimonies about the pogrom which have been preserved until now. The memory of the Jedwabne murders was nevertheless all too quickly buried in the national unconscious, only to come to light again after the publication of Gross's book.

I would like to dwell for a moment on this instance of delayed 'revelation' Gross himself experienced when investigating the events of Jedwabne, a revelation which arrived through the detour of disbelief, doubt and miscomprehension. What is most surprising about his account is that Gross, Professor of Politics at New York University, graduate of Warsaw and Yale, and author of numerous publications on Polish society in the Second World War period, is presumably well versed in reading, analysing and making sense of archival materials, including personal accounts and testimonies. Yet when faced with the scraps of the Jedwabne story, Professor Gross is unable immediately to grasp the significance of the events. Interestingly, Gross's narration is steeped in religious rhetoric: and indeed his inability to 'see', confessed here three separate times, seems to be an inversion of Peter's triple denial of 'truth' (while Peter *denies* three times that he knows Jesus, and for the sake of his own safety, resorts to a lie, Gross seems unable to *take in the truth* he is confronted with). His description of the actual moment of seeing 'when the veil finally falls from our eyes' resonates with religious undertones: it could be read as referring to an instance when the Holy of Holies, the sacred place of the Temple, is revealed to the gaze of the eyes which, in Judaism, must never focus on the sacred image.[7] Elizabeth Grosz explains that in the Hebraic tradition

> [s]ight does not reveal the other, nor command the subject's response. ... This aversion to privileging the visual has major implications not only for modes of representation and depiction available to the Jew but also for notions of knowledge, which, in the Hellenic tradition have been so reliant on metaphors derived from the privilege of vision – 'insight', 'reflection', 'enlightenment', 'clarification'. These imply a knowledge that is 'seen', 'regarded' as tangible correspondence, the correspondence between word and thing – very different from the disputational and insecure status the Jew accords to knowledge as 'interpretation'. (1993: 67)

The fact that Gross resorts to religious tropes in order to convey his bemusement, his use of the image of the veil which conceals not God but rather an atrocity committed on His children, and the failure of the other's voice to make the story fully understandable (Gross admits to having been familiar beforehand with some accounts of the Jedwabne crime), imply perhaps a doubt cast on the Hebraic model of cognition. In the Hebraic tradition, the visual is inadequate as a source of knowledge, and has to be supplemented with, or even superseded by, the voice of the other, an approach that considerably differs from the Hellenic/Platonic model, in which replicas and copies represent the hidden truth. At the moment when the available words do not seem to reveal anything, Gross takes recourse to image, reconstruction, representation: knowledge here comes through an act of seeing the event performed before his own eyes. He can only internalize the knowledge about what happened by committing a sacrilege from which there is no return: 'when the veil finally drops from our eyes' we have no choice but to face the horror we have finally allowed ourselves to see.

The story of Jedwabne – singular in the multiplied tragedy of some 1600 individuals who perished but also universalized by being a reiteration of numerous acts of anti-Jewish violence occurring throughout Europe under the Nazi occupation – can only be approached 'at one remove', through the mediation of cinematic material (for Gross) or through the staging of media debates (for a number of Poles who beforehand both *knew* and *did not know* about the pogrom). The 'revelation' of Jedwabne takes place as a result of what could be described as the initial violation of the Hebraic tradition of knowledge as 'interpretation'; instead, knowledge is only gained here through representation, through reenactment, through sight. And yet, it is precisely 'interpretation' that Gross turns to once 'the veil has fallen', and it is his 'interpretation' of the 'events' that he is mainly criticized for. (He has been accused by historians of 'interpreting the facts too freely', of misinterpreting the witnesses' accounts and of providing his own 'version' of the events.) The story of Jedwabne thus constitutes an aporia of knowledge: it is a place where the Hebraic and Hellenic traditions embrace each other, in their mutual insufficiency and failure, in the face of 'the inconceivable which had happened'. In order to begin to make sense of the unimaginable, recourse needs to be taken to both revelation and interpretation, to image and voice.

IS THERE SUCH A THING AS COLLECTIVE RESPONSIBILITY?

In order to attempt to reconstruct the events of the Jedwabne tragedy in search of some forms of knowledge, remembrance and forgiveness, we must situate these events in the context of the current ideas regarding Poland and Polishness. It is quite significant that a number of Polish historians, social scientists and other representatives of the intelligentsia have accused Gross and his supporters of unfair generalizations regarding the crime and have voiced objections as to any attempts to 'stretch national responsibility' on to the whole of the Polish nation. That the latter phrase, indicating a physical effort of moulding and channelling the unwieldy burden of responsibility, resonates as awkwardly in Polish as it does in English should not really surprise us: language, and specifically, the dominant discourse of national identity, seems to have been suddenly 'burdened' with a new set of significations to which it has to readjust itself in order to be able to name the unnameable. The detectivist 'Who did it?' aspect of the debate I mentioned earlier, focused on establishing 'the real perpetrators of the crime', is framed by the logic of undivided rational subjectivity, and yet it is precisely this very idea of the subject as unified and responsible to and for itself that is being questioned in these debates. This is not an attempt on my part to contribute to the attempts to deny, dilute or 'stretch out' responsibility but rather to propose a new framework for thinking about (Polish) national identity, collective and individual. Protesting against 'being burdened' with collective responsibility, some defenders of 'truth' refuse to see that they are *already* burdened with it, that they have been carrying it on their shoulders – as a secret, loss or remorse – for a long time. However, it is the precise location and naming of this weight that is causing so much discomfort, so much wriggling, in these debates. The 'Who did it?' investigation can thus be seen as an attempt to close the gap between the idea of Polishness – one that many Poles hold dear, and which they are prepared to defend against 'foreign hostile elements' – and its image; it is an attempt to make the self whole again.

The 'revelation' of Jedwabne incises and cuts through the convoluted folds of Polishness. It also exposes some of the mechanisms involved in the production of the idea of national unity which has to bar, exclude and anni- hilate any forms of alterity that threaten it. This is not an intent on my part to position the Jew as 'intrinsically other' – Hannah Arendt claims that such a positioning, accompanied by thinking in terms of a radical 'self/other' sep- aration, is in fact the sine qua non condition for the birth of anti-Semitism (1973: xii). Rather than trace the working of violence on a straightforward trajectory *from* self *to* other, much less on that from other to self, I want to look at 'the very attempt to delineate the borders that separate self *from* other' (de Vries and Weber, 1997: 2), an attempt which for Hent de Vries and Samuel Weber is synonymous with a violent act. Here violence is not seen as something 'befalling' its victims from without but is instead related to 'what is generally presupposed to be its other: the "inviolate" self' (1997: 2). This is probably why Arendt vehemently dismisses the transhistorical narrative of Jewish martyrology, based on the belief 'that Jewish people had always been the passive, suffering object of Christian persecution, [which] actually amounted to a prolongation and modernisation of the old myth of chosenness' (1973: xiii). According to Arendt, since the nineteenth-century Jewishness has become only a 'psychological quality', 'an involved personal problem' (66). It is not insignificant that in *The Origins of Totalitarianism*, which is where the above analysis is developed, Arendt focuses mainly on the more or less assimilated and secularized Jews of Western Europe, only to mention in passing that the political significance of the Eastern European conditions, 'although they constituted the essence of the Jewish mass ques- tion', 'was limited to backward countries where the ubiquitous hatred of Jews made it almost useless as a weapon for specific purposes' (29). While she declares Western anti-Semitism a serious and complex phenomenon which requires in-depth investigation and analysis, she is not prepared to devote too much time to either its Eastern counterpart or, indeed, to the Jews themselves inhabiting the 'backward' Eastern European countries. Opposing both Jewish homogeneity and the grand theory of anti-Semitism, she in fact consolidates Jewishness as a Western European experience, secu- larized and strongly rooted in the bourgeois social order. There is no room for the story of the Jedwabne Jews and their Polish neighbours in the pages of *The Origins of Totalitarianism*.

Eva Hoffman's *Shtetl: The Life and Death of a Small Town and the World of Polish Jews* provides a useful counterpart to Arendt's book. Less a histo- riographic treatise than a micrological analysis of the complex textures of Polish–Jewish everyday life, *Shtetl* is a memorial to both East European

Jewry and the Polish–Jewish neighbourly relations that also perished in the Shoah. Hoffman – a Polish Jew who immigrated to Canada at the age of thirteen and who currently lives in London – addresses the two narratives that have enveloped the Polish–Jewish relations since the Second World War: that of alleged Polish anti-Semitism and of 'Polish resentment of the exaggerated charges and at the world's forgetfulness of Poland's own struggle for survival during the war, and its immense losses' (1998: 5). Strongly opposing the theory of Poles' natural inclination towards anti-Semitism and their willing participation in the genocide, she does not though pass over the complicated and painful histories of the relationships between ethnic Poles and Jews (who were also, in their majority, Polish citizens), nor does she attempt to 'absolve' or 'condemn'. Instead, she is set on moving beyond stereotypical representations fostered by mutual accusations, reproaches and grudges in order to 'complicate and historicise the picture'. Hoffman delineates the intricacies of the Polish–Jewish coexistence over the centuries, which she describes as 'a long experiment in multiculturalism *avant la lettre*' (9), as follows:

> [F]or about six hundred years Poland was one of the most important centres of Jewish life in the world. The Jews started settling there as early as the eleventh century, and they started arriving in larger numbers in the fourteenth. By the late seventeenth century, nearly three-quarters of the world's Jewry lived in the Polish-Lithuanian Commonwealth. In the eighteenth century, before the partitions, Jews constituted about 10 per cent of Poland's population, which made them that country's largest minority. Before World War II, they may have grown to as much as 13 per cent. … The question of the proper relationship between the two peoples was a matter of ongoing debate throughout Polish history, and the proposed answers varied on both sides of the ethnic divide. (9–11)

Can the Jedwabne tragedy be seen as an inevitable part of this mixture? Does the multiplicity of influences and outlooks explain what happened there on 10 July 1941? Will we have to understand it as an outcome of historical circumstances? And, if we reject an attempt to explain history through its alleged natural development and inevitable teleology, will we be able to understand Jedwabne 'otherwise', without trying to rationalize it, but also without confining it to the category of the incomprehensible? The traditional scientific tools, designed to establish and interpret the facts, are likely to prove unsatisfactory in our search for some 'other' forms of understanding.

NATIONAL MEMORY AND NATIONAL FORGETTING

In her article 'Witnessing Otherness in History', Kelly Oliver tells a story of psychoanalyst Doris Laub interviewing an eyewitness to the Auschwitz uprising in which prisoners set fire to the camp. The testimony was discredited by a number of historians because the witness reported four chimneys going up in flames and exploding, while evidence showed that in fact only one chimney had been destroyed. The testimony to something so radical and unimaginable as the occurrence of resistance in Auschwitz was thus initially occluded by debates about facts and figures. As Oliver reports, 'While the historians were listening to hear confirmation of what they already knew, the psychoanalysts were listening to hear something new, something as yet beyond comprehension' (2001: 41).

A similar situation occurred after the publication of Gross's *Neighbors* in Poland. The stories narrated by both Gross and the primary witness of the Jedwabne tragedy, Szmul Wasersztajn, have been discredited by historians because the numbers were found to be inexact – there were doubts as to the names and exact number of people who perished in the barn, and over who had been executed in Jedwabne earlier that day. A criticism of this kind can be interpreted as an (unconscious?) attempt to prevent facing and coming to terms with the unimaginable. Exposed to the trauma of the Jedwabne massacre that leaves many Poles gasping – angry with the fact that Polishness is being slandered yet again, disbelieving what they are hearing – and to some other traumatic revelations from the nation's past, we have to supplement the methods and approaches of the historian with those developed by the psychoanalyst, the philosopher and the cultural critic. Because, the primary problem we are dealing with here is not the presence of a fact, and the material evidence confirming it, but rather a multiple loss – both of individual lives (be it 1600 or 'only' 480)[8] and of a chunk of Polish national identity and memory that was wiped out in the aftermath of the Shoah. As Polish cultural anthropologist Joanna Tokarska Bakir observes, 'Our memory is the place from which Jews are missing' (2001, unpag.).

And it is precisely the Jewish shtetl, a small town like Jedwabne and many others, summoning 'poignant, warm images of people in quaint black garb, or Chagall-like crooked streets and fiddlers on thatched roofs' for some and 'pogroms and peasant barbarism' for others (Hoffman 1998: 11), that, according to Hoffman, serves as a most powerful metaphor for loss. Polish shtetls belong to the category of 'ghost towns', towns that only enter our world 'once they refuse to remain dead' (Marchitello, 2001a: 141). Hoffman explains that, until the twentieth century, the rural shtetl, situated worlds apart from more cosmopolitan and business-driven towns like Cracow or Łódź inhabited by Hasidic Jews, secularists, wealthy industrialists and assimilated professionals, retained its deeply religious and traditional character. A close-knit community in which Jews lived side by side with the local population, the Polish shtetl was constituted out of two poor, traditionalist, and fairly incongruous subcultures: Orthodox Jews and premodern peasants. Hoffman writes:

> Morally and spiritually, the two societies remained resolutely separate, by choice on both sides. Yet they lived in close physical proximity and, willy-nilly, familiarity. ... This was where both prejudices and bonds were most palpably enacted – where a Polish peasant might develop a genuine affection for his Jewish neighbor despite negative stereotypes and, conversely, where an act of unfairness or betrayal could be most wounding because it came from a familiar. As an example of Polish–Jewish relations during World War II, the shtetl offered the most extreme scenario. The villages and small towns were where Jews and Poles were at their most exposed and vulnerable, and where ongoing political conflicts were at their sharpest. This was where Jewish inhabitants experienced acts of the most unmediated cruelty from their neighbors – and also of most immediate generosity. In the dark years of the Holocaust, the shtetl became a study in ordinary morality tested, and sometimes warped, by inhuman circumstances. (1998: 12–13)

What does this context tell us? Does it actually facilitate explanation; does it help us understand what really happened in Jedwabne? Or does it highlight even more the incomprehensibility of the pogrom, of the neighbourly crime occurring under the dark umbrella of wider socio-political conflicts in Europe and yet painfully specific and singular? If we continue to ask questions about the crime, the investigation of facts and numbers (How many people died in the pogrom? Who executed it?) has also to involve the examination of *who*, or *what*, it is that actually perished in Jedwabne on 10 July 1941. In our investigations we have to pay heed to Arendt's warnings against the essentialization of Jewishness as standing for both chosenness and martyrology, as a sign of absolute alterity which cannot be comprehended or accounted for. And yet we should perhaps also be aware that, when talking about European Jews, and particularly about Jewish shtetl communities in Central and Eastern Europe, we are faced with an absence, a lacuna which calls to us for a response, while at the same time defying imagination and representation.

This call for a response is also a call to responsibility: as David Carroll observes in his foreword to Lyotard's *Heidegger and the 'jews'*, "'The jews" are the debt Western thought rarely acknowledges and never can repay; "they" are the irrefutable indication of the fact of obligation itself' (Carroll, 1990: xii). Lyotard's 'the jews' are an approximation at bridging the gap between Jewishness as an idea, the other of Hellenic thought, and the reality of lived lives, without attempting to close it off altogether. He inscribes the problematic of 'the jews' in 'the contradictory feeling of "presence" that is certainly not present, but which precisely needs to be forgotten to be represented' (Lyotard, 1990: 4). Further on, Lyotard links the question of 'the jews' with the idea of the sublime, conceptualized as 'perhaps the only mode of artistic sensibility to characterise the modern' (Lyotard, 1991: 93). This does not of course mean that Lyotard confines Jewishness into an impossible aesthetics – he rather exposes the insufficiency of traditional aesthetic categories and their explosion by the ethico-political. The sublime – like 'the jews' (using an analogy which nevertheless bears traces of irreducible difference) – does not provide any positive representation; instead, it testifies that there is something that cannot be represented, that there *is something* rather than *nothing*. If 'the jews' are the concealment that 'lets something else show', 'not without resemblance to that of the "veiling unveiling" in Heidegger' (Lyotard, 1990: 4), Gross's surprise at the testimonies and legal records of the Jedwabne tragedy, his deferral in facing and acknowledging the true weight of the atrocities, can thus be seen as vacillation between the inability to really see the imprescriptible, and a duty to convey it, to give it a name.

But perhaps his hesitation and 'triple denial' are also an attempt to protect the forgotten as a hidden anxiety that keeps haunting Polish national memory? Lyotard argues that acts of remembrance involving public displays of national guilt and erection of memorials all contribute to the politics of forgetting; they create conditions for 'moving on' and leaving the troubled past behind, thus 'cancelling' it and burying it for good. Gross's decision to have the book published may have been accompanied by the realization that it would lead to a national self-questioning and the examination of the nation's past deeds. And yet, there was a danger involved that, by giving Poles *Neighbors*, Gross was contributing to the process of Poland's self-purification, that by 'remembering' Jedwabne and some other instances of Polish anti-Semitism and by creating conditions for talking about 'it', the loss in Polish national identity will be superficially recuperated, and that the national psychoanalysis will be terminated with a few rough stitches that will nevertheless create pretence of a 'cure'. This would explain to some extent Gross's initial reluctance to 'see' and 'understand' the events. His narrative of Jedwabne is thus not only a sacrilege of allowing oneself to see the unrepresentable, and resorting first to image in order to see it with his own eyes, and then to writing in order to preserve the lost memory, it is also a betrayal of memory-as-haunting, as absent presence.[9] By giving Poles the story of Jedwabne, an unrequested and unthanked-for gift but thus a 'true gift', Gross has in fact distributed a *Gift*, a poisonous *pharmakon* that can also have curative properties.[10] Penetrating the tissue of the Polish nation, the Gift of the Jedwabne story seems both interminable (i.e. excessively generous, with no expenses spared) and incurable, as Poles will never be able to stop talking about 'it'. The question of Polish anti-Semitism, always already overflown by the immeasurable terror of life and death, will have to go on as a question, because 'psychoanalysis, the search for lost time, can only be interminable, like literature and like true history' (Lyotard, 1990: 20).

NARCISSISM, ALTERITY AND NATIONAL IDENTITY: ETHICS 'UNDER DURESS'

The story of Polish anti-Semitism, if there ever is, or was, one story, must touch upon this double bind involved in Lyotard's notion of 'the jews' – it is a story of both absolute alterity and incised selfhood, of communal psychosis and singular desire. The death of the Jedwabne Jews in a neighbour's barn, to some extent paradigmatic of death in a camp, can perhaps be interpreted as an attempt to 'enclose' alterity, to put an end to it. It was an act of 'devouring the Jews' live, internalizing them by an inverted reenactment of anti-Semitic stories claiming that Jews use the blood of Christian children to make their bread. However, the act of taking one's neighbours hostage was also a most bizarre act of neighbourly hospitality, manifested not only in a desire to open one's doors to the stranger but also to close the door behind him, to keep him in his 'new' place, to make him stay.[11] Elizabeth Grosz argues that the Jew (similar in her interpretation to Lyotard's 'the jews' – as an idea of radical heterogeneity and the familiar neighbourly presence) 'represents a resistance to the norms governing the citizen, the neighbour, and the (Hellenic/Christocentric) subject' (1993: 61).[12] But what kind of resistance to the neighbourly norms does the Jew offer and what are these norms actually? By resisting domestication, perhaps 'the jews' are also exposing the precariousness of a neighbourly community and the pervertibility of the hospitality upon which it is allegedly based? Never at home wherever they are, 'the jews' seem to be impossible neighbours, posing a challenge to the idea of neighbourliness seen as consolidation of identity devoid of difference, the identity of the selfsame.[13]

Can we thus suppose that the neighbours of Jedwabne attempted to eliminate a threat to their fantasy of neighbourliness, to close the door to the other within *oneself*? The tragedy of Jedwabne in which neighbours killed neighbours presents itself as either a logical impossibility or an act of self-killing, self-implosion. Homi K. Bhabha argues that 'the ambivalent identifications of love and hate occupy the same psychic space; and paranoid projections "outwards" return to haunt and split the place from which they are made' (1990: 300). However, the narcissistic confinement of the wounded self accompanied by the aggressivity projected onto the other results in 'the unbearable ordeal of the collapse of certainty' and the enhancement of narcissistic neurosis, if the 'self' and 'other' are found to be inhabiting the same territory, if they form constitutive parts of one national discourse.

If, as Howard Marchitello argues, the other can be described as 'the relationship between space and time' (2001a: 125), the staging of the murder in which the infinite alterity of the neighbour – 'the Stranger who disturbs the being at home with oneself [le chez soi]' (Levinas 1969: 39) – is both annihilated and incorporated, necessitates a rethinking of our relationship to space and time. This rethinking may also allow us to delineate some new ways of conceptualizing history and ethics.[14] Pogroms in general, and Jedwabne specifically, constitute a spatio-temporal disturbance, an ethical situation of being faced with infinite alterity in which ethics yields to pervertibility (see Bennington, 2000: 72). If alterity elicits a response, the rightness of this response cannot be prescribed: it can only be encountered, faced. I would like to stress here that it is not my claim that ethics died in pogroms, in Jedwabne, in Auschwitz – even if some of the actors of those events failed to welcome the alterity that threatened to violate the illusionary wholeness of the selfsame.[15] Jedwabne should not thus be interpreted as a failure of ethics *per se* but rather as a failure to act ethically (whereby the possibility of this failure is also a condition and guarantee of ethics). But Jedwabne did perhaps involve the failure of language, of the discourse of national identity which could not think 'Polishness' as overflowing the traditional model of space, or reconcile the concept of sameness underpinning the idea of citizenship with the intrinsic alterity inhabiting it.

As well as being the problem of collapsed space Jedwabne also brings up issues of interrupted time. We can refer here once again to Giorgio Agamben's doubts regarding the public demonstrations of guilt and the collective pleas for forgiveness. Agamben fears that manifestations of this kind can easily be turned into an attempt to seal off the past through an accomplishment of the closure of what Derrida calls 'the imprescriptible' (i.e. the event for which we have no name, and which we cannot really forgive, since only those who had perished in it would have the authority to legitimate its forgiveness). In his short essay 'On Forgiveness' (2001) Derrida inscribes the ethical problematic of forgiveness related to historical atrocities in the aporia between singularity and universality: it is a way of saying *I do understand* WHAT *happened but I do not understand* HOW *it could have happened.* The latter part of the phrase raises questions about general conditions of history; it is an expression of an anxiety about the future and a concern not to let it happen again. Thus a willingness to learn a lesson from history and a plea for forgiveness must be seen as situated at an aporia between responsibility for the past and for the future. (As explained previously, a lot of effort in the public debate on Jedwabne in Poland has gone towards stabilizing this aporia, towards enclosing it in a reenactment of the 'barn scene' by drawing a demarcation line between zones of responsibility.) If the tragedy of Jedwabne can be seen as a lesson, its teaching must involve a certain openness springing from vigilance. Kelly Oliver insists that vigilance, understood as 'both keeping watch and responding to something beyond your own control' (2001: 46), must always accompany the process of working-through the history of otherness. However, her Levinas-inflected notion of vigilance, even though inhering the limitations of the self, is still goal-orientated; it consists of a 'movement beyond ourselves towards otherness', where the identitarian categories must be in place for this movement to be instantiated. Derrida's account of awaiting the monster (1995: 386) and Lyotard's notion of the sublime seem to be more radical, but also more unstable proposals for facing the unknown. Rather than being a positive programme of movement beyond oneself, they name an ethical situation in which the self is already held hostage to what questions and ultimately pulverizes it, to what may or may not be there, to what may not de-MONSTR-ate itself at all (see Derrida, 1995: 386–7). Of course, this possibility of the appearance of the other, and of the arrival of justice, coupled with the terror of nothingness, can never be resolved – it has to be constantly, obsessively and intermittently revisited. This kind of vigilance as situatedness rather than prior decision necessarily involves the possibility of violence and of the pervertibility of justice (even if not of its ultimate collapse). But, as de Vries and Weber put it, 'the most mystified form of "violence" might turn out, paradoxically perhaps, to be what seeks to eliminate or to delegitimize violence entirely' (1997: 2).

Poland's efforts to 'join Europe' should not therefore be seen as a promise of a new chapter of national history, one that requires the closure of her past and the healing of her wounds. These efforts to be part of the European Union have to be inextricably linked with an examination of the wounded self: it is a question of realizing that joining the European structures will not make her wounds disappear, that Poland will always bear her lack, her mark of absence – her anti-Semitism, her Jews, her shtetls. Indeed, Poland's aspirations to 'join Europe', to some extent springing from the nation's desire to exorcize the phantom of the communist past and to 'start again', are not out of tune with the general trajectory of Europe, which has always identified itself with 'the figure of the *Western* heading' (Derrida, 1992c: 25) and 'a point of departure for discovery, invention, and colonisation' (Derrrida, 1992c: 20). The attempt to 'join Europe' is closely linked with a desire to become part of an advance towards the future unity that for Derrida always already involves an advance on the other: 'to induce, seduce, produce, and conduce, to spread out, to cultivate, to love or to violate, to love to violate, to colonise, and to colonise itself' (Derrida, 1992c: 49). This does not of course mean that Poland should turn back on the European heading, and foreclose the possibility of 'colonising itself' once and for all, no matter how tempting this option may be for some representatives of the Catholic far right. Rather, the question of 'joining' must involve an exploration of how to 'advance' differently, how to reconcile the advance for joining with a call for justice, and, last but not least, how to incise, rip open and deflate her own rigid ideas of Polish history, memory and identity on its route towards 'full membership'.

Notes

1 For a comprehensive collection of journalistic and academic essays (both in Polish and English) on the Jedwabne tragedy see the website of Pogranicze, the publisher of Gross's *Sąsiedzi*, http://www.pogranicze.sejny.pl. There are a number of articles on Jedwabne gathered into a volume *Thou Shalt Not Kill: Poles on Jedwabne* edited by

Więź and available in English at http://free.ngo.pl/wiez/jedwabne/, accessed on 11 March 2004.

2   A commission of Catholic and Jewish scholars was set up in 1999 to examine the 12 volumes of the work *Actes et Documents du Saint Siège relatifs à la seconde guerre mondiale*, which includes all the documents of the Vatican archives during the Second World War. It was originally composed of three Catholic scholars and three Jewish scholars; one of the Catholics left later. The commission was particularly interested in studying the role of Pope Pius XII and the Holy See in Europe during Hitler's Third Reich, especially because the Church has now begun work toward beatifying Pius (the first step towards sainthood). Members had been working with 11 volumes of archive documents that the Vatican published from 1965 to 1981, but wanted access to the rest of the documentation. Dissatisfied with the inaccessibility of some archival materials, in July 2001 the commission decided to suspend its work. Father Gumpel, the German Jesuit in charge of gathering documents to support the beatification of Pius XII, accused some Jewish historians of having 'a clear propagandistic goal to damage the Holy See' as they pressed for access to its Second World War archives. He argued: 'Every scholar knows that no archive can be consulted if the documents are not catalogued and classified' and that 'all the material referring to the pontificate of Pius XII will be made available, as soon as possible, not only to them but to all scholars'. Michael Marrus, a Jewish commission member, said he was dismayed by Father Gumpel's statement. 'We have tried in a very respectful way, in a very restrained way, to make the case that scholars needed access to this material', he said. 'There is no effort that I know of to disparage the Catholic Church or to conduct a negative campaign that Father Gumpel alludes to.' See http://www.bc.edu/bc_org/research/cjl/news/gumpel.htm, accessed on 1 March 2004.

3   After acknowledging that the tragedy of Jedwabne was not a fabrication, 'the national debate' in Poland focused on measuring the degree of forgiveness that should be dispensed. The guilt (both in its legal and religious sense) was then situated within the discourse of economics. Questions were raised about the justness of substituting 'a bunch of hooligans' for 'the whole of Poland', about the irreconcilability of individual and collective conscience and about the alleged Jewish 'guilt' in the events (formulated in the accusation of the 'But they were communists!' type).

4   In *Adieu: To Emmanuel Levinas* Derrida transforms the two mathematical assumptions underlying ethics and politics, which for Levinas remain incommensurable (ethics belongs to the realm of the infinite; politics to the 'earthly' realm of the State, with its laws, procedures and tyrannies), into a figure of a 'hiatus'. He argues:

> The border between the ethical and political [in Levinas] loses for good the indivisible simplicity of a limit. No matter what Levinas might have said, the determinability of this limit was never pure, and it never will be. It would be possible to follow this inclusion of excess, or this transcendence in immanence, through subsequent texts such as 'Beyond the State in the State' or 'The State of Caesar and the State of David'. A hyperbolic transgression brings about a disjunction in the immanence to self. In each case, this disjunction has to do with the pre-originary ex-propriety or ex-appropriation that makes of the subject a guest [*hôte*] and a hostage, someone who is, *before* every invitation, elected, invited, *and* visited in his home of the other, who is *in his own home in the home of the other*, in a given at home, an at home that is given or, rather, loaned, allotted, advanced before every contract, in the 'anachronism of a debt preceding a loan. (1999a: 99)

> The Catholic perception of God as both merciful and just constitutes a similar hiatus, bringing together the logic of infinity and accountancy, of celestial beyond-measure and earthly payback.

5   The translation of Gross's *Sąsiedzi* into English, undertaken by the author himself, has actually resulted in a slightly different version of the book. Perhaps unsurprisingly, given the different cultural backgrounds of Polish and Anglo-American readers, in the English version of the book Gross introduced some changes in sentence order, in the amount and kind of detail provided and in the endnotes. For the purposes of this chapter, I sometimes refer to the Polish version of the book and provide my own translation into English. I do this in a few cases in which the English version replaces the figurative language employed in the Polish original with a more 'restrained, or non-figurative' discourse. The reader will be able to tell which version I am quoting from by looking at the year of publication provided in brackets: 2000 refers to the Polish edition, 2001 to the English one.

6   The first part of the phrase, '*when the veil finally falls from our eyes* and we realise that what has so far been unimaginable is precisely what happened' (2000: 15–16; emphasis added), has been translated by Gross into English as '*once we realize* that what seems inconceivable is precisely what happened' (2001: 22; emphasis added). However, for the sake of my argument regarding the significance of the image of the veil in the revelation of truth and the construction of historical knowledge I have decided to retain the original Polish metaphor. The theologically inflected metaphors of unveiling the infinite and of the impossibility of 'closure' (for more on these concepts see Derrida 1976: 14; 1978: 250) also play a significant part in the 'Introduction' chapter in the English edition, one that is absent from the Polish original. Gross writes there:

> In an important respect, however, this is a rather typical book about the Holocaust. For, as is not true of historical studies we write about other topics, I do not see the possibility of attaining closure here. In other words, the reader will not emerge with a sense of satisfied yearning for knowledge at the conclusion of reading; I certainly did not do so at the conclusion of writing. I could not say to myself when I got to the last page, 'Well, I understand now', and I doubt that my readers will be able to either. (2001: 12)

7   Derrida explains the link between infinity and closure in language, a relation that for him has a religious character, as follows: 'The sign and divinity have the same place and time of birth. The age of the sign is essentially theological. Perhaps it will never *end*. Its historical closure is, however, outlined' (1976: 14).

8   In December 2001 the Institute of National Memory (IPN) in Poland, following earlier exhumations conducted in Jedwabne in the summer, completed the investigation into the number of Jewish victims murdered on 10 July 1941. It was concluded that the main grave contained 300–400 bodies, while the other, smaller one, 30–50 bodies. Additionally, in the pile of rubble nearby fragments of bones and teeth (including children's milk teeth) belonging to at least 33 people had been found. Even though the figures confirmed by IPN turned out to be lower than those originally given by Gross in *Neighbors* (c. 480 and not 1600 victims), the evidence provided by the Institute of National Memory has foreclosed the possibility of denying, or diminishing, the scope and significance of the Jedwabne tragedy. Suddenly the supporters of what Dorota Kolodziejczyk calls 'the mathematical fraction' (i.e. those prepared to face the tragedy only from the perspective of 'numbers') have been deprived of the main line of their argument. *Gazeta Wyborcza* online service 19 December 2001. Accessed on 17 January 2002, http://wyborcza.gazeta.pl/info/artykul.jsp?dzial=010101&xx=612617.

9   Lyotard writes, 'All memory, in the traditional sense of representation, because it involves decision, includes and spreads the forgetting of the terror without origin that motivates it' (1990: 28).

10 In his essays *Given Time* and *The Gift of Death*, Derrida challenges our everyday understanding of the gift as something we possess on reception, or something we pass on

to another person, usually in association with some kind of celebration. Traditionally, gifts are exchanged both in private – on birthdays, Christmases, St Valentine's days, etc. – and in public – on state visits of different ranks. It is precisely this exchange-ability of the gift that Derrida exposes as contradictory to the very essence of the idea of 'giving' when he says: '[The gift] must not circulate, it must not be exchanged, it must not in any case be exhausted, as a gift, by the process of exchange, by the move-ment of circulation of the circle in the form of return to the point of departure' (1992b: 7). Working against the logic of debt and gratitude supporting the circle of symbolic exchange, the gift disrupts traditional economy. To retain its status of a gift (rather than a token for a grace or favour, be it a lover's affection, international co-operation or a feel-good factor), it has to remain unspeakable, or even inconceivable, which saves it from being reduced to the familiar economy based on the exact calculation of gains and losses. The possibility of rejection constitutes the very essence of the gift. (I discuss Derrida's notion of the gift in the context of ethics in Zylinska (2001: 88–97).)

11 In *Politics of Friendship* (1997b) Derrida expounds friendship as a political concept and points to the links between the notions of hospitality and hostility in Western political thought.

12 In a similar vein, Lyotard argues that

'The jews' are the irremissible in the West's movement of remission and pardon. They are what cannot be domesticated in the obsession to dominate, in the compul-sion to control domain, in the passion for empire, recurrent ever since Hellenistic Greece and Christian Rome. 'The jews', never at home wherever they are, cannot be integrated, converted, or expelled. They are also always away from home when they are at home, in their so-called own tradition, because it includes exodus as its beginning, excision, impropriety, and respect for the forgotten. (1990: 22)

13 Derrida recognizes that 'because being at home with oneself ... supposes a reception or inclusion of the other which one seeks to appropriate, control, and master according to different modalities of violence, there is a history of hospitality, an always possible perversion of *the* law of hospitality' (2001: 17).

14 For an interesting discussion of 'an alternative approach to history' which rethinks historical events in terms of, and in relation to, 'the non-synchronic temporality that Levinas associates with the ethical relation to the other', and in which history 'gains ethical significance not from "beyond" but from "within," on the basis of a re-thought understanding of temporality', see Krzysztof Ziarek (2001).

15 See *Ethics After the Holocaust* (Roth, 1999) for a polyvocal debate on some possible ways of practising ethical thinking in the aftermath of the Shoah.

7

Ethics and Technology

To articulate a prosthesis means, on the one hand, to bring to light the artificiality of what is supposed to emulate the real and, on the other, to bend, twist or adjust the connection between two bodily organs. The figure of what we might call 'double articulation', prosthesis has always been associated with both silence and speech. A perfect prosthesis can 'pass' for the lost bodily part it replaces, and thus remains invisible and unspeakable. But, as David Wills explains in his eponymous book on prosthesis, in its first appearance in English in 1553 the word 'prosthesis' stood for 'an addition of a syllable to the beginning of a word' (1995: 218), designating an interruption and simultaneous extension of the body of language. Focusing on the discursive arrangements around the practice of torture which depended on both bodily extensions and verbal excess, Wills draws attention to the element of violence that prosthesis inextricably entails. Physical violence is a manifestation (or an extension, a substitute, or, indeed, prosthesis) of power exerted on weak but unsubmissive bodies which are then prosthesized (extended, adjusted, bent, etc.) in an attempt to deprive them of their integrity and inviolability. But prosthesis also involves another kind of bodily disintegration: it violates the logic of totality which underlies modern concepts of identity and selfhood.[1] A prosthetic extension reveals a lack in the corpus to which it is attached, the very need for, or even a possibility of, such an attachment or extension indicating an original incompleteness, or perhaps unboundedness, of the self. It is in this sense that prosthesis becomes an important figure in ethical ruminations.

PROSTHETICS AND ETHICS

Many traditional forms of ethical thinking in Western philosophy are organized around the concept of prosthesis. As John Wild argues in his Introduction to Emmanuel Levinas's *Totality and Infinity*, 'There is a strong tendency in all human individuals and groups to maintain this egocentric attitude and *to think of other individuals either as extensions of the self, or as alien objects to be manipulated* for the advantage of the individual and social self' (Wild: 1969: 12; emphasis added). But I want to suggest in this chapter that it is possible – even necessary – to conceptualize prosthesis beyond self-possession and autonomy. Looking at different ways in which the self negotiates its relationships with alterity and exteriority, I want to position prosthesis as an articulation of connections and slippages *between* the self and its others. Prosthetics will thus stand for me for an ethical way of thinking about identity and difference.

While I am particularly interested in changes in the concepts of identity and difference that have been provoked by recent developments in technology, I do not subscribe to the linear model of the development of the human, from the 'natural man' to the 'posthuman cybernetic organism'. Samuel Weber has argued in his reading of Heidegger's 'Die Frage nach der Technik' that technology and nature are in fact two processes of *poiēsis* (i.e. bringing-forth, or creation) which function according to the same mechanism. However, Weber moves beyond the everyday understanding of technology as relating to contemporary advances in media, communication and medicine, to embrace its meaning of 'technique, craft, or skill'. If 'the innermost principle of "nature" is its impulse to open itself to the exterior, to alterity', technology-as-a-technique has to be seen as one form of nature, or even described as 'more natural than nature itself' (1996: 67). Inspired by Weber's argument, Catherine Waldby suggests that the very relationship between technology and the human has a prosthetic character: 'modern technics is never simply at the disposal of "Man" but sets Man up and replaces and displaces him in dynamic ways' (2000: 42).[2] In this sense the term 'the posthuman', which is frequently used in cyber-discourses, should be seen as a different view of subjectivity, one that 'thinks of the body as the *original prosthesis* we all learn to manipulate' (Hayles, 1999: 3; emphasis added), and not the next stage on the evolutionary ladder. Contemporary experiments in cosmetic and corrective surgery, organ transplants, genetics and cloning – to name but a few contentious areas where such prosthetic couplings are currently taking place – have brought to the fore the instability of the relationship between nature and technics, but they have also foregrounded their mutual interdependence. These conceptual changes are transforming the ways in which we define identity, allowing for the emergence of less bounded and more connected models of human subjectivity. They also create possibilities for reconsidering the relationship between what belongs to the self and what does not, thus calling for a rethinking of the ethical relationship between the self and its others.

In this chapter I intend to interpret this newly emergent view of the human as always already 'intrinsically other', i.e. existing in relation to, and dependent on, its technology, from the perspective of Emmanuel Levinas's ethics of responsibility for the alterity of the other – which constitutes one of the most significant interventions into debates over ways of approaching alterity – in order to develop what I describe as the prosthetic ethics of welcome. Rather than propose a grand theory of ethics, I want to explore singular ethical moments in the practices of two artists: the Australian performance artist Stelarc and the French performance artist Orlan.[3] Opening their bodies to the intrusion of technology and acquiring some forms of body extension, Stelarc and Orlan raise the issues of hospitality and welcome, of embracing incalculable difference, in a radical way. In this context, prosthesis can be interpreted as an ethical figure of hospitality, of welcoming an absolute and incalculable alterity that challenges and threatens the concept of the bounded self. But Orlan's and Stelarc's art will not be seen only as an illustration of a ready-made ethical theory: it is the performative aspect of their artistic practices, where 'performativity must be understood not as a singular or deliberate "act", but, rather, as the reiterative and citational practice by which discourse produces the effects that it names' (Butler, 1993: 2), that will be seen as a (necessarily precarious) legislation of an ethics of welcome. Even though neither artist defines their work as having an explicitly ethical character, I want to argue that their bodily experimentation challenges the possessive individualism which is characteristic of the capitalist model of selfhood, delineating instead the contours for what Celia Lury describes as 'prosthetic culture' (1998: 1). It is not necessarily through art that fixed identity can be challenged, but artistic practices of this kind foreground the broadly enacted performativity of identity, as well as preparing the grounds for the rethinking of identitarian relationships in our culture.

WELCOMING THE ALIEN: EMMANUEL LEVINAS'S ETHICS

The identity of humanity is a differential relation between the human and technics, supplements and prostheses. (The seeming logic of this sentence, defining the human partly by relation to itself, works precisely to dislodge the concept of the human from any identity whose 'origin' is not always split, supplementary.) Technics and the human have to be thought on the basis of 'an oppositional différance' that necessarily displaces our concepts of both. (Clark, 2000: 247)

The alterity which the self encounters in the world can be both animate and inanimate, material and immaterial. Whatever its form, Emmanuel Levinas – the philosopher whose writings constitute a starting point for the ethical ruminations included in this book – argues that 'Western philosophy coincides with the disclosure of the other where the other, in manifesting itself as a being, loses its alterity' (1986: 346). The question of subjectivity and identity is really close to Levinas's heart; indeed, one of his major works, *Totality and Infinity*, has been positioned as 'a defence of subjectivity'.[4] But what he aims to achieve with his critique of totality delineated in this book is propose a new way of approaching the concepts of subjectivity and self-hood. For Levinas, the self is always already a response to the arrival of the other, whose demand is infinite and who for ever remains 'infinitely other', 'with an alterity constitutive of the very content of the other' (1969: 39).[5] Ethics stands for an embrace of this alterity, for a welcome extended to it, for a granting of permission to be disturbed in the skin of one's own home. Responsibility, which is one of the key terms of Levinas's ethics, does not mean that the other cannot be ignored, scorned or even annihilated, but rather that he or she has to be acknowledged and addressed (responded to) in one way or another. As Simon Critchley explains, ethics, for Levinas, 'is not an obligation toward the other mediated through the formal and procedural universalization of maxims or some appeal to good conscience; rather – and this is what is truly provocative about Levinas – ethics is lived in the sensibility of a corporeal obligation to the other' (1999: 64). In order to convey the significance of the bodily dimension in an ethical encounter, Levinas terms this arrival, or apparition, of the other before the self *the face*. The face does not, however, stand for 'an amalgamation of facial features'; it escapes vision and, 'rather than showing itself, the face speaks, addressing me as its interlocutor' (Glowacka, 2003: unpag.).

To render the dynamics of this encounter, Levinas has recourse to the images of rupture and overspilling. 'The other who manifests himself in the face as it were breaks through his own plastic essence, like someone who opens a window on which his figure is outlined. His presence consists in divesting himself of the form which, however, manifests him' (1986: 351). What we experience here is an act of displacement, a breaking out of the plasticity of essence toward the insubstantiality of air. Levinas's other inter-rupts his own alleged completeness and separability; he amputates himself from the window which constitutes a part of his being and reaches out to the self. It is here that the contamination between the ideas of identity and alterity in Levinas's thought is rendered manifest. It seems to me that the Levinasian encounter with the other inscribes itself in Wills's idea of a prosthetic relationship, which he defines as 'displacement, replacement, standing, dislodging, substituting, setting, amputating, supplementing', and as 'articulations between matters of two putatively distinct orders' (1995: 9–10). This encounter 'is necessarily a transfer into otherness, articulated through the radical alterity of ablation as loss of integrity' (Wills, 1995: 13). This moment of displacement and rupture is also constitutive of selfhood as relationality without reciprocity, as the accomplishment of my position on earth (see Levinas, 1969: 128). In this way, ethical perspective opens up between the self and the other, even though, let me repeat, there is no guar-antee that the self will respond ethically to this situation. It is 'because the self is sensible, that is to say, vulnerable, passive, open to wounding, outrage and pain' that, as Critchley argues, 'it is capable and worthy of ethics' (1999: 64), but, we have to remember, it is not sentenced to the performance of an ethical act. The ethical condition arises out of this *possibility* of acknowl-edging and welcoming the alterity that, according to Levinas, is always already part of the self's experience.

ETHICAL CONFUSION AND 'GOOD SCANDAL': THE PROVOCATIONS OF ORLAN AND STELARC

In what follows I want to argue that the sentient self in Orlan's and Stelarc's performances is articulated (in the double sense of being expressed and connected) in a way that foregrounds its openness to 'wounding, outrage and pain'. Indeed, outrage has been a frequent reaction to both Orlan's surgeries and Stelarc's 'body shamanism'.[6] As Jane Goodall remarks,

> Both artists have achieved notoriety for taking risks in deliberately spectacular ways. They are creators of *scandal*, in the original sense of the term as σκάνδαλον, a trap or stumbling block, metaphorically interpreted as a moral snare causing perplexity and ethical confusion (*OED*). Some forms of risk-taking may be scandalous, but scandal in this sense tests the moral ground and puts morality itself at risk. (2000: 153)

Interestingly, for Goodall, the scandalous nature of Orlan's and Stelarc's work does not erase the possibility of reading it in an ethical context. Instead, she describes their bodily experiments as a 'good scandal – one which generates complex confusions around high-intensity issues and cannot be resolved through the simple assertion of precepts' (154). I would not like to treat the notion of a good scandal as a positively valued state of events, dialectically opposed to the 'original', bad situation of moral confusion. Its 'goodness' results for me from the impossibility of providing a consistent, totalizing narrative about the events in question. In this sense, Orlan's and Stelarc's performances inscribe themselves in the logic of the *differend*, which Jean-François Lyotard defines as 'a case of conflict between (at least) two parties, that cannot be equitably resolved for lack of a rule of judgement applicable to both arguments' (1988: xi). For Lyotard, differends, which are born from encounters between phrases of heterogeneous regimens, are unavoidable in our everyday life. The occurrence of differends in discourses about art, nature, politics, ethics or morality – something that is so vividly manifested in different, irreconcilable responses to Orlan's and Stelarc's work – is also a guarantee of the emergence of an ethical dimension; that is, a need to respond to the often uncomfortable 'otherness' of their performances. This ethical dimension can be either embraced and explored from the perspective of respect for what often seems shocking and incomprehensible, or absorbed by the totalizing logic which yearns for the undisturbed unity of the self without the other.

The scandal the two artists often provoke can be attributed to the obligation they put on otherwise complacent selves, making them face the unspeakable and thus challenging them in their self-knowledge and self-sufficiency. Inspired by Levinas's philosophy of alterity, Lyotard explains the nature of this scandal as follows: 'obligation should be described as a scandal for the one who is obligated: deprived of the "free" use of oneself, abandoned by one's narcissistic image, opposed in this, inhibited in that, worried over not being able to be oneself without further ado' (1988: 109-10). Acknowledging further that these doubts can only be voiced by a 'far too human, and humanist' self, Lyotard goes on to ask the following question: 'Can we begin with the dispersion, without any nostalgia for the self?' The scandal of an ethical relationship as illuminated by Levinas consists for him in the recognition that '*The ego does not proceed from the other; the other befalls the ego*' (110; emphasis in original). Here, the alterity of the other presents itself, first, as irreducible to the I, to its dreams, fears and expectations, and, second, as arriving unexpectedly and taking the I by surprise, thus depriving it of mastery and self-possession.

I want to postulate here that the identity of both Orlan's and Stelarc's 'performing I' is prosthetic, foregrounding and enacting the 'radical recontextualisation' of the self through the processes of artificiality and contrivance (see Wills, 1995: 45). It is some of the ways in which Orlan and Stelarc expose the non-mastering relationship of the self to alterity (see Wills, 1995: 26) – a relationship that calls us to respond to this scandal of heterogeneity, dispersal and confusion – that I will investigate in the next two sections of this chapter.

'I IS AN OTHER': ORLAN'S PROSTHETIC SELFHOOD

The work of the French performance artist Orlan, who has been involved in remodelling her face over and over again to conform with different standards of beauty and thus problematize their 'natural' character, is an example of such a non-mastering relationship with alterity. In her 1998 project entitled *Self-Hybridations*, Orlan digitally constructed a series of portraits, 'adorning' her face with elements from the pre-Columbian cultures, which, as the artist herself says, 'have a relationship with the body which is particularly disturbing for us, which completely challenges us and which is very intense. ... This is the idea of entering into the skin of the other' (Ayers, 2000: 177). The photographs representing Orlan's face equipped with the large nose of King Wapacal or carrying a superimposed Olmec mask – the production of which involves skull deformation, as well as scar-like drawings – can be seen as a continuation of the artist's earlier project *Interventions*. Initiated in 1990, *Interventions* consisted of a series of cosmetic surgeries, by means of which Orlan self-mockingly modelled herself on selected mythological figures: she acquired the nose of Diana, the mouth of Boucher's Europa, the chin of Botticelli's Venus and the eyes of Gérôme's Psyche. However, the final result was no more important than the actual operation-performance, conducted by 'surgeon-sculptors' (Armstrong, 1997: 4) in co-operation with the artist herself.

But Orlan objects to having her work reduced to the problematics of identity.[7] In interviews and conferences she asserts the directedness and vocation of her artistic I, which she sees, in a somewhat Mephisthophelean fashion, as involved in a 'struggle against the innate, the inexorable, the programmed, Nature, DNA (which is our direct rival as far as artists of representation are concerned), and God!' (Orlan, 1996: 91). She announces further: 'My work is blasphemous. It is an endeavour to move the bars of the cage, a radical and uncomfortable endeavour!' (91). In this way, Orlan inscribes her project in a certain teleology of liberation, facilitated and authorized by the artist as an agent of social change and a source of moral anxiety. During her surgeries Orlan is only partially anaesthetized, which allows her to maintain control and direct the performance from her operating table. And yet, the boundaries of her carefully contrived 'I' suddenly open up with her announcement that 'I is an other' (*'Je est un autre'*) (91).

Interestingly, a number of interpreters of Orlan's *oeuvre* display a similar ambiguity regarding the artist's identity and its possible conceptualization. Sarah Wilson, for example, claims that, ever since Orlan's series of *'tableaux vivants'* staged in 1968 and parodying the Venuses of Manet and Velásquez, the artist 'was always, insistently, herself' (1996: 10). Wilson does not question Orlan's intention of single-handedly challenging God, Nature and DNA: indeed, the declaration of prosthetic selfhood, translated into English by Wilson as 'I am [*sic*] an other', becomes for her the realization of the dream of ultimate fulfilment and plenty. Seen in this way, Orlan not only fights God, she becomes God, 'sacred and profane, Alpha and Omega' (Wilson, 1996: 16). And yet Wilson's article, significantly titled *'L'histoire d'O*, Sacred and Profane', opens with an assertion, 'Orlan is O, "The O in open. *The O of the other*"' (1996: 8; emphasis added). Michel Onfray, in turn, interprets Orlan's surgeries as springing from a desire 'to bridge the abyss between what one feels oneself to be and what, in reality, one shows'. According to him, Orlan manages to 'correct and transcend' human alienation 'by making the inside and outside match' (1996: 35). Orlan's totalization of identity, her de-prosthesization of selfhood, signifies for Onfray an ethical undertaking of attempting to overcome the fragmentation that is characteristic of 'our nihilistic, postmodern age' (34). Making 'the signifier, the face, coincide with the signified, the soul' (35), Orlan's work is turned here into a magic cure against 'this spreading desert, void of intellectual resistance'; it is elevated to the position of a moral agent who will cleanse 'matter forsaken, execrated and soiled by the market by invoking the possibility of sculpting it as only an artist can'. Stefan Morawski, author of *The Troubles with Postmodernity* and exponent of the thesis of the 'aestheticisation of everyday life', shares Onfray's diagnosis of our contemporary ailments, but offers a completely different reading of Orlan's work. In 'A Symptomatic Case of Self-Mystification', Morawski asks: 'What is the sense of her art?', only to conclude that in our 'Tower of Babel' 'the values have vanished and lay [*sic*] entangled on the scales' (1996: 203). Since, according to Morawski, Orlan attacks 'both culture, metaphysical needs and nature (which, after all, is the basis of sexual differences and identity)' (199), the possibility of identifying an ethical dimension in Orlan's work is for him totally foreclosed.

What emerges from the above discussions is that Orlan's work can be simultaneously interpreted as a 'good' and 'bad scandal', revealing a differend (itself a prosthetic figure, a figure of 'double articulation') between the heterogeneous discourses employed for its analysis. I do not intend to resolve this conflict here. I am more interested in the very possibility of continuing to comment on Orlan's performances without attempting to close off the differend by 'usurping' her work for some pre-defined purpose (e.g. salvation or castigation). At this point I would like to return to Orlan's declaration 'I is an other', and to relate it to Derrida's interpretation of the relationship between selfhood and otherness as delineated by Levinas. My reason for turning to these two thinkers is that the 'staple' cultural studies questions concerning identity, difference and their possible (ir)reconciliation, which I am discussing here in relation to Orlan, have been addressed in a most rigorous and provocative way in their work.

The ethics of welcome and hospitality, a recurring thread in Derrida's writings, is based on the disavowal of the subject–object distance upon which Western philosophy has based its understanding of alterity. Derridean hospitality – delineated as an *extension* of Levinas's ethics of obligation towards the alterity of the other – implies the possibility, and danger, of the intrusion of the unpresentable, of what we cannot yet know or name, into the confined territory of the self. Instead of protecting itself against the unknown, the self extends a prosthetic invite to the always already monstrous (in the sense of 'showing itself as something that is not yet shown') other, and thus recognizes the necessary doubling – but also splitting – of identity. However, as Derrida observes, for any action, any decision, to take place, 'it must be made by the other in myself' (1999b: 67; see also 1999a: 23). A decision made by the self which does not have any doubts regarding its rightness and which is fully in control of what it is doing is not a decision: this kind of decision has already been, in a way, pre-decided. The self, the host awaiting the arrival of the other, is at the same time 'a hostage insofar as he is the subject put into question' (Derrida, 1999a: 56).

From this perspective, Orlan's attempts to 'move the bars of the cage' through her performances – even if enveloped in the rhetoric of self-liberation – become a simultaneous attack on the idea of the self that maintains a fantasy of autonomy and solipsism, a self that sees itself as separate from the innate, from Nature and from DNA. Orlan's fight against the self's components (which are here projected as its absolute 'others') and her attempts to de-prosthesize selfhood in order to achieve a state of perfect closure, work only when this self is opened to the intrusion of incalculable alterity. Significantly, one of the operations Orlan underwent for her *Interventions* series involved inserting two cheek implants onto her temples, 'giving a sort of naughty Pan "horned" look' (Millard, 1996: 52). By shifting the corporeal boundaries in this way, Orlan makes us realize that 'Nothing "fits" any longer. ... The inside no longer lies patiently within the outside, contained and stable, and a guarantee that the world is just the world' (Adams, 1996: 156-7). I do not interpret Parveen Adams's conclusion as a reinforcement of the evolutionary narrative of technological development, but rather as an acknowledgement of the idea that selfhood can only come from 'the other' (both human – i.e. spectator audience, a surgeon-intruder; and non-human – i.e. a cheek implant, an anaesthetic injection), and thus is intrinsically prosthetic. By allowing for this sort of bodily intervention Orlan embraces the possibility of the unpredictable transformation that inevitably challenges the humanist discourse of identity. Perhaps even against herself, and in contradiction with her modernist concept of artist as public con-science and scandal-monger, Orlan performs what Timothy Clark calls a 'deconstruction of the Aristotelian system', where technology is perceived as 'extrinsic to human nature as a tool which is used to bring about certain ends' (2000: 238). By allowing 'the unforeseen [to disrupt] the very criteria in which it would have been captured' (Clark, 2000: 250), Orlan enacts what we could term 'the exhaustion' of the discourse of 'identity without difference' which is not able to convey the unforeseen and the 'not-yet'.

This sense of unpredictability and 'not-yet' is clearly visible in the open-endedness of Orlan's project, which always involves the possibility of an accident and failure. As Barbara Rose observes,

> each time [Orlan] is operated on, there is an increased element of risk. She insists on being conscious to direct and choreograph the actions, so the operations take place under local rather than general anaesthesia. The procedure, known as an epidural block, requires a spinal injection that risks paralysing the patient if the needle does not hit its mark exactly. With each successive surgical intervention and injection, the danger is said to increase. ... To at least some degree she risks deformation, paral-ysis, even death. (1993: 82–7)

The recognition of this dimension of mortality in Orlan's work has impor-tant ethical consequences. I am not primarily concerned here with the issue of medical ethics which is frequently raised in the context of surgical interventions into the body, their scope and justification, but rather with the ultimate performance of the ethics of hospitality in this particular art-ist's body. If, as Levinas argues, 'I am responsible for the other insofar as he is mortal' (quoted in Derrida, 1999a: 7), Orlan can be said to instantiate what Levinas terms 'the passage to the ethical'. By embracing mortality as an unavoidable part of the performance, Orlan undertakes responsibility for the other *in* her, for her death *and* life. Undermining the perception of death as a 'termination of life', she foregrounds death as an unavoidable element – perhaps also the most significant incarnation – of the self's relationship with incalculable and infinite alterity. Her sacrifice goes beyond the logic of capitalist spending, which depends on the equal calculation of gains and losses. Indeed, it is only in the light of the possibility of deformation and annihilation that her decision of self-offering gains an ethical character. Its ethicity follows neither the Judaeo-Christian tradition of martyrdom as part of a redemptive project (even if the artist does actually resort to the rhetoric of self-sacrifice when announcing that she is 'giving her body to art'), nor the sacrificial economy of biovalue which designates some bodies as less valuable than others (Waldby, 2000: 52): it is death *as such* (i.e. the unpresentable, rather than 'a passage to eternity', 'the end-product of life', etc.) that needs to be responded to and chosen. Through the extension of her body towards absolute alterity, Orlan challenges the confinement of moral agency to an autonomous and bounded self.

'THE INFORMATION IS THE PROSTHESIS': STELARC'S BODILY EXTENSIONS

PHANTOM LIMB/VIRTUAL ARM
Amputees often experience a phantom limb. It is now possible to have a phantom sensation of an additional arm – a virtual arm – albeit visual rather than visceral. The Virtual Arm is a computer-generated, human-like universal manipulator interactively controlled by VPL Virtual Reality equipment. Using data gloves with flexion and position-orientation sensors and a GESTURE-BASED COMMAND LANGUAGE *allows real-time intuitive operation and additional extended capabilities. (Stelarc's website)*

Stelarc's performances have always focused on the idea of prosthesis: from external bodily extensions such as the Third Hand or Extended Arm, to internal prostheses such as the Stomach Sculpture, where the body 'becomes a host not for a self or soul, but simply for a sculpture' (Stelarc's website). One of his experiments involved developing the Movatar project – that is, an avatar taking over the human body, which then functions as a prosthesis for this avatar. As the artist himself explains,

> Motion Capture allows a physical body to animate a 3D computer-generated virtual body to perform in computer space or cyberspace. ... Consider, though, a virtual body or an avatar that can access a physical body, actuating its performance in the real world. If the avatar is imbued with an artificial intelligence, becoming increasingly autonomous and unpredictable, then it would become more an AL (Artificial Life) entity performing with a human body in physical space. (Stelarc's website)

While differing as to the degree and scale in which the body is extended, augmented and transformed, all these performances seem to have been inspired by the idea of openness, of welcoming the unpredictable and the unknown. This kind of transaction, intended to 'explore alternate, intimate and involuntary interfaces with the body' (Stelarc's website), does not come without a loss: but what Stelarc renounces in his prosthetic performances is not agency as such – that would only reinforce the humanist, agent-driven notion of selfhood he does not subscribe to – but rather *the idea of the self* as an autonomous agent. Stelarc's declarations that accompany his artistic practices do not share Orlan's language of self-sacrifice and artistic vocation. By dispassionately referring to his body as 'the body', Stelarc foregrounds the 'originary prosthecity' of selfhood and its situatedness in the network of relations that criss-cross the envelope of the skin.

This abandonment of the idea of self-as-agent, as skin-bounded and will-controlled, creates an ethical opening in the discourse of subjectivity which traditionally singles out the individual at the cost of suppressing an incalculable alterity it might encounter. However, Stelarc does not announce this withdrawal of agency in advance, but rather performs it through his prosthetic manoeuvres. His performances connect, divide, transmute and cut across the strict conceptual boundaries on which the discourse of 'identity without alterity' has relied. Stelarc's prostheses do not merely extend the body perceived as a bounded whole: the Extended Arm or the Movatar make the real arm or the neural system look like prosthetic devices.[8] 'ALTERING THE ARCHITECTURE OF THE BODY RESULTS IN ADJUSTING AND EXTENDING ITS AWARENESS OF THE WORLD' (Stelarc's website). As a result, the body is not seen here as an envelope for a soul or agency but rather as a sequence of co-dependent additions and replacements. In fact, the metaphysical perception of the self as a sum of bodily parts plus 'something else' (psyche, soul, practical reason) can itself be described as a prosthesis, an extension of the corporeal towards the spiritual, a bridge between materiality and ideality. Howard Caygill argues that 'The redesign that Stelarc envisages entails a thorough reconsideration of prosthesis. Instead of regarding the prosthesis as a supplement to the human body, it is now seen as already an integral part of its organisation and consequently as a site for its potential reorganisation' (1997: 48).

What I have termed here, after the French philosopher Bernard Stiegler (1998), the 'originary prosthecity' of Stelarc's performances is a reworking, in the context of technology and experimentation, of the thesis of 'originary alterity' that underpins Levinas's ethical thinking. The very positing of this thesis, and, consequently, the description of Stelarc's work as an ethical opening to the alterity of technology enabled by his prosthetic performances, itself amounts to a prosthetic manoeuvre. As Joanna Hodge argues, the thesis of originary alterity is 'not a thesis, since it hypothesises the instability of the site at which it is posited. ... The self-identity presupposed by the positing of theses is a prosthetic move, necessary but illegitimate in advance of the production of an argument for the validity of argument' (2000: 183). She explains further: 'Originary prosthecity is the thesis which declares the unjustifiability of theses, except in terms of carrying the discussion from where it starts to where it ends in a way which lends it sense and significance and which shows the necessary polemical nature of any determination of meaning and order' (192). It is thus perhaps inevitable that any discussion of Stelarc's artistic practice should inscribe itself in the logic of Lyotard's differend I referred to in the earlier part of this chapter – a (Levinas-inflected) concept that validates the paradoxical thesis of 'the unjustifiability of theses', without relieving us of the responsibility to keep the differend open, to continue talking. From the perspective of the differend, the ethical character of Stelarc's performances can never be unambiguously asserted or denied, but this need not stop us from trying to consider the possibility of ethics erupting within artistic discourses, especially those that often lend themselves to negative and accusatory readings.

As Levinas's ethics rooted in his notion of originary alterity remains prone to 'the unjustifiability of theses', it cannot be enclosed in a book of conduct. It does not consist of rules and regulations, which should not lead to a conclusion that his ethics is unfounded. It springs precisely from the recognition of, and respect for, the other, whose alterity cannot be reduced to the ideas elaborated and mastered by the self. The self is not for Levinas a 'microcosm in miniature': it emerges only in contact with, or as a response to, the other who is both a stranger and 'in all essential aspects like me'. It can thus be concluded that ethics is here an *inevitable* consequence of this recognition of the 'thereness' of the other. Its inevitability does not mean that the other cannot be annihilated or devoured, but rather that it is necessary to respond to alterity in one way or another. Indeed, this pervertibility of ethics is also its first and foremost condition.[9]

Stelarc's performance of prosthetic selfhood can thus perhaps be described as the abandonment of the idea of self-possession and self-mastery. It creates a space for an encounter with, even intrusion of, what is radically different from the self and yet what remains, paradoxically, in some sort of relationship with the self. By denying the mastery of the self (of the artist, *auteur*, creator, demiurge), Stelarc does not give up what he previously possessed: he rather resigns from a certain idea of not only the performance artist but also the human as *only singular* and autonomous. His 'hospitality' – to borrow Derrida's term, which he employs to describe precisely this kind of ethical opening – should not, however, be interpreted as an act of good will but rather as a compulsion to respond to the inevitability of ethics and a decision not to commit violence against it.

Stelarc himself willingly embraces the rhetoric of hospitality in his performances, describing the body as a 'host – not only for technology, but also for remote agents' (1997b: 66). His 'Stomach Sculpture' project, in which a dome capsule built of quality metals was inserted into his body and then arrayed with switches on the control box and documented by means of video endoscopy equipment, is one example of such unconditional hospitality. As the artist himself puts it,

It is time to recolonise the body with MICROMINIATURISED ROBOTS to augment our bacterial population, to assist our immunological system and to monitor the capillary and internal tracts of the body. ... SPECK-SIZED ROBOTS ARE EASILY SWALLOWED, AND MAY NOT EVEN BE SENSED! At a nanotechnology level, machines will inhabit cellular spaces and manipulate molecular structures. (1997a: 248–9)

This interpenetration between human and machine is for Stelarc a promise of new forms of hospitality and intimacy: 'The body has been augmented, invaded and now becomes a host – not only for technology, but also for remote agents' (1997b: 66). Opening his body to the intrusion of technology and thus shifting the locus of human agency, Stelarc renounces the possibility of knowing the consequences of his connected performances in advance. By abandoning the desire to master the house of his own body and opening himself to the (perhaps hostile) intrusion of the guest, Stelarc performs the most ethical act of what Derrida terms 'unconditional hospitality', where

> unconditional hospitality implies that you don't ask the other, the newcomer, the guest, to give anything back, or even to identify himself or herself. Even if this other deprives you of your mastery of your home, you have to accept this. It is terrible to accept this, but that is the condition of unconditional hospitality: that you give up the mastery of your space, your home, your nation. (Derrida, 1999b: 70)

But this openness towards alterity is not a passive enterprise. Even though the self cannot rely on a book of laws and rules for its conduct, the welcome it extends towards the other – to retain its openness and not to fossilize into a predictable and measurable 'gift' – has to be constantly revisited. In this sense, Stelarc's continual rethinking of the ways in which prosthetic relationships can be recast in his performances can be interpreted as a responsible response to ethics itself, a response which arises out of the duty towards unassimilable difference. Geoffrey Bennington confirms that

> an ethical act worthy of its name is always *inventive*, and inventive not at all in the interests of expressing the 'subjective' freedom of the agent, but in response and responsibility to the other. ... I can in fact 'express myself', exercise my freedom, only in this situation of response and responsibility with respect to the always-already-thereness of the other text as part of a 'tradition' to which I am always already indebted. (2000: 68)

Stelarc's inventiveness leads him constantly to run up against the limits of the physical and the corporeal in search of its possible extension and of what he terms 'the telematic scaling of subjectivity'. Perhaps we could go so far as to suggest that his performances enact a kind of 'connected Levinasianism', one that arises out of a specific historical moment in the development of technology that embraces the everyday in numerous ways. As email communication, online shopping and virtual friendships are becoming a prominent part of many people's lives, Stelarc proposes a way of encountering the alterity of technology that moves beyond both technophilia and technophobia. Recognizing a certain unavoidability of prosthetic connections facilitated by the Internet and cyberspace, he predicts that 'bodies will generate phantom partners, not because of a lack, but as an extending and enhancing addition to their physiology' (1997b: 69). Exposed to the multiplicity of agents, the body has to develop a kind of 'fluid and flowing awareness that dims and intensifies as they are connected and disconnected' (69). An ethical response of this kind presents itself a non-hysterical acceptance of a necessity.

'A SPECIES FOR WHICH WE DO NOT YET HAVE A NAME'

Orlan's and Stelarc's performances not only foreground the originary prosthecity of identity but also embrace the intrinsic monstrosity of the human that becomes ever so visible in 'the technological age'. To describe their artistic projects as 'monstrous' does not amount to reducing them to 'bad scandal' or horror. A monster, according to Derrida, 'shows itself [*elle se montre*] – that is what the word monster means – it shows itself in something that is not yet shown and that therefore looks like a hallucination ... it frightens precisely because no anticipation had prepared one to identify this figure' (1995: 386). The prosthetic ethics of welcome cannot thus be learnt in advance, because an encounter with alterity (which we can supplement – even if not substitute – here with prosthecity or monstrosity) is always singular and irreplaceable. But its uncertain occurrence and unpredictable form do not diminish our responsibility to respond to what shows itself as incalculably different. As this alterity transcends our discursive mastery, the ethical moment of being faced with incalculable difference, with 'a species for which we do not yet have a name', presents itself as inevitable.

Notes

1   A number of philosophers and sociologists argue that 'identity' can be described as a modern invention. As Zygmunt Bauman asserts,

> To say that modernity led to the 'disembedding' of identity, or that it rendered identity 'unencumbered', is to assert a pleonasm, since at no time did identity 'become' a problem; it was a 'problem' from its birth – was *born as a problem* (that is, as something one needs to do something about, as a task), could exist only as a problem; it was a problem, and thus ready to be born, precisely because of that experience of

under-determination and free-floatingness which came to be articulated *ex post facto* as 'disembeddedment'. (1996: 18–19)

Cultural studies' long-standing engagement with the problem of identity can be envisaged as a response to this feeling that 'one needed to do something about it'; that it was a task a 'committed' socio-political discipline could not ignore. This engagement has involved the problematization of 'identity' as fixed and the interrogation of the ideological and psychic mechanisms involved in its production. It is thus perhaps unsurprising that identity – along with the different forms of political, national, racial, sexual and bodily (mis- and dis-)identification associated with it – should function as one of the organizing concepts in this book.

2   I develop this point further in the last chapter of the book, drawing on Bernard Stiegler's notion of 'originary prosthecity' and exploring it in the context of the concept of the cyborg and its early twenty-first-century mutations.

3   Readers who are not familiar with Orlan's and Stelarc's work might want to consult their websites: http://www.orlan.net; http://www.stelarc.va.com.au. For an extended discussion of Orlan's and Stelarc's artistic projects in an ethico-political context see my edited collection *The Cyborg Experiments: the Extensions of the Body in the Media Age* (Zylinska, 2002a).

4   Levinas writes there: 'If the same would establish its identity by simple *opposition to the other*, it would already be a part of a totality encompassing the same and the other' (1969: 38).

5   For a deconstruction of this notion of absolute alterity and dissymmetry between self and other see Derrida's 'Violence and Metaphysics: An Essay on the Thought of Emmanuel Levinas' included in *Writing and Difference* (1978). The fact that he sees problems with the absoluteness of Levinas's distinction does not, however, stop Derrida from embracing Levinas's ethical thinking in both his early and late works – even if it comes with a question mark posed over the 'absoluteness' of this 'absolute' difference. It is precisely in the contamination of this dissymmetry, and in the need for some form of economic calculation and economic community between self and other, that Derrida situates the possibility of politics. As I have admitted many times throughout the course of this book, I usually read Levinas through a Derridean lens.

6   For an interpretation of Stelarc's work in the context of shamanism and Western ritual see Marsh (1993: 96–140).

7   When discussing her project *Refiguration/Self-Hybridation* with Robert Ayers, Orlan explains:

Here we're quite a long way from the problem of identity. These are images that I put before the public, which could find takers in our society, and which, in the end, present themselves as being 'acceptable' as a type of face that doesn't, strictly speaking, refer to identity. Of course there's an inference in relation to what *I* am, but no, this isn't work concerned with identity. You could put it like this: it's simply the idea of saying that beauty can take on an appearance that is not usually thought of as beautiful. (Ayers, 2000: 180)

8   This process of the destabilization of boundaries is not specific to technology-based art. Donna Haraway argues that a number of recently developed scientific prostheses do much more than augment or enhance human capabilities: they question the utilitarian conception of technology and call for a radical rethinking of human–machine interaction: 'The "eyes" available in modern technological sciences shatter any idea of passive vision; these prosthetic devices show us that all eyes, including our own organic ones, are active perceptual systems, building in translations and specific *ways* of seeing, that is, ways of life' (1991: 190).

9   '[T]his pervertibility is the positive condition (to be affirmed, then) of all the "positive" values (the Good, the Just, and so on) ethics enjoins us to seek' (Bennington, 2000: 72).

8

Bio-*Ethics and Cyberfeminism*

(YET MORE) QUESTIONS OF CULTURAL IDENTITY

Questions of identity and difference, of kinship and belonging, have always featured prominently on the cultural studies agenda. However, the 1990s saw 'a veritable explosion' of debates around identity, coupled with a 'searching critique' of the concept itself (Hall, 1996a: 1). Collections such as *'Race', Culture and Difference* (Donald and Rattansi, 1992), *Questions of Cultural Identity* (Hall and du Gay, 1996), *Identity and Difference* (Woodward, 1997) or *Identity: A Reader* (du Gay *et al.*, 2000) remain a testimony to the tension between the understanding of identification as an 'interminable process of becoming' on the one hand, and the pluralization of clearly distinguishable identity positions which does not entail any specific critique of identity as such on the other. Aware of this co-existence within cultural studies of foundational and anti-foundational positions on identity, Stuart Hall remains adamant that it is only through an engagement with what he terms 'the deconstructive critique' that 'the question of identity' can be addressed in a responsible and politically enabling way. He argues 'Identity is ... a concept – operating "under erasure" in the interval between reversal and emergence; an idea which cannot be thought in the old way, but without which certain key questions cannot be thought at all' (1996a: 2).

As the reader will be aware by now, the 'key questions' that are the focus of this book concern politics and ethics: the possibility of the transformation of the social and our ability to live with forms of alterity we can neither ultimately comprehend nor master. And it is precisely through a deconstruction-inspired investigation of different forms of identity and identification, of being and becoming, that I have so far attempted to approach these questions. While I intend to continue with this line of enquiry in the closing pages of the book, I also want to take the question of 'human identity' further and explore some new forms of emergence and life associated with what we can describe as 'the biotechnological age'. It is thus not so much the human as the cyborg – a cybernetic organism which hybridizes carbon and silicon, genetic code and computer code – that will be central to my politico-ethical investigations in this chapter.

SOFTENING THE CYBORG

The fascination with 'the cyborg' as a new form of being was perhaps symptomatic of the 'explosion' of discourses around identity and identification that took place in cultural studies in the 1990s. Inspired by Donna Haraway's celebrated 'A Cyborg Manifesto', cultural theorists took up the concept of the cyborg as a metaphor for the transformed relationship between humans and technology in late capitalist societies. An offspring of the militarism of the Space Wars era, the cyborg was adopted as a figure of transgression that allowed for the rethinking of the conceptual boundaries between virtuality and materiality, mechanism and vitalism, culture and nature, mind and body. And yet not enough attention was often paid on a philosophical level to *how* these boundaries where actually being transgressed and what consequences this transgression had for the socio-political system within which they were established. The specificity of Haraway's socialist feminist project and its links with what some US theorists call 'progressive politics' thus risked being lost amidst the overenthusiastic celebration of the 'transgressed boundaries' and 'potent fusions' that the cyborg allegedly offered.[1]

One intellectual project that took on board both the political consequences of Haraway's 'Manifesto' and the critical engagement with the new technologies of late capitalism became known under the playful name of 'cyberfeminism'. Embracing the traditional feminist concern with the construction of gender, 1990s cyberfeminism drew its inspiration from the deconstructive modes of thinking: the feminist philosophy of Luce Irigaray and the performative theory of sex and gender as elaborated by Judith Butler, as well as the 'situated' epistemologies of Haraway herself. There was something blasphemous about cyberfeminists building their strategies of intervention into the culture of technoscience on irony and parody, on 'humour and serious play', but blasphemy also meant 'taking things very seriously' (Haraway, 1991: 149). In other words, early cyberfeminists were no technophobes – they did not eschew technoscientific enquiry for the sake of a return to 'nature'; instead, they fought for women's entry into the masculinized world of technoscience on their own terms, and for a more 'situated' version of cyborg ontologies. Writers such as Claudia Springer, Zoe Sofoulis, Sadie Plant and A.R. Stone turned their attention to *the matter* of the cyborg's body, and its relation to, and alteration by, technology. In this way, they challenged the cyborg's alleged overcoming of 'meat' (as evidenced, for example, in the writings of the 'father' of cyberspace, William Gibson), its sexualization-beyond-matter and its enactment of the militaristic fantasies of corporate capitalism.

The importance of the cyberfeminist perspective for imagining new models of corporeality in the world in which information sciences remain one of the dominant scientific paradigms should not be underestimated. I want to come back to this point later on in this chapter, but for the moment let me just point out that, with the increased interest of many scientists in some other, 'softer' and 'wetter' forms of technology, the emphasis in the study of different forms of interaction between technology and the human has shifted over the last few years. As scientific research into the hierarchical, systemic formations of artificial intelligence has led to investigations of more 'bottom up' technologies and forms of emergence described as 'artificial life' (Kember, 2003), the 1990s cyborg looks increasingly like Arnold Schwarzenegger's Terminator from *Rise of the Machines*: it has become an 'old model', slightly gauche in its military origin and machinic pathos. I would therefore like to suggest that in the early twenty-first century the term 'cyborg' should perhaps rather refer to those biotechnological, transgenic, soft hybrids which put into question the origin and nature of 'life itself' – OncoMouse™, Dolly the sheep, inhabitants of the *SimLife* computer game designed as a 'genetic playground' – rather than the animated machines of the previous decades.

In an attempt to explore some of the consequences the emergence of these new ontological formations has for our conceptions of ethics and politics, I want to take a look at a number of such emergent 'soft cyborgs' in this chapter. Two questions will inform my investigations: 1. Do 'soft cyborgs' have bodies? 2. Can these 'soft cyborgs' be seen as 'others' who are worthy of ethical respect? Drawing on the cyberfeminist critique of disembodied information in cybernetics and molecular biology as well as the feminist investigation of gendered power relations in the sciences, I will attempt to outline a (modest) proposal for a feminist cyberbioethics. Significantly, for Haraway the political position delineated in her 'Manifesto' also has clear ethical undertones. She argues that blasphemy (by which she means an illicit, passionate and intellectually rigorous invasion of science by feminist scholars) 'protects one from the moral majority' within – be it the ethos of socialist feminism or technoscientific capitalism – 'while still insisting on the need for community'. And it is in its desire to envisage some new modes of (insubordinate) being in the techno-world, and to come to terms with its alterity, that cyberfeminism becomes an interesting intellectual and ethico-political proposition for me. Hybridizing historical, philosophical and scientific trajectories (the history of biosciences, Derridean deconstruction, Levinasian ethics, recent developments in genetic technology) in a perhaps illicit way, I want to take issue with some of the more established ways of thinking about bioethics that have been developed within the corporate world of biotechnosciences, as well as some of the theories of bioethics within traditional moral philosophy. It is in the unavoidable tension between an infinite (ethical) responsibility to respond to difference, and a finite (political) desire to reduce or annihilate some forms of difference in order to make our own lives liveable, that the feminist cyberbioethics I propose here will be situated.

BIOETHICS BETWEEN CORPORAL AND CORPORATE
OBLIGATIONS

As Helga Kuhse and Peter Singer explain in the Introduction to their anthology *Bioethics*, the term 'bioethics' 'was coined by Van Rensselaer Potter, who used it to describe his proposal that we need an ethic that can incorporate our obligations, not just to other humans, but to the biosphere as a whole' (1999: 1). Although ecological concerns are not foreign to many bioethicists, nowadays the term is used 'in the narrower sense of the study of ethical issues arising from the biological and medical sciences' (1). A branch of applied ethics, bioethics is most commonly seen as requiring the formal logic, consistency and factual accuracy that set a limit to the subjectivity of ethical judgements. In most cases, however, the requirements of formal reasoning have to be reconciled, in one way or another, with 'practical constraints'. Kuhse and Singer postulate 'universal prescriptivism' – prescribing universalizable judgement for all possible circumstances, including hypothetical ones – as a promising alternative to both ethical subjectivism and 'cultural relativism'.[2] This concept is not based on any notion of a pre-given 'universal good', but rather on what we might term the methodical calculation of goods under given socio-political circumstances. In this way, Jeremy Bentham's and John Stuart Mills's utilitarianism, whose ethical principles were aimed at ensuring the 'greatest surplus of happiness', is modified: the idea of maximizing net happiness is abandoned for the sake of a more modest attempt to satisfy the greatest number of desires and preferences.[3] (Neo)utilitarian positions of this kind inform a great number of debates among contemporary bioethicists.[4]

Singer himself is one of the most pre-eminent proponents of this position. His thought-provoking book, *Rethinking Life and Death: the Collapse of Our Traditional Ethics* (1994), launches an attack on the human-centred Western moral tradition, counterposing it with neo-Darwinism, which deprives humans of the privileged place in the universe and undermines the ontological distinction between human and nonhuman animals. But this is not the most innovative aspect of his thesis – after all, similar positions have been put forward by more radical advocates of the ecologist and animal liberation movements. Singer is at his most original when he introduces the distinction between a 'human being' and a 'person', with only the latter, characterized by rationality and self-awareness, being worthy of ethical respect. He includes nonhuman animals such as great apes in the category of 'persons', while also believing that 'whales, dolphins, elephants, monkeys, dogs, pigs and other animals may eventually also be shown to be aware of their own existence over time and capable of reasoning' (1994: 182).[5] The sheer fact of 'life' (be it human or animal), for Singer, is not a universal value per se which should be protected at all cost.

In his attempt to 'rewrite the commandments' of traditional Western ethics, which tend to have religion as their (direct or indirect) inspiration,

Singer comes up with 'a new ethical outlook'. This he formulates in five principles: 1. Recognize that the worth of human life varies; 2. Take responsibility for the consequences of your decisions; 3. Respect a person's desire to live or die; 4. Bring children into the world only if they are wanted; 5. Do not discriminate on the basis of species (1994: 189–206). While his 'new ethical outlook' raises radical questions for the principle of the sanctity of human life, his concept of the 'person' only extends the notion of the human as a rational being worthy of ethical respect. For Singer, the 'new humans' are still skin-bound, carbon-based singular entities, and thus his bioethical propositions are merely an updated version of traditional, moral theories. This position – shared, among others, by E. O. Wilson and Richard Dawkins – does not leave any room for the investigation of sociobiology as a constructed practice which is linked to different forms of technoscience and technopolitics.[6] Although Singer does encourage his readers to interrogate the boundaries (or better, temporalities) of life and death, he does not really investigate the philosophico-political model (i.e. the political philosophy of self-interest and possessive individualism) which underlies his notion of the human. Indeed, there is not much recognition in his work given to the fact that life sciences such as biology and primatology, rather than being just a mirror reflection of capitalist social relations, actively reproduce them (see Haraway, 1991: 44). In Singers's moral universe there is no room for the investigation of wider political processes or cultural influences. His is an ethics of (and for) the individual who has to make rational moral choices as if he could always be carved out from the network of relations and flows of capital. Nor does Singer offer a recognition of the dimension of antagonism that organizes the social, because wider socio-political processes are seen as irrelevant when it comes to making moral judgements. No 'horizon of justice' against which moral decisions need to be made exists for him; instead what we are left with is just a rational working out of rules, a process of calculation where values can be compared for the sake of elaborating the common good.

In her *Modest_Witness@Second_Millennium* Haraway takes bioethics as precisely such a 'technical discourse about values clarification and choice' to task (1997: 109). Commenting on a US high school textbook, *Advances in Genetic Technology*, she points out that ethical analysis as envisaged there is supposed to mime scientific analysis: 'both are based on sound facts and hypothesis testing; both are technical practices' (109). The 'career section' of the book explains that 'most people working in bioethics have a "terminal degree", which is the highest (usually doctoral) academic degree offered in their discipline' (109). And thus the business of bioethics is not only a moral discourse; it is, first and foremost, a serious enterprise which needs to be properly authorized and controlled, while also concealing its own embeddedness in power structures. The academicization of bioethics goes hand in hand with its corporatization.[7] Haraway argues that 'ethics is now a literal industry, funded directly by the new developments in techno-science. Ethics experts have become an indispensable part of the apparatus of technoscience-production' (109). Haraway's work has been invaluable in diagnosing problems concerning the biotech industry, and especially in tracing the connections between bioethics as a neo-Darwinian philosophy that brings together organic and social processes on the one hand, and the corporate structures of the biotech industry on the other. But even though she speaks for 'engagement' and 'commitment' in technoscience (112), Haraway does not develop any consistent ethical proposal, or even give us any specific ethical pointers.

DO SOFT CYBORGS HAVE BODIES?

Entering at the point where Haraway leaves off, my proposal for a feminist cyberbioethics is intended as a response to ethical challenges posed by 'virtual bodies' born out of the biotechnological practices of the dawn of the twenty-first century. For the purposes of this chapter, my investigation will be anchored in three different corporeal formations, whose hybridity and technicity, manifested in their multi-parented origin, calls for an investigation of the 'nature of their nature'[8]: OncoMouse™ – the first patented, genetically manipulated mouse that carries an activated oncogene; the Massachusetts 'nude' mouse with a prosthetic human ear on its back; and the human hand gripping a computer mouse, i.e. a human–machine interface whose main goal is to translate the hand's motion into signals that a computer can use. My turning to mice here is an attempt to evoke the logic of human-nonhuman separation, in which 'animal' becomes 'an appellation that men have instituted, a name they have given themselves the right and the authority to give to another living creature' (Derrida, 2002: 393). For a long time mice as objects of experimentation have functioned as tools in the development of biotechnoscience; they have served humans in their progression toward better health, wealth and self-knowledge. Considered a 'pest' that deserves to be trapped, killed and disposed of, they have become sanitized in the purity of the laboratory in which their bodies have acquired a sacrificial character. As is perhaps evident from the three 'examples' listed above (although I should mention here that my feminist cyberbioethics does not proceed by exemplarity, as it will hopefully become clear later on), mine are not any usual 'mice'. They are chimeras, hybrid monsters, whose bodies are nodes in the flows of genomics and cybernetics, biotechnology and technocapitalism. Rather than as 'examples', I thus see them as experimental figures in a test run for the ethical project in which the well- (and ill-)being of the human is always already linked with that of other living creatures.

OncoMouse™, 'a technobastard' (Haraway, 1997: 78), is for Haraway a synecdoche for all technoscience (22); it is a sentient transgenic being whose suffering matters for the cyberfeminist ethical project. Inscribed in the networks of the corporate biotech industry (from the Harvard research laboratories, which 'developed' this 'soft cyborg', to the DuPont medical enterprise, which bought and patented it), it makes us address the question of 'life' in the context of issues of property, agency, heredity and owner-ship. A creature whose death becomes not only the inevitable end but also the very justification of its existence, OncoMouse™, according to Haraway, raises the fundamental ethical question: '*Cui bono?*', which Haraway trans-lates as: 'For whom does OncoMouse™ live and die?' (1997: 113). I want to pair OncoMouse™ here with another figure, one whose biocapital(ist) 'gift' does not involve the ultimate sacrifice required of OncoMouse™. This is the Massachusetts mouse, which becomes a host for regrowing human organs such as ears and noses. In this case, a biodegradable mould covered with human cartilage cells is implanted into the back of the animal. Its blood helps the cartilage cells grow and eventually replace the fibres of the mould. Apparently, after the new ear is removed from the mouse, the hairless rodent remains alive and healthy.

My third techno-corporeal formation, the computer mouse, designed by Douglas Engelbart in the 1960s and patented in 1970, represents 'the becoming-virtual of the finger' (Doyle, 2003: 50). In connection with a human hand that is clasped around it, the computer mouse is doubled as an avatar on the other side of the screen. A figure of optimization and progress, of connectivity and body–mind expansion, the mouse-hand assemblage is nevertheless haunted by the possibility of damage (that is, cumulative trauma disorder known as Repetitive Strain Injury affecting tendons, nerves, muscles and other soft body tissues) that is linked to its 'overuse'.

I call these three mouse formations 'soft cyborgs' due to their kinship with the earlier discourses and material practices of the cybernetic organ-isms 'devised' by Manfred E. Clynes and Nathan S. Kline,[9] as well as due to their positioning in the networks of 'soft technologies' of the biotech industry. My mice participate in multiple events of technoculture that radi-cally shift not only the boundaries of the human as the living, feeling and thinking organism, but also the idea of 'life' as we know it. 'Life' becomes 'enterprised', flowing through the multinational channels of capital in which species acquire the status of brand names (Haraway, 1997: 12). Soft cyborgs' uncertain ontology and the epistemological challenges they pose create fun-damental problems for the traditional moral principles that would be derived from human rationality and rooted in the idea of the *human* common good. The prosthetic mice of this chapter enter a non-phylum kinship with a number of other cyborg figures of the twenty-first-century biotech culture; they help us envisage ethical events without ultimately prescribing the format of their occurrence. The *monstr-osity* of these 'soft cyborgs', de-*mon-strates*, or reveals itself 'as something that is not yet shown'.[10] As a result, it disables the possibility of running an ethical programme that could be applied to specific 'cases', as the cases themselves are still very much 'in the making'. 'Applied bioethics', understood as the application of the previously agreed moral principles informed by rational argument and based on biological knowledge, can thus be seen as in fact threatening to close off ethical enquiry which concerns encounters between organisms and life forms that defy traditional classification.

This is why I attempt to look elsewhere for a philosophical paradigm that will help me address the ethical challenges posed by 'soft cyborgs'. Drawing its impulse from Levinas's conceptualization of ethics as responsibility for the incalculable alterity of the other (and from Derrida's rereading thereof), my feminist cyberbioethics is non-systemic. In other words, it does not provide a set of rules and regulations which would be developed through speculative thinking and then applied to specific cases. Instead, it consists of a content-free, specific obligation that (radically) other beings – which I describe here as 'soft cyborgs' – impose on my body, and a need to respond to this obligation. The body is not defined here as an opposite of a mind or soul but as that by which the self is susceptibility itself; it is the site of our obligation.[11] The encounter with beings of uncertain, material–virtual corporeality, calls on us to reassess our understanding of the body and its embodiment, its matter and tissue, its life source and life flows, its codes. By asserting their kinship with information and communication technologies and systems, that is, their virtuality, I am not denying the material embededness of soft cyborgs. On the contrary, I follow N. Katherine Hayles's definition of virtuality as the 'the cultural perception that material objects are interpenetrated by information patterns' (1999: 14). The corporeal boundaries of soft cyborgs are not erased in this project; however, they are characterized by an openness to the 'flows of information, from the DNA code to the global reach of the World Wide Web' (Hayles: 1999, 14).[12] For Hayles, embodiment names precisely this relationality between biology and information through which organisms emerge and transmute in time. Their boundaries remain unfixed: they only materialize in social interaction. It is worth pointing out here that the perception of bodies as merely graspable but reprogrammable objects, as 'rearrangeable packets of DNA' (Tomasula, 2004: 254) – a perception that has accompanied the coming together of molecular biology and the biotech industry – in fact entails a disavowal of the processual 'nature of their nature'. It forecloses on the analysis of the proximity, connectivity and intimacy *between* cells, organs and bodies. Richard Doyle foregrounds this need for taking connectivity into account in the emergence of life when he observes, in his commentary on the work of biologist Marcello Barbieri, that DNA information is necessary but not sufficient for the emergence of life, and that 'organisms have always been networks' (2003: 23). Significantly, Haraway warns us that the redefinition of bodies and organisms as 'biotic components', or cybernetic information-processing devices, instigated by the developments in molecular biology and information sciences, should be subject to cyberfeminist critique. She is interested in exploring what kind of regulatory powers define the corporal/corporate networks in which bodies-as-communication-systems function, and who is in charge of this 'informatics of domination'. While not denying the usefulness of the metaphor of connectivity in envisaging new cyborg couplings in the world, Haraway nevertheless postulates that the networks of technoscience and biocapital within which cyborg bodies are inscribed should not be seen as a re-naturalized household for these 'biotic components', and that (socialist) feminists should attempt to delineate some new systems of connections between them.

Embodiment is thus fundamental to 'cyborg encounters' which are to be considered in an ethical context.[13] This position takes issue with the cybernetic-biotechnological model of the world which is seen as mathematical in its essence, where phenomenological experience is only an illusion (Hayles, 1999: 232). Hayles positions the body as an unstable battleground for the new definition of the (post)human, where the earlier cybernetic perspective of disembodied information competes against more recent models of human–machine, carbon–silicon interaction (or what I describe here as 'soft cyborgs'). Like Hayles, I am not prepared to give in to the story of necessary disembodiment in informatics and genetics, to the mechanic tale in which the body is a mere container for 'life' understood as information. Even if there is 'no absolute demarcation between bodily existence and computer simulation', between biological organism and cybernetic mechanism (Hayles, 1999: 3); besides, even if embodiment is indeed an accident of history rather than an inevitability of life, the instances of the corporeal embodiment of information (or the erasure thereof) have an ethical significance. Were we to contend that embodiment was not essential to being human, that it was possible to 'upload' the human to a cybernetic system that would be free from the trappings of carbon-based life, such a position (represented, among others, by Marvin Minsky) would merely reiterate a transcendental masculine fantasy of overcoming the dirtiness of the flesh and 'jacking into' a different – spiritual, nonmaterial – universe.

Rooted in Levinas's rereading of Husserl and Heidegger, my feminist cyberbioethics adopts a phenomenological perspective, while also remaining aware of the mediation processes involved in the sensate construction of our epistemologies. Already in Levinas the sentient self is not the origin of knowledge and meaning in the world – its subjectivity only comes from infinite difference. The paradise of solitude and self-possession is only a fantasy, from which one gets expelled by the alterity of the other. As Levinas argues in *Totality and Infinity*: 'Life is a body, not only lived body [corps propre], where its self-sufficiency emerges, but a cross-roads of physical forces, body-effect' (1969: 164). This conceptualization of the body as the sequence of processes, flows and levels of complexity, rather than an entity, is also evident in some forms of cyberfeminism that engage with cybernetics and molecular biology, information technologies and genetics. According to Haraway, 'bodies are nodes in webs of integration' (1997: 142). Defined in terms of its dynamics, the phenomenological (techno)body is thus best characterized in terms of what it *does*, not what it *is*.[14]

I am thus coming to bioethics from a different perspective than Singer's utilitarianism. My ethical position is not rooted in the 'self' but rather in what Levinas terms 'the infinity of the other'. For Levinas, the self cannot be the arbiter of the world's happiness and justice because justice, judgement and the good can only ever come from the other. As he explains in *Otherwise Than Being*,

> the Good is not presented to freedom; it has chosen me before I have chosen it. No one is good voluntarily. ... What is exceptional in this way of being signalled is that I am ordered toward the face of the other. In this order which is an ordination the non-presence of the infinite is not only a figure of negative theology. All the negative attributes which state what is beyond the essence become positive in responsibility, a response answering to a non-thematizable provocation and thus a non-vocation, a trauma. (1998: 11–12)

Ethics is therefore not the result of a rational reflection that a fully formed ego can make; it involves the singularity of obligation placed on the 'ordinated' self, which only ever arises in the accusative (i.e. *soi*) as a response to a demand. Even though his philosophy does not espouse the idea of applicability that shapes the discourses of bioethics as an applied branch of moral philosophy, I believe Levinas can help us think about bioethical issues in a more interesting, productive and perhaps even more 'responsible' way.

However, an attempt to read Levinas in the context of bioethics, soft cyborgs and mice probably amounts to a blasphemous (cyberfeminist?) gesture. After all, for Levinas it is indubitably the *human* other that is worthy of ethical consideration – an approach that is 'a matter of serious concern' not just for me but also for Derrida. In a presentation given at the Cerisy conference *L'Animal autobiographique* in 1997, and later transformed into the essay 'The Animal That Therefore I Am (More to Follow)', Derrida takes up the subject of the 'Ends of Man' to pose some serious ethico-political question for the concept of the 'animal' as man's subservient and inferior other. In particular, Derrida finds it hard to accept that the 'animal', a 'catch-all concept', names

> *all the living things* that man does not recognize as his fellows, his neighbors, or his brothers. And that is so in spite of the infinite space that separates the lizard from the dog, the protozoon from the dolphin, the shark from the lamb, the parrot from the chimpanzee, the camel from the eagle, the squirrel from the tiger or the elephant from the cat, the ant from the silkworm or the hedgehog from the echidna. (2002: 402)

In his revisiting of the bestiary which, he argues, inhabits 'the origin of philosophy', Derrida looks at both living and extinct creatures, real and mythical ones (his own cat, the Cheshire Cat from *Alice in Wonderland*, the Greek chimera – 'more than one animal in one', biblical ass and ram sacrificed on Mount Moriah, the horse, ox and reindeer employed in 'land exploitation'), as well as the 'joint developments [in the course of the last two centuries] of zoological, ethological, biological, and genetic *forms of knowledge* and the always inseparable *techniques* of intervention with respect to their object, the transformation of the actual object, its milieu, its world, namely, the living animal' (2002: 394).

Let me remark here in passing that my incorporation of Derrida's discussion of the 'animal' into a bioethical debate about what I term 'soft cyborgs' is not a category mistake. For Haraway, '[t]he cyborg appears precisely where the boundary between human and animal is transgressed' (1991: 152). In Derrida's own bestiary, which he introduces in 'The Animal That Therefore I Am (More to Follow)', the distinction between real and mythical animals, as well as that between organisms and machines, undergoes a process of deconstruction. He questions what it means to be a 'living animal' and what forms of life (and death) these critters can take, by taking issue with the philosophical treatment of the animal – from Descartes's and Lacan's perception of the animal as a creature with no power to respond, through to Heidegger's dismissal of it as 'poor in the world', a being without, or even outside, *Dasein*. Then Derrida adopts this definition of the animal as a being unable to use language reciprocally, and thus also incapable of pretending, lying, covering its tracks and erasing its own traces, as a new alternative for defining a limit between creatures. It is at this point that he embarks on a brief intellectual exercise, a philosophical joke, we might say, and conjures up a hybrid being, which he calls animal-machine: 'an animal of reading and rewriting' (406), a creature with unlimited appetite that gnaws at signs as soon as they appear in writing. This is precisely one example of an animal that is capable of deleting words, of erasing traces, and thus of subverting the philosophers' numerous principles of distinction between human and animal. Like a computer virus, this 'quasi-animal', a figment of Derrida's imagination, is put to work by Derrida in Heidegger's texts by deleting all words that Heidegger wants to liberate from the metaphysics of being ('spirit', '*Dasein*', 'animal', etc.).

Infecting everything one writes, the animal–machine thus becomes yet another figure in Derrida's repository of *différance*, a term that introduces radical alterity into the very process of writing, that plants nonsense into the very act of sense-making, that instantiates death at the very core of life. 'An animal which is capable of deleting (thus of erasing a trace ...)' (2002: 407), of striking out being, Derrida's machine-animal can perhaps be said to be related to my soft cyborgs, biological creatures of uncertain provenance whose very being is a technology of (DNA) writing. Biology itself, we have to remember, 'is already a writing system whose re-presentation of itself disrupts the purity and integrity imputed to it' (Kirby, 1999: 27). This means that every living creature can be seen as inhabited by the animal–machine, which carries with it the possibility of DNA reinscription, of code error, of genetic miscalculation.

I should perhaps explain here that my turning to Levinas and Derrida in my ethical enquiry (rather than, for example, Spinoza, Deleuze, Badiou or Negri, as is so often the case in techno-philosophical enquiries about bodies and machines) springs from a conviction that the deconstruction-inspired philosophy of difference has not yet run out of steam and that there are still some stakes in exploring incalculable alterity. I propose an engagement with *multiplicities of life*, with different forms of genetic organisms and the connections within and between them, through deploying the notion of alterity, which will disable us from making an argument about them through analogy. Naturally, this perspective involves to some extent reinstating, at least temporarily, the difference between man and animal, alongside differences between animal and machine, flesh and metal, materiality and virtuality, as well as a myriad other differences that our soft cyborgs both trouble and spring from, without at the same time attempting to close these differences all too hastily. To deny these differences, to wipe out the historical circumstances that have authorized them, would be an act of critico-ethical irresponsibility. And thus, when talking about multiplicities of life, I have no interest in propagating a seamless continuity of all species and life forms, or what Derrida calls a simplistic 'biologistic continuism' (2002: 398). Such an attitude would not only mean 'blinding oneself to so much contrary evidence' but would also involve the suspension of all attention given 'to difference, to differences, to heterogeneities and abyssal ruptures' that deconstrutive thinking has been associated with.[15]

Embedded in the corporeal networks of technoscientific capitalism, differences between species and life forms do not, however, all carry equal value. When postulating 'the end of man' and 'Western humanism' as concepts legislating our current thinking about the world, Haraway at the same time warns us that 'we risk lapsing into boundless difference and giving up on the confusing task of making partial, real connection. Some differences are playful; some are poles of world historical systems of domination. "Epistemology" is about knowing the difference' (1991: 160–1). Ethics, one might add, is about *not* knowing this difference *in advance*, without the painstaking effort of going through the history of domination in technoscience, through the networks of power that arrange these differences into hierarchies, through the specific events and instances in which differences between beings are (mis)recognized. What I am proposing here, then, is that it is our task and our responsibility to investigate these networks, and to look closely at the relations they enable or enforce.

And yet we have to be aware that the incalculable alterity of the other that makes a demand on my being-in-the-world always exists in a tension with the practical – moral, political – contextualization of this incalculable demand. Levinas himself claims that, as soon as ethics enters the material world, it needs to coexist with politics, with calculation, with the need to choose between different competing demands at any one time. He explains: 'I don't live in a world in which there is but one single "first comer"; there is always a third party in the world; he or she is also my other, my neighbor. Hence it is important to me to know which of the two takes precedence. Is the one not the persecutor of the other? Must not human [and other – J.Z.] beings, who are incomparable, be compared?' (Robbins: 165-6). This need for calculation, for a 'practical resolution' to ethical dilemmas, does not make the infinite horizon of justice instantiated by the alterity of the other disappear. But it does point to the fact that violence is inevitable in ethical experience – a realization that should not relieve us from the responsibility of attempting to minimize this violence, to answer in the best possible way to contradictory demands in a way that will not merely involve applying a ready-made moral rule (e.g. maximizing net happiness in the world or satisfying the greatest number of desires and preferences).

MICE EXPERIMENTS

To pick up this thread of difference (which is never stable, fixed or one) between man and animal, or, more broadly, between human and non-human, I would like to look a little closer at my (hybrid) mice and propose a little experiment. This does not mean that it is the mice that will be experimented on. Instead, I want to recuperate the double meaning of the Latin *experimentum*, which stands not only for *test* or *trial* (and I am not ready to specify who will actually undergo this trial here, partly because such a simple 'who?' question cannot yet be answered in any straightforward manner), but also for *experience*. Indeed, the primordial level of lived experience is the starting point for my bioethical investigations; and it is an encounter with radical difference that constitutes the point of emergence for my feminist cyberbioethics. Alphonso Lingis explains in the Introduction to Levinas's *Otherwise Than Being* that 'The relationship with alterity is ... presented by Levinas both as an experience and as an a priori to all experience, on the "hither side" even of the a prioris that make experience possible' (Lingis, 1998: xxviii). In Levinas the self must receive its subjectivity from alterity, but this exposedness to alterity is primordial; it precedes openness to the sensible, given beings. This relationship with alterity is also ethical – it is a bond imposed upon me, an obligation or ordination about which I spoke earlier. The other is thus experienced 'as a contestation of my appropriation of the world, as a disturbance in the play of the world, a break in its cohesion' (Lingis, 1998: xxix). While ethical experience thus imprints itself on me, it might be said I am put on *trial*, I am being *test*ed to see whether

I am ready to take up this responsibility for which I have been chosen (see Levinas, 1998: 13).

Before we discuss the consequences of this (somewhat violent) 'ethical takeover' for our ideas of the human, I would like to talk about one particular experience, not a major event in the media sense, but just an everyday occurrence: an encounter between Derrida and his cat. (This is reported in his essay 'The Animal That Therefore I Am ...' .) Wondering around his apartment in his full nakedness, the celebrated French philosopher finds himself caught naked, in silence, by the gaze of the animal. 'What animal? The other' (2002: 372). He has trouble overcoming his embarrassment, but is also 'ashamed for being ashamed'. This brief instance of uneasiness leads Derrida, the philosopher who never seems to be at leisure, to the striking realization that the animal brings man to the consciousness of his nakedness, of his sex, of property, propriety and impropriety, of good and evil. That's right, Derrida's cat makes him aware of good and evil. Because 'the property unique to animals and what in the final analysis distinguishes them from man, is their being naked without knowing it' (2002: 373). Clothing is a property of humans, 'one of the "properties" of man', inseparable from the other forms of property and propriety such as language, *logos*, reason, the gift, mourning. In case we were to conclude that through this argument Derrida just reaffirms the moral superiority of humans, let us remember that the consciousness of nakedness, of lack and the need for clothing comes from the other – and here this other is not Levinas's God, or even another human being treated as *if he were God*, but rather a cat. Could it also be an (onco)mouse?

Perhaps we should be more careful and speak about morality rather than ethics emerging in an encounter with the animal. The need for clothing, ornament, artifice, *tekhnē* (which, let us not forget, is frequently translated as either technology or art, and in which, from Aristotle through to Heidegger, resounds an echo of bringing-forth, creation, and revealing) is triggered off by shame. But shame arises as a response to the demand on the being of the human placed by the alterity of the other (animal–chimera–monster–soft cyborg). If we were to use a shortcut (although one has to be careful with these), we could say that artifice, ornament or *tekhnē*, but also custom and/as morality, arises in response to an ethical demand, or that (even more briefly) technics is an ethics.

Thus the question posed in the opening of this chapter, 'Are soft cyborgs worthy of ethical respect?', now seems misguided in its premises, as the very possibility of its formulation relies on the presumed superiority of the (hu)man to the forms of alterity – nonhuman, animal – that (s)he has the right and authority to control and dominate. The cyberanimal, the onco-techno-mouse, pushes us to envisage a new relation between human and technics, in which a technical 'object' (say, a computer mouse) cannot be just a utensil. There is no simple end–means relation between 'man' and 'his' technologies (see Stiegler, 1998: 21). Instead, for the philosopher Bernard Stiegler, who anchors his investigation of technology in Derrida's deconstructive thinking as well as the non-humanist paleontology of André Leroi-Gourhan, the 'nature' of the human is produced only *as* and *through* technicity. Hominization is a moment of rupture, a process of exteriorization in which the skeletal being raises on two feet and reaches for what is outside him (tools, language) (1998: 141). This process of exteriorization marks the appearance of the technical. 'Or again: the human invents himself in the technical by inventing the tool …' (141). The moment of technicity, a 'putting-out-of-range-of-oneself' (146) is a moment in which the (not yet formed) self reaches for an alterity it does not know. It is thus perhaps not too much of a leap to suggest that the self, in its 'originary' relation with technics, is instituted as ethical. The strict distinctions between human and machine, as well as between human and animal, carbon and silicon, organic and non-organic, material and virtual, become less relevant. However, what interests me here is not so much the liquid(iz)ation of these distinctions as their multiplication, as well as the emergence of the forms of connectivity between them. The nature of these relations, connections and differences is perhaps undecidable. And yet in this very undecidability inheres an injunction to choose, to answer the question of being.

Thus, even though the conceptual boundary between humans and soft cyborgs that I posited at the beginning of this chapter looks increasingly unstable, I do not just want to repeat Haraway's conclusion from the end of her 'Manifesto' that 'we are they' (1991: 180) – a conclusion that, incidentally, seems to exist in a logical contradiction with her earlier formulation: 'We can be responsible for machines; *they* do not dominate or threaten us' (180). Reneging on the possibility of transcendental agency but failing to explore any other possibilities for an ethical impulse and ethical action, Haraway ends up embracing the humanist values she contested earlier (see Zylinska, 2001: 132; Marsden, 1996: 14). As humans and machines collapse into a fluid epistemology in which difference is overcome for the sake of rebellious politics, it is not clear any more who encounters, responds to, and is responsible for whom in an ethical encounter and, what's more important, why it should matter at all. To avoid some of these problems Haraway runs up against in her work, the new cyberbioethics I propose here will need to remain rooted in the concept of the human. And yet 'the human' should not be seen as an essential value or a fixed identity but rather as a strategic *quasi*-transcendental point of entry into debates on the relationship between humans and technology. I believe ethical thinking in terms of originary technicity that brings forth the very concept of the human[16] – as an ethical response to otherness – allows us to affirm the significance of the question of responsibility, without needing to rely on the prior value system that legislates it.

So, to reiterate Derrida's question, what does it mean to be naked before an animal? Is this an ethical question (as well as being, as Derrida has argued, a question *about* ethics)? And what if we cannot even decide if the animal is alive? Or whether it is human? Or machinic? Material? Virtual? Can 'one' be naked before a computer mouse? What does it mean if my hand is already gently gripping its plastic body, while I am positioned, naked, before my computer screen? What if the computer is connected to the net? And I am being looked at by the eye of the webcam? What kind of ethical questions am I posed with here? Is 'using' a computer mouse ethically neutral? Who does the mouse connect me to? What kinds of flows of technology, capital, desire, fantasy, projection and imagination are instantiated with a gentle click on its nose? (What do I know about my Internet Service Provider to whom I remain inextricably linked? Is it a he or an it, for example? Does it *matter?*) My own Packard Bell(e) mouse (did I mention that for me, a Polish speaker, the mouse always remains a 'she'?) hails from China. Do I know what it *really* means? What sort of connectivity does it instantiate, what other bodies, cultures, labours, markets does it link me to? Should I know?

And what if the mouse itself is naked? Another one of my soft cyborgs is the Massachusetts 'nude' mouse well known for its lack of immune system, which means that the mouse is less likely to reject human skin tissue when the organ regrowth takes place. And so it is a perfect host, an incarnation of an ethical principle of hospitality which unconditionally welcomes the other. But Derrida has instructed us that this unconditional hospitality, though necessary as a horizon of justice, is also an act of madness, as well as violence – towards one's own self-preservation, health, property, economics. Is the nude Massachusetts mouse with an ear on its back an exemplum of ethicality and generous sacrifice, or a painful reminder of our own ethical faultiness, our scrabble for self-preservation and self-possession? (We have already ruled out the possibility of treating 'her' as a mere tool for human 'use'.) Should we read anything into the fact that there is a monstrous prosthetic *ear* attached to its back rather than any other bodily organ? The ear is always that of the other (ear) (Royle, 2003: 64); it is one organ we cannot voluntarily close. Instead, it is always 'ready' to receive, even if its 'owner' isn't. The very possibility of speaking and writing, and thus of language, comes from the ear (Royle, 2003: 64). But what does it mean if this gift comes from a nude mouse? Can 'it' give 'us' language? Also, what does it mean to carry an ear on one's back? Is the ethics of the listening spine a variation of the Levinasian ethics of the listening eye, another hybrid transgenic bodily organ which displaces the primacy of the human gaze in establishing the relationship with the other?

Then there's OncoMouse™, a patented Christ-like figure, who dies so that I do not have to. Taking our cancer on herself, OncoMouse™ is a spectre that both saves us from death and haunts us with mortality. It is the undead, '[n]ot dead, but not living' (Derrida and Stiegler, 2002: 123). How can we relate to this life (and death) form? Are we already related? In his conversation on spectrality with Bernard Stiegler, Derrida argues that respect for the alterity of the other which I do not know in advance 'dictates respect for the non-living, for what it's possible is not alive' (Derrida and Stiegler, 2002: 123). This is not just to say that OncoMouse™, a soft cyborg, deserves to be respected by *us humans*. Rather, OncoMouse™'s kinship with death opens up an ethical horizon for us, *it makes ethics possible*. Echoing his argument from *Specters of Marx*, Derrida argues:

> There is no respect, and, therefore, no justice possible, without this rela-
> tion of fidelity or of promise, as it were, to what is no longer living or
> not living yet, to what is not simply present. There would be no urgent
> demand for justice, or for responsibility, without this spectral oath. And
> there would be no oath, period. Someone pointed out to me that the word
> 'specter' is the perfect anagram of respect. ... Respect would be due the
> law of the other, who appears without appearing and watches or concerns
> me as a specter. (Derrida and Stiegler, 2002: 123–4)

OncoMouse™'s life and death haunt the labs and accountants' offices at Harvard and DuPont, hovering over the courtrooms where 'she' was patented 'for the benefit of Man' (and a wholesome profit of a few men and women). But how does one calculate the price of life and death? Is patenting a way of exorcizing mortality, controlling it, keeping it under wraps? Of attempting to own and annihilate it?

We are posed with so many questions here, while even more are waiting to be asked – and it is only three little mice that have triggered all these. Formulating a feminist cyberbioethics is not proving an easy task. But perhaps we already are *in ethics*: we are responding to an ethical injunction that soft cyborgs – be it transgenic and silicon mice or numerous other creatures for which we perhaps do not even have a name – impose on our humanity (or better, imprint on our bodies) and demand from us a choice, a decision, a judgement. They serve as a warning to humans not to *hog* the space of the world, not to ignore the breaks in its cohesion, not to turn a deaf ear to its *différance*. Put otherwise, soft cyborgs foreground what we could term – paraphrasing Stiegler – 'the originary virtuality' of the human, where the virtual names both a technical ensemble and a technical condition, a corporeal being-in-and-through technology (see Richardson and Harper, 2002). What soft cyborgs seem to disable, in turn, is systemic ethics run as a programme, already tested, just ready to be applied, with 'other crea-tures and species' seen only as extensions of the human that deserve ethical respect by analogy. So, perhaps against some odds, I would like to sum up the ethical speculations developed in this chapter by delineating the fol-lowing proposal below.

A MODEST PROPOSAL FOR FEMINIST CYBERBIOETHICS

The feminist cyberbioethics I propose:

1. Is non-systemic; it is an ethics of hybrids that is hybrid in its origin.
2. Does not move from normative assumptions about morality to their practical application.[17] Rather, informed by deconstructive logic, it shows that between normativity and application, between theory and practice, there exists a certain degree of contamination. (Normativity does not stand here for a set of norms decided in advance; it is an infinite ethical horizon of justice against which singular decisions have to be made always anew.)
3. Problematizes the distinction between human and animal, but also that between human and machine, carbon and silicon, vitalism and mechanism. Drawing on deconstruction and cultural studies' critique of identity, it thinks of the human as always already existing in a prosthetic relationship to its technologies.[18]
4. Does not just ask *what* and *whose life* is worth living. It takes seriously research into cybernetics and molecular biology which interrogates not only the boundaries of the human but also the notion of 'life itself'.
5. Remains critical of the disembodiment of information and 'life' in cybernetics and molecular biology. It considers ethical beings as embodied as well as embedded in the material networks of capital, energy, labour and technoscience, and does not see these networks as race- or gender-neutral.[19]
6. Goes beyond utilitarianism and contractualism which still put the good of the human (be it in its 'extended' or 'contracted' form) as central to ethical investigations.
7. Is post-Kantian (but in a different sense than some forms of more traditional moral philosophy). While it takes from Kant the non-metaphysical foundation for ethics, it does not locate its ethical impulse in the self but rather in what Levinas terms the 'infinite alterity of the other'. And yet Levinas's work is not taken on board uncritically: feminist cyberbioethics does not accept the Levinasian premise that ethical status should only be owed to humans. (See 3. and 4. above.)
8. Considers the point of entry for moral subjects as always situated *between* ethics and politics.

Notes

1   For a (not entirely unsympathetic) critique of Haraway's notion of the cyborg see Jill Marsden, 'Virtual Sexes and Feminist Futures: the Philosophy of "Cyberfeminism"' (1996). Zoe Sofoulis provides an evaluation of the critical (mis)readings of the 'Manifesto' in her article 'Cyberquake: Haraway's Manifesto' (2003).

2   As Kuhse and Singer explain, 'The effect of saying that an ethical judgement must be universalizable for hypothetical as well as actual circumstances is that whenever I

make an ethical judgement, I can be challenged to put myself in the position of the parties affected, and see if I would still be able to accept that judgement' (1999: 3). This ethical position has been developed by the Oxford philosopher R. M. Hare, but we can hear in it echoes of Kant's moral philosophy. For Kant, morality has to come from our reason, rather than from any external concept of the good, and it does not involve any principles that would not be subject to universalization. We can see the working of his categorical, universal imperative in the so-called 'Formula of the End in Itself', which demands that we treat 'humanity in your own person or in the person of any other never simply as a means but always at the same time as an end' (quoted in O'Neill, 1993: 178). Postulating respect for other persons, Kant's ethics stems from the (rational) self which is *naturally* conducive to moral judgement. While a number of contemporary consequentalists, such as R. M. Hare, are more interested in 'practical' resolutions to moral dilemmas, for Kant there are inviolable rules which cannot be changed even if the moral majority would like them to be 'adjusted'.

3   This ethical position can be described as 'consequentialism', and is based on the view that the rightness of an action depends on its consequences.

4   Other philosophical positions that play a significant role in bioethics today involve a Kant-inflected belief in the inviolable moral principles formulated in the categorical imperative; the Aristotelian ethics of the good based on certain adopted views of 'human nature'; Christian ethics of natural good and evil regulated by the idea of God; and, last but not least, ethical positions that are not based on any principles or rules but rather on an idea of what it means to be a 'good person' (and more narrowly, a 'good doctor', 'good researcher', 'good academic').

5   Singer writes:

> Why should we treat the life of an anencephalic human child as sacrosanct, and feel free to kill healthy baboons in order to take their organs? Why should we lock chimpanzees in laboratory cages and infect them with fatal human diseases, if we abhor the idea of experiments conducted with intellectually disabled human beings whose mental level is similar to that of the chimpanzees?
>
> The new vision leaves no room for the traditional answer to these questions, that we human beings are a special creation, infinitely more precious, in virtue of our humanity alone, than all other living things. In the light of our new understanding of our place in the universe, we shall have to abandon that traditional answer, and revise the boundaries of our ethics. One casualty of that revision will be any ethic based on the idea that what really matters about beings is whether they are human. This will have dramatic effects, not only on our relations with nonhuman animals, but on the entire traditional sanctity of life ethic. (1994: 183)

6   For example, the feminist critic of science Evelyn Fox Keller claims that 'The body of modern biology, like the DNA molecule – and like, too, the modern corporate or political body – has become just another part of an informational network, now machine, now message, always already ready for exchange, each for the other' (1994: 321).

7   Witness an excerpt from an article by Carl Elliott titled 'Not-So-Public Relations: How the drug industry is branding itself with bioethics', which was posted to the Feminist Approaches to Bioethics mailing list <FABLIST@LIST.MSU.EDU> on 20 December 2003:

> The drug industry has even managed to turn peer-reviewed scientific literature into a sophisticated marketing device. It has long been known that corporate-funded research studies are more likely than impartial studies to favor the products of their corporate sponsor. But only recently has evidence emerged to suggest how many 'scientific' studies have actually been ghostwritten by specialized PR firms – 'medical communications' agencies – that represent the drug industry. These firms then

pay well-known academic researchers to sign on as authors. Often these academic researchers are not even allowed to see the raw data upon which the published studies are based. A recent article in the *British Journal of Psychiatry* examined articles on Pfizer's antidepressant Zoloft (sertraline) whose authorship had been coordinated by the communications agency Current Medical Directions. When checked against the raw data, which had come to light in a lawsuit, it became clear that the studies authored by Current Medical Directions omitted or greatly minimized Zoloft's side effects, including the risk of suicidal acts. Yet these studies outnumbered 'traditionally authored' articles, were published in more prestigious journals and were cited by other researchers at a much higher rate.

8 In *Modest Witness* Haraway proposes the term 'the new nature of no nature' (1997: 108), by which she means that 'nature is a technics through and through' (109). According to her, OncoMouse™ teaches us that 'universal nature' is itself fully artificial. However, Haraway's is a somewhat linear story of an escape, or removal, from nature, the proximity with which was allegedly at one time assured, and which used to be 'natural'. I believe that with his concept of 'originary prostheticity' Bernard Stiegler (1998) offers a more interesting, and less problematic in philosophico-temporal terms, take on the relationship between humans and technics.

9 Clynes and Kline first used the term 'cyborg' to describe a rat with an osmotic pump under its skin designed to permit continuous injections of chemicals at a slow controlled rate into an organism without any attention on the part of the organism (see Clynes and Kline, 1995).

10 A monster, according to Derrida, 'shows itself [*elle se montre*] – that is what the word monster means – it shows itself in something that is not yet shown and that therefore looks like a hallucination, … it frightens precisely because no anticipation had prepared one to identify this figure' (1995: 386). I discuss Derrida's notion of monstrosity in relation to technology and ethics in the previous chapter.

11 Levinas writes:

> To hold on to exteriority is not simply equivalent to affirming the world, but is to posit oneself in it corporeally. … To assume exteriority is to enter into a relation with it such that the same determines the other while being determined by it. … The way in which the same is determined by the other, and which delineates the plane in which the negating acts themselves are situated, is precisely the *way* designated above as 'living from …'. It is brought about by the body whose essence is to *accomplish* my position on earth, that is, to give me as it were a vision already and henceforth borne by the very image that I see. (1969: 127–8)

12 In the article 'Flesh and Metal: Reconfiguring the Mindbody in Virtual Environments', which is a follow-up to her book, *How We Became Posthuman*, N. Katherine Hayles argues that bodies remain in relation with information technologies, and that it is precisely this relationality that characterizes embodiment:

> Instead of the Cartesian subject who begins by cutting himself off from his environment and visualizing his thinking presence as the one thing he cannot doubt, the human who inhabits the information-rich environments of contemporary technological societies knows that the dynamic and fluctuating boundaries of her embodied cognitions develop in relation to other cognizing agents embedded throughout the environment. Among which the most powerful are intelligent machines.
>
> In these views, the impact of information technologies on the mindbody are [is? – J.Z.] always understood as a two-way relation, a feedback-loop between biologically evolved capabilities and a richly engineered technological environment. (2004: 233)

13 This is not to say that, for example, an 'online' encounter cannot be considered ethical or that physical proximity is necessary, only that the body *matters* in these encounters.

14 The concept of the 'dynamic body' is put forward in the Introduction to Robert Mitchell and Phillip Thurtle's collection, *Data Made Flesh: Embodying Information* (2004). Nevertheless, the body is still characterized in ontological terms: what seems to matter more to the editors is what this newly evolved body *is like* rather than what it *does* (see 2004: 3–4).

15 Derrida argues: 'The discussion becomes interesting once, instead of asking whether or not there is a discontinuous limit, one attempts to think what a limit becomes once it is abyssal, once the frontier no longer forms a single indivisible line but more than one internally divided line, once, as a result, it can no longer be traced, objectified, or counted as single and indivisible' (2002: 398).

16 There is a performative logic involved in the production of the concept of the human. I discuss performativity and reflexivity in 'A User's Guide' (Chapter 1) and draw on it in several other chapters.

17 In the Introduction to *Bioethics: a Philosophical Introduction*, a book that presents a more traditional account of positions in bioethics which are rooted in analytical moral philosophy, Stephen Holland states: 'a grasp of normative moral theory is required to address practical ethical problems' (2003: 4). While logical within its own parameters, this statement foregrounds the view of ethics as expertise rooted in (pre-decided) moral norms that can then be applied to specific cases.

18 This mode of thinking goes further than the 'extension' (e.g. to include animals) or 'contraction' (e.g. to exclude anencephalic infants) of the notion of 'person' as a being worthy of moral status in analytical philosophy (see Holland, 2003: 17–18). In my feminist cyberbioethics the self has always been 'extended', i.e. prosthetically dependent on and constituted by, its technological 'others'. (For a discussion of humans' 'originary prosthecity' see Stiegler (1998).)

19 'Of course, who controls the interpretation of bodily boundaries in medical hermeneutics is a major feminist issue' (Haraway, 1991: 169).

Bibliography

Adams, Parveen (1996) *The Emptiness of the Image: Psychoanalysis and Sexual Difference* (London and New York: Routledge).

Agamben, Giorgio (1998) *Homo Sacer: Sovereign Power and Bare Life*, trans. Daniel Heller-Roazen (Stanford: Stanford University Press).

— (1999) *Remnants of Auschwitz: The Witness and the Archive*, trans. Daniel Heller-Roazen (New York: Zone Books).

Ang Ieng (2000) 'Identity Blues' in *Without Guarantees: In Honour of Stuart Hall*, eds Paul Gilroy, Lawrence Grossberg and Angela McRobbie (London: Verso).

Arendt, Hannah (1973) *The Origins of Totalitarianism* (new edn) (New York: Harcourt Brace).

Armstrong, Rachel (1997) 'What Is Sci-Fi Aesthetics?' *Art and Design: Sci-Fi Aesthetics* 12: 9/10 (September/October): 3–5.

Ashfield, Andrew and de Bolla, Peter (eds) (1996) *The Sublime: A Reader in British Eighteenth-Century Aesthetic Theory* (Cambridge: Cambridge University Press).

Austin, J. L. (1962) *How To Do Things with Words* (Cambridge, MA: Harvard University Press).

Ayers, Robert (2000) 'Serene and Happy and Distant: An Interview with Orlan' in *Body Modification*, ed. Mike Featherstone (London, Thousand Oaks, New Delhi: Sage).

Badiou, Alain (2001) *Ethics: An Essay on the Understanding of Evil*, trans. Peter Hallward (London and New York: Verso).

Baudrillard, Jean (2002) *The Spirit of Terrorism*, trans. Chris Turner (London and New York: Verso).

Bauman, Zygmunt (1996) 'From Pilgrim to Tourist – or a Short History of Identity' in *Questions of Cultural Identity*, eds Stuart Hall and Paul du Gay (London, Thousand Oaks, New Delhi: Sage).

Bennett, Tony (1998) *Culture: A Reformer's Science* (London, Thousand Oaks, New Delhi: Sage).

Bennington, Geoffrey (2000) 'Deconstruction and Ethics' in *Deconstructions: A User's Guide*, ed. Nicholas Royle (Basingstoke and New York: Palgrave).

Bhabha, Homi, K. (1990) 'DissemiNation: Time, Narrative, and the Margins of the Modern Nation' in *Nation and Narration*, ed. Homi Bhabha (London and New York: Routledge).

Bloom, Harold (1994) *The Western Canon: The Books and School of the Ages* (New York: Harcourt Brace).

Bowman, Paul (2001) 'Between Responsibility and Irresponsibility: Cultural Studies and the Price of Fish', *Strategies: Journal of Theory, Culture & Politics* 14: 2 (November): 277–91.

Burke, Edmund (1967) *A Philosophical Enquiry into the Origin of Our Ideas of the Sublime and the Beautiful* (Oxford: Blackwell).

Butler, Judith (1990) *Gender Trouble: Feminism and the Subversion of Identity* (New York and London: Routledge).

— (1993) *Bodies That Matter: On the Discursive Limits of 'Sex'* (New York and London: Routledge).

— (1997) *Excitable Speech: A Politics of the Performative* (New York and London: Routledge).

— (2000) 'Ethical Ambivalence' in *The Turn to Ethics*, eds Marjorie Garber, Beatrice Hanssen and Rebecca L. Walkowitz (New York and London: Routledge).

— (2002) *Antigone's Claim: Kinship Between Life and Death* (New York: Columbia University Press).

— (2004) *Precarious Life: The Powers of Mourning and Violence* (London and New York: Verso).

Butler, Judith, Laclau, Ernesto, and Žižek, Slavoj (2000) *Contingency, Universality, Hegemony: Contemporary Dialogues on the Left* (London and New York: Verso).

Campbell, David (1999) 'The Deterritorialization of Responsibility: Levinas, Derrida, and Ethics after the End of Philosophy' in *Moral Spaces: Rethinking Ethics and World Politics*, eds David Campbell and Michael J. Shapiro (Minneapolis and London: University of Minnesota Press).

Campbell, David and Shapiro, Michael J. (1999a) 'Introduction: From Ethical Theory to the Ethical Relation' in *Moral Spaces: Rethinking Ethics and World Politics*, eds David Campbell and Michael J. Shapiro (Minneapolis and London: University of Minnesota Press).

Campbell, David and Shapiro, Michael J. (eds) (1999b) *Moral Spaces: Rethinking Ethics and World Politics* (Minneapolis and London: University of Minnesota Press).

Caputo, John D. (1993) *Against Ethics: Contribution to a Poetics of Obligation with Constant Reference to Deconstruction* (Bloomington: Indiana University Press).

Carroll, David (1990) 'Foreword: The Memory of Devastation and the Responsibilities of Thought: "And let's not talk about that"' in Jean-François Lyotard, *Heidegger and the 'jews'* (Minneapolis: University of Minnesota Press).

Caruth, Cathy (1995) *Trauma: Explorations in Memory* (Baltimore and London: Johns Hopkins University Press).

— (1997) 'Traumatic Awakenings' in *Violence, Identity and Self-Determination* eds Hent De Vries and Samuel Weber (Stanford: Stanford University Press).

Caygill, Howard (1997) 'Stelarc and the Chimera: Kant's Critique of Prosthetic Judgement' *Art Journal* 56: 46–51.

Chalier, Catherine (2002) *What Ought I to Do? Morality in Kant and Levinas*, trans. Jane Marie Todd (Ithaca and London: Cornell University Press).

Chanter, Tina (1995) *Ethics of Eros: Irigaray's Rewriting of the Philosophers* (New York and London: Routledge).

Chow, Rey (1998) *Ethics after Idealism: Theory – Culture – Ethnicity – Reading* (Bloomington and Indianapolis: Indiana University Press).

Clark, Timothy (2000) 'Deconstruction and Technology' in *Deconstructions: A User's Guide*, ed. Nicholas Royle (Basingstoke and New York: Palgrave).

Clynes, Manfred E. and Kline, Nathan S. (1995) 'Cyborgs and Space' in *The Cyborg Handbook*, eds Chris Hables Gray *et al.* (New York and London: Routledge).

Cohen, Stanley (2002) *Folk Devils and Moral Panics: The Creation of Mods and Rockers* (3rd edn) (London and New York: Routledge).

Connolly, William E. (1999) 'Suffering, Justice, and the Politics of Becoming' in *Moral Spaces: Rethinking Ethics and World Politics*, eds David Campbell and Michael J. Shapiro (Minneapolis and London: University of Minnesota Press).

Critchley, Simon (1992) *The Ethics of Deconstruction: Derrida and Levinas* (Oxford: Basil Blackwell).

— (1999) *Ethics – Politics – Subjectivity* (London: Verso).

— (2002) 'Ethics, Politics and Radical Democracy: a History of a Disagreement' *Culture Machine* 4. http://culturemachine.tees.ac.uk/Cmach/Backissues/j004/Articles/critchley.htm

— (2003) 'Why I Love Cultural Studies' in *Interrogating Cultural Studies: Theory, Politics and Practice*, ed. Paul Bowman (London and Stirling, VA: Pluto Press).

Crowther, Paul (1989) *The Kantian Sublime: From Morality to Art* (Oxford: Clarendon Press).

Davis, Todd F. and Womack, Kenneth (eds) (2001) *Mapping the Ethical Turn: A Reader in Ethics, Culture, and Literary Theory* (Charlottesville: University of Virginia Press).

Dawkins, Richard (1998) *Unweaving the Rainbow* (Harmondsworth: Penguin).

de Bolla, Peter (1989) *The Discourse of the Sublime: Readings in History, Aesthetics and the Subject* (Oxford: Basil Blackwell).

Derrida, Jacques (1976) *Of Grammatology*, trans. Gayatri Chakravorty Spivak (Baltimore and London: Johns Hopkins University Press).

— (1978) *Writing and Difference*, trans. Alan Bass (London and Henley: Routledge & Kegan Paul).

— (1987) *The Truth in Painting*, trans. Geoff Bennington and Ian McLeod (Chicago and London: University of Chicago Press).

— (1988) *Limited Inc* (Evanston, IL: Northwestern University Press).

— (1990) 'Force of Law: "The Mystical Foundation of Authority"' *Cardozo Law Review: Deconstruction and the Possibility of Justice* 11: 5–6: 920–1045.

— (1991) 'Interpretations at War: Kant, the Jew, the German' *New Literary History* 22: 39–95.

— (1992a) 'Before the Law' in *Jacques Derrida: Acts of Literature*, ed. Derek Attridge (New York and London: Routledge).

— (1992b) *Given Time: I. Counterfeit Money*, trans. Peggy Kamuf (Chicago and London: University of Chicago Press).

— (1992c) *The Other Heading: Reflections on Today's Europe*, trans. Pascale-Anne Brault and Michael B. Naas (Bloomington and Indianapolis: Indiana University Press).

— (1992d) 'Ulysses Gramophone: Hear Say Yes in Joyce', trans. Tina Kendall, in *Jacques Derrida: Acts of Literature*, ed. Derek Attridge (New York and London: Routledge).

— (1994) 'The Deconstruction of Actuality: An Interview with Jacques Derrida', *Radical Philosophy* 68 (Autumn): 28–41.

— (1995) 'Passages – from Traumatism to Promise' in *Points ... Interviews, 1974–1994 Jacques Derrida*, ed. Elizabeth Weber (Stanford: Stanford University Press).

— (1996) 'As If I Were Dead: An Interview with Jacques Derrida' in *Applying: To Derrida*, eds Joan Brannigan *et al.* (London: Macmillan).

— (1997a) 'Perhaps or Maybe: Jacques Derrida with Alexander Garcia Düttman' in *Responsibilities of Deconstruction PLI: Warwick Journal of Philosophy*, eds Jonathon Dronsfield and Nick Midgley 6 (Summer): 1–18.

— (1997b) *Politics of Friendship*, trans. George Collins (London and New York: Verso).

— (1999a) *Adieu: To Emmanuel Levinas*, trans. Pascale-Anne Brault and Michael Naas Stanford: (Stanford University Press).

— (1999b) 'Hospitality, Justice and Responsibility: a Dialogue with Jacques Derrida' in *Questioning Ethics: Contemporary Debates in Philosophy*, eds Richard Kearney and Mark Dooley (London and New York: Routledge).

— (2000) *Of Hospitality: Anne Dufourmantelle Invites Jacques Derrida to Respond*, trans. Rachel Bowlby (Stanford: Stanford University Press).

— (2001) *On Cosmopolitanism and Forgiveness*, trans. Mark Dooley and Michael Hughes (London and New York: Routledge).

— (2002) 'The Animal That Therefore I Am (More to Follow)', trans. David Wills, *Critical Enquiry* 28 (Winter): 369–418.

Derrida, Jacques and Stiegler, Bernard (2002) *Echographies of Television*, trans. Jennifer Bajorek (Cambridge: Polity).

Devenney, Mark and Zylinska, Joanna (eds) (2001) *Cultural Studies: Between Politics and Ethics Strategies. Journal of Theory, Culture and Politics* 14: 2 (November).

de Vries, Hent (1997) 'Violence and Testimony: On Sacrificing Sacrifice' in *Violence, Identity and Self-Determination*, eds Hent de Vries and Samuel Weber (Stanford: Stanford University Press).

de Vries, Hent and Weber, Samuel (1997) 'Introduction' in *Violence, Identity and Self-Determination*, eds Hent de Vries and Samuel Weber (Stanford: Stanford University Press).

Donald, James and Rattansi, Ali (eds) (1996) *'Race', Culture and Difference* (London, Thousand Oaks, New Delhi: Sage, with the Open University).

Doyle, Richard (2003) *Wetwares: Experiments in Postvital Living* (Minneapolis and London: University of Minnesota Press).

du Gay, Paul, Evans, Jessica and Redman, Peter (eds) (2000) *Identity: A Reader* (London, Thousand Oaks, New Delhi: Sage, with the Open University).

During, Simon (1999) 'Introduction' in *The Cultural Studies Reader* (2nd edn), ed. Simon During in (London and New York: Routledge).

Elsaesser, Thomas (2001) 'Postmodernism as Mourning Work', *Screen* 42: 2 (Summer): 193–201.

Felman, Shoshana and Laub, Dori (1992) *Testimony: Crises of Witnessing in Literature, Psychoanalysis, and History* (New York and London: Routledge).

Ferguson, Marjorie and Golding, Peter (1997) 'Cultural Studies and Changing Times: An Introduction' in *Cultural Studies in Question*, eds Marjorie Ferguson and Peter Golding (London, Thousand Oaks, New Delhi: Sage).

Flax, Jane (1998) [1995] 'Race/Gender and the Ethics of Difference' *Ethics: The Big Question*, ed. James P. Sterba (Malden and Oxford: Blackwell).

Foucault, Michel (1984) *The History of Sexuality: An Introduction*, trans. Robert Hurley (Harmondsworth: Penguin Books).

Fox Keller, Evelyn (1994) 'The Body of a New Machine: Situating the Organism between Telegraphs and Computers' *Perspectives on Science* 2: 3: 302–23.

Freud, Sigmund (1985) 'Civilization and Its Discontents' in *The Pelican Freud Library*, vol. 12: *Civilization, Society and Religion*, trans. J. Strachey (Harmondsworth: Penguin).

Garber, Marjorie, Hanssen, Beatrice and Walkowitz, Rebecca L. (eds) (2000) *The Turn to Ethics* (New York and London: Routledge).

Garnham, Nicholas (1997) 'Political Economy and the Practice of Cultural Studies' in *Cultural Studies in Question*, eds Marjorie Ferguson and Peter Golding (London, Thousand Oaks, New Delhi: Sage).

Gee, Sue (1995) *Spring Will Be Ours* (London: Arrow).

Gilbert, Jeremy (2001) 'A Certain Ethics of Openness: Radical Democratic Cultural Studies', *Strategies: Journal of Theory, Culture & Politics* 14: 2 (November): 189–208.

Gilroy, Paul (2000) 'The Sugar You Stir …' in *Without Guarantees: In Honour of Stuart Hall*, eds Paul Gilroy, Lawrence Grossberg and Angela McRobbie (London and New York: Verso).

Giroux, Henry A. (1992) *Border Crossing: Cultural Workers and the Politics of Education* (New York and London: Routledge).

— (2000a) 'Cultural Politics and the Crisis of the University', *Culture Machine* 2. http://culturemachine.tees.ac.uk/Cmach/Backissues/j002/Articles/art_giro.htm

— (2000b) *Impure Acts: The Practical Politics of Cultural Studies* (New York and London: Routledge).

— (2000c) 'Public Pedagogy as Cultural Politics: Stuart Hall and the "Crisis" of Culture' in *Without Guarantees: In Honour of Stuart Hall*, eds Paul Gilroy, Lawrence Grossberg and Angela McRobbie (London and New York: Verso).

Glowacka, Dorota (2003) '"Anarchic Vision": Ocular Constructions of Race and the Challenge of Ethics', *Culture Machine* InterZone (May). http://culturemachine.tees.ac.uk/InterZone/Glowacka.htm

Goodall, Jane (2000) 'An Order of Pure Decision: Un-Natural Selection in the Work of Stelarc and Orlan' in *Body Modification*, ed. Mike Featherstone (London, Thousand Oaks, New Delhi: Sage).

Gross, Jan Tomasz (2000) *Sąsiedzi: historia zaglady żydowskiego miasteczka* (Sejny: Pogranicze). Subsequently published in English (2001) as *Neighbors: The Destruction of the Jewish Community in Jedwabne, Poland* (Princeton and Oxford: Princeton University Press).

Grossberg, Lawrence, Nelson, Cary and Treichler, Paula (eds) (1992) *Cultural Studies* (New York and London: Routledge).

Grosz, Elizabeth (1993) 'Judaism and Exile: The Ethics of Otherness' in *Space and Place: Theories of Identity and Location*, eds Erica Carter, James Donald and Judith Squires (London: Lawrence & Wishart).

Halberstam, Judith (1998) *Female Masculinity* (Durham, NC, and London: Duke University Press).

Hall, Gary (2002) *Culture in Bits: The Monstrous Future of Theory* (London and New York: Continuum).

Hall, Stuart (1996a) 'Introduction: Who Needs "Identity"?' in *Questions of Cultural Identity*, eds Stuart Hall and Paul du Gay (London, Thousand Oaks, New Delhi: Sage).

— (1996b) 'Race, Culture, and Communications: Looking Backward and Forward at Cultural Studies' in *What Is Cultural Studies?*, ed. John Storey (London: Arnold).

— (1999) 'Cultural Studies and Its Theoretical Legacies' in *The Cultural Studies Reader* (2nd edn), ed. Simon During (London and New York: Routledge).

Hall, Stuart and du Gay, Paul (eds) (1996) *Questions of Cultural Identity* (London, Thousand Oaks, New Delhi: Sage).

Hall, Stuart *et al.* (1978) *Policing the Crisis: Mugging, the State, and Law and Order* (Basingstoke and London: Macmillan).

Haraway, Donna J. (1991) *Simians, Cyborgs and Women: The Reinvention of Nature* (London: Free Association Books).

— (1997) *Modest_Witness@Second_Millennium. FemaleMan©_Meets_OncoMouse*™ (New York and London: Routledge).

Hayles, N. Katherine (1999) *How We Became Posthuman* (Chicago and London: University of Chicago Press).

— (2004) 'Flesh and Metal: Reconfiguring the Mindbody in Virtual Environments' in *Data Made Flesh: Embodying Information*, eds Robert Mitchell and Phillip Thurtle (New York and London: Routledge).

Hebdige, Dick (1988) *Hiding in the Light* (New York and London: Routledge).

Hodge, Joanna (2000) 'Forays of a Philosophical Feminist: Sexual Difference, Genealogy, Teleology' in *Transformations: Thinking Through Feminism*, eds Sara Ahmed *et al.* (London and New York: Routledge).

Hoffman, Eva (1998) *Shtetl: The History of a Small Town and an Extinguished World* (London: Secker & Warburg).

Holland, Stephen (2003) *Bioethics: A Philosophical Introduction* (Cambridge: Polity).

hooks, bell (1999) 'A Revolution of Values: The Promise of Multicultural Change' in *The Cultural Studies Reader* (2nd edn), ed. Simon During (London and New York: Routledge).

Jameson, Fredric (1991) *Postmodernism, or, the Cultural Logic of Late Capitalism* (London and New York: Verso).

Johnson, Barbara (2000) 'Using People: Kant with Winnicott' in *The Turn to Ethics*, eds Marjorie Garber, Beatrice Hanssen and Rebecca L. Walkowitz (New York and London: Routledge).

Johnson, Richard (1995) 'What Is Cultural Studies Anyway?' in *A Cultural Studies Reader: History, Theory, Practice*, eds Jessica Munns and Gita Rayan (London and New York: Longman).

Kant, Immanuel (1952) *The Critique of Judgement*, trans. James Meredith (Oxford: Clarendon Press).

Kellner, Douglas (1997) 'Overcoming the Divide: Cultural Studies and Political Economy' in *Cultural Studies in Question*, eds Marjorie Ferguson and Peter Golding (London, Thousand Oaks, New Delhi: Sage).

— (undated) 'Cultural Studies and Ethics', available on his website at http://www.gseis.ucla.edu/faculty/kellner/papers/CSETHIC.htm

Kember, Sarah (2003) *Cyberfeminism and Artificial Life* (London and New York: Routledge).

Kirby, Vicky (1999) 'Human Nature', *Australian Feminist Studies* 14: 29: 19–29.

Kuhse, Helga and Singer, Peter (eds) (1999) *Bioethics: An Anthology* (Oxford: Blackwell).

LaCapra, Dominick (1998) *History and Memory after Auschwitz* (Ithaca, NY, and London: Cornell University Press).

Laclau, Ernesto (1990) *New Reflections on the Revolution of Our Time* (London and New York: Verso).

— (2002) 'Ethics, Politics and Radical Democracy: A Response to Simon Critchley', *Culture Machine* 4. http://culturemachine.tees.ac.uk/Cmach/Backissues/j004/Articles/laclau.htm

Laclau, Ernesto and Mouffe, Chantal (1985) *Hegemony and Socialist Strategy* (London and New York: Verso).

Levinas, Emmanuel (1969) *Totality and Infinity: An Essay on Exteriority*, trans. Alphonso Lingis (Pittsburgh: Duquesne University Press).

— (1986) 'The Trace of the Other', trans. Alphonso Lingis in *Deconstruction in Context*, ed. Mark C. Taylor (Chicago: University of Chicago Press).

— (1989a) 'Ethics as First Philosophy' in *The Levinas Reader*, ed. Sean Hand (Blackwell: Oxford).

— (1989b) 'Substitution' in *The Levinas Reader*, ed. Sean Hand (Blackwell: Oxford).

— (1998) *Otherwise Than Being: Or Beyond Essence*, trans. Alphonso Lingis (Pittsburgh: Duquesne University Press).

Levinas, Emmanuel and Kearney, Richard (1986) 'Dialogue with Emmanuel Levinas' in *Face to Face with Levinas*, ed. Richard A. Cohen (Albany: SUNY Press).

Lingis, Alphonso (1998) 'Translator's Introduction' in Emmanuel Levinas, *Otherwise Than Being: Or Beyond Essence*, trans. Alphonso Lingis (Pittsburgh: Duquesne University Press).

Lury, Celia (1998) *Prosthetic Culture* (London and New York: Routledge).

Lyotard, Jean-François (1988) *The Differend*, trans. Georges Van Den Abbeele (Manchester: Manchester University Press).

— (1990) *Heidegger and the 'jews'*, (trans. Andreas Michel and Mark S. Roberts (Minneapolis: University of Minnesota Press).

— (1991) *The Inhuman*, trans. Geoffrey Bennington and Rachel Bowlby (Cambridge: Polity Press).

McRobbie, Angela (1992) 'Post-Marxism and Cultural Studies: A Postscript' in *Cultural Studies*, eds Lawrence Grossberg, Cary Nelson and Paula Treichler (New York and London: Routledge).

— (1994) *Postmodernism and Popular Culture* (London and New York: Routledge).

Marchitello, Howard (2001a) 'Heterology and Post-Historicist Ethics' in *What Happens to History: The Renewal of Ethics in Contemporary Thought*, ed. Howard Marchitello (New York and London: Routledge).

Marchitello, Howard (ed.) (2001b) *What Happens to History: The Renewal of Ethics in Contemporary Thought* (New York and London: Routledge).

Marsden, Jill (1996) 'Virtual Sexes and Feminist Futures: The Philosophy of "Cyberfeminism"', *Radical Philosophy* 78 (July/August): 6–16.

Marsh, Anne (1993) *Body and Self: Performance Art in Australia 1969–92* (Melbourne: Oxford University Press).

Michnik, Adam (2001) 'Rachunek polskiego sumienia', *Rzeczpospolita* 5 (September): 207.

Millard, Rosie (1996) 'Pain in the Art', *Art Review* May: 52–3.

Mitchell, Robert and Thurtle, Phillip (2004) 'Introduction. Data Made Flesh: The Material Poiesis of Informatics' in *Data Made Flesh: Embodying*

Information, eds Robert Mitchell and Phillip Thurtle (New York and London: Routledge).

Morawski, Stefan (1996) 'A Symptomatic Case of Self-Mystification', trans. M. B. Guzowska, *Magazyn Sztuki/Art Magazine* 10: 2: 196–203.

Morgan Wortham, Simon and Hall, Gary (2002) 'Responding: Interview with Samuel Weber', *South Atlantic Quarterly* 101: 3 (Summer): 695–724.

Mouffe, Chantal (2000) *The Democratic Paradox* (London and New York: Verso).

Munns, Jessica and Rajan, Gita (eds) (1995) *A Cultural Studies Reader: History, Theory, Practice* (London and New York: Longman).

Oliver, Kelly (2000) 'Witnessing Otherness in History' in *What Happens to History: The Renewal of Ethics in Contemporary Thought*, ed. Howard Marchitello (New York and London: Routledge).

O'Neill, Onora (1993) 'Kantian Ethics' in *A Companion to Ethics*, ed. Peter Singer (Oxford: Blackwell).

Onfray, Michel (1996) 'Surgical Aesthetics' in *Orlan: This is my body ... This is my software*, ed. Duncan McCorquodale (London: Black Dog Publishing).

Orlan (1996) 'Conference' in *Orlan: This is my body ... This is my software*, ed. Duncan McCorquodale (London: Black Dog Publishing).

O'Shea, Alan (1998) 'A Special Relationship? Cultural Studies, Academia and Pedagogy', *Cultural Studies*: 12: 4: 513–27.

Philo, Greg and Miller, David (2001) 'Cultural Compliance' in *Market Killing*, eds Greg Philo and David Miller (Harlow: Longman).

Readings, Bill (1996) *The University in Ruins* (Cambridge, MA, and London: Harvard University Press.

Reid, Roddey and Traweek, Sharon (2000) 'Introduction: Researching Researchers' in *Doing Science + Culture*, eds Roddey Reid and Sharon, Traweek (New York and London: Routledge).

Richardson, Ingrid and Harper, Carly (2002) 'Corporeal Virtuality: The Impossibility of Fleshless Ontology', *Body, Space and Technology Journal* 2: 2. http://www.brunel.ac.uk/depts/pfa/bstjournal/

Rifkin, Adrian (2003) 'Inventing Recollection' in *Interrogating Cultural Studies: Theory, Politics and Practice*, ed. Paul Bowman (London and Sterling: Pluto Press).

Robbins, Jill (ed.) (2001) *Is It Righteous To Be? Interviews with Emmanuel Levinas* (Stanford: Stanford University Press).

Rorty, Richard (1996) 'The Inspirational Value of Great Works of Literature', *Raritan* 16: 1: 8–17.

Rose, Barbara (1993) 'Is It Art? Orlan and the Transgressive Act', *Art in America* 81: 2 (February): 82–7.

Roth, John K. (ed.) (1999) *Ethics after the Holocaust: Perspectives, Critiques, and Responses* (St Paul, MN: Paragon House).

Roy, Arundhati (2002) *The Algebra of Infinite Justice* (London: Flamingo).

Royle, Nicholas (2003) *The Uncanny* (Manchester: Manchester University Press).

Singer, Peter (1994) *Rethinking Life and Death: The Collapse of Our Traditional Ethics* (Oxford: Oxford University Press).

Slack, Daryl Jennifer (1996) 'The Theory and Method of Articulation' in *Stuart Hall: Critical Dialogues in Cultural Studies*, eds Kuan-Hsing Chen and David Morley (London and New York: Routledge).

Slack, Jennifer Daryl and Semati, M. Mehdi (2000) 'The Politics of the "Sokal Affair" ' in *Wild Science: Reading Feminism, Medicine and the Media*, eds Janine Marchessault and Kim Sawchuk (London and New York: Routledge).

Slack, Jennifer Daryl and Whitt, Laurie Anne (1992) 'Ethics and Cultural Studies' in *Cultural Studies*, eds Lawrence Grossberg, Cary Nelson and Paula Treichler (New York and London: Routledge).

Sofoulis, Zoe (2003) 'Cyberquake: Haraway's Manifesto' in *Prefiguring Cyberculture: An Intellectual History*, eds Darren Tofts *et al.* (Cambridge, MA, and London: MIT Press).

Sokal, Alan and Bricmont, Jean (1998) *Intellectual Impostures* (London: Profile Books).

Sophocles (2000*) The Three Theban Plays*, ed. Bernard Knox, trans. Robert Fagles (New York: Penguin).

Steele, Tom (1997) *The Emergence of Cultural Studies 1945–65: Cultural Politics, Adult Education and the English Question* (London: Lawrence & Wishart).

— (1999) 'Marginal Occupations: Adult Education, Cultural Studies and Social Renewal' in *Teaching Culture: The Long Revolution in Cultural Studies*, eds Nannette Aldred and Martin Ryle (Leicester: NIACE).

Stelarc (1997a) 'From Psycho to Cyber Strategies: Prosthetics, Robotics and Remote Existence', *Cultural Values* 1: 2: 241–9.

— (1997b) 'Parasite Visions: Alternate, Intimate and Involuntary Experiences', *Art and Design: Sci-Fi Aesthetics* 12: 9/10 (September/October): 66–9.

Stiegler, Bernard (1998) *Technics and Time, 1: The Fault of Epimetheus*, trans. Richard Beardsworth and George Collins (Stanford: Stanford University Press).

Storey, John (ed.) (1996) *What Is Cultural Studies? A Reader* (London: Arnold).

Striphas, Ted (1998) 'Introduction. The Long March: Cultural Studies and Its Institutionalization', *Cultural Studies* 12: 4: 571–94.

Thompson, Keith (1998) *Moral Panics* (London and New York: Routledge).

Tokarska Bakir, Joanna (2001) 'Obsesja niewinnosci', *Gazeta Wyborcza*, 12 January.

Tomasula, Steve (2004) 'Gene(sis)' in *Data Made Flesh: Embodying Information*, eds Robert Mitchell and Phillip Thurtle (New York and London: Routledge).

Turner, Graeme (2002) *British Cultural Studies: An Introduction* (3rd edn) (London and New York: Routledge).

Waldby, Catherine (2000) *The Visible Human Project: Informatic Bodies and Posthuman Medicine* (London and New York: Routledge).

Warszawski, David (2000) 'Responsibility and the Lack of Responsibility' in *Thou Shalt Not Kill: Poles on Jedwabne, Wiez*, http://free.ngo.pl/wiez/jedwabne

Weber, Max (1930) *The Protestant Ethic and the Spirit of Capitalism*, trans. Talcott Parsons (London: Unwin University Books).

Weber, Samuel (1996) *Mass Mediauras: Form, Technics, Media*, ed. Alan Cholodenko (Stanford: Stanford University Press).

— (1997) 'Wartime' in *Violence, Identity and Self-Determination*, eds Hent de Vries and Samuel Weber (Stanford: Stanford University Press).

— (2002) '*War, Terrorism, Spectacle*: On Towers and Caves', *South Atlantic Quarterly* 101: 3 Summer: 449–58.

West, Cornel (1999) 'The New Cultural Politics of Difference' in *The Cultural Studies Reader* (2nd edn), ed. Simon During (London and New York: Routledge).

Wild, John (1969) 'Introduction' in Emmanuel Levinas, *Totality and Infinity: An Essay on Exteriority* (Pittsburgh: Duquesne University Press).

Wills, David (1995) *Prosthesis* (Stanford: Stanford University Press).

Wilson, Sarah (1996) '*L'histoire d'O*, Sacred and Profane' in *Orlan: This is my body ... This is my software*, ed. Duncan McCorquodale (London: Black Dog Publishing).

Woodward, Kathryn (1997) *Identity and Difference* (London, Thousand Oaks, New Delhi: Sage, with the Open University).

Young, Robert (1996) 'Colonialism and Humanism' in '*Race*', *Culture and Difference*, eds James Donald and Ali Rattansi (London, Thousand Oaks, New Delhi: Sage, with the Open University).

Ziarek, Ewa Plonowska (2001) *An Ethics of Dissensus: Postmodernity, Feminism, and Radical Democracy* (Stanford: Stanford University Press).

Ziarek, Krzysztof (2001) 'The Ethos of History' in *What Happens to History: The Renewal of Ethics in Contemporary Thought*, ed. Howard Marchitello (New York and London: Routledge).

Zylinska, Joanna (2001) *On Spiders, Cyborgs and Being Scared: The Feminine and the Sublime* (Manchester: Manchester University Press).

— (ed.) (2002a) *The Cyborg Experiments: The Extensions of the Body in the Media Age* (London and New York: Continuum).

— (2002b) *The Ethico-Political Issue, Culture Machine* 4. http://culturemachine.tees.ac.uk/Cmach/Backissues/j004/journal.htm

Index

Note: 'n.' after a page number refers to a note on that page.